ERASING THE HUMAN

COLLAPSE OF THE POSTCOLONIAL WORLD AND THE REFUGEE IMMIGRATION CRISIS

ERASING THE HUMAN:
COLLAPSE OF THE POSTCOLONIAL WORLD AND THE REFUGEE IMMIGRATION CRISIS

HATEM BAZIAN

CLARITAS
BOOKS

1 2 3 4 5 6 7 8 9 10

CLARITAS BOOKS

Bernard Street, Swansea, United Kingdom
Milpitas, California, United States

CLARITAS
BOOKS

© CLARITAS BOOKS 2021

First Published in April 2021

Typeset in Minion Pro 14/11

Erasing the Human: Collapse of the Postcolonial
World and the Refugees-Immigration Crisis

By Hatem Bazian

A CIP catalogue record for this book is available from the British Library

ISBN: 978-1-80011-995-6

"O My servants! I have forbidden dhulm (oppression) for Myself, and I have made it forbidden amongst you, so do not oppress one another." 40 Hadith Nawawi

"Beware of the supplication of the oppressed, for the supplication of the oppressed is answered." Al-Muwaṭṭa

The book is dedicated to the oppressed facing erasure while continuing to resist despite walls of violence, indifference and the deafening silence.

To the indigenous people,

To the enslaved Africans and their descendants who are struggling to end racism in all its forms,

To women confronting multiple erasures, objectification, demonization, commodification and trafficking across the world,

To those who faced the ravages of colonization and post-colonization,

To victims of war, economic and environmental injustice in the Global South,

To the immigrants, and refugees across the globe,

To the lost their lives in the Mediterranean, on the US south borders and every corner of the globe,

To victims of child labor toiling to satisfy the vanity of the rich and powerful across the world, and

To the people who strive daily to bring meaning and love into each and every household.

Contents

Introduction

Palestine's colonization, displacement, and refugee camps are part of a narrative and a reality that I grew up with and witnessed daily on a firsthand basis. In Amman, Jordan, my family lived just outside Jabal Al-Hussein camp, a refugee camp set up by the United Nations Relief and Works Agency (UNRWA) after the 1948 Nakba[1] (the Catastrophe) to house Palestinians who were forced out of their homeland.[2] The Nakba witnessed the forceful expulsion of more than 750,000 Palestinians to the surroundings countries, including a large number to Jordan. In the aftermath of the 1967 Six-Day War, referred to as Al-Naksa (the Setback) in Palestinian history books, another large group of Palestinian refugees were forced into exile, making their way to Egypt, Jordan, Lebanon, Syria, and other countries.

Palestinian refugees in Jordan live both inside the ten different UNRWA-run camps as well as outside and within major cities across the country because not everyone who left Palestine from 1948 to the present is recorded or recognized as a refugee. Consequently, Palestinians constitute around 65 percent of Jordan's population and primarily work in the private business and professional sectors.

Growing up in Amman, I was used to the Al-Hussein camp being part of my daily life. Every morning, my daily chore before going to school was to take my mother's homemade bread to the communal oven, which was located inside the camp, a ten-minute walk from home. This was one of the most rewarding and nutritious chores to have since carrying the freshly baked Arabic bread on my head on the way back included devouring it—priceless.

My mother's weekly vegetable, meat, and grocery shopping was always done in the camp's bustling markets, and I always accompanied her to carry whatever was bought. I remember we had a long-standing credit relationship with a number of merchants in the camp that knew everyone in my family by name. Whenever a crisis or a shortage of an item came about in Amman due to the many conflicts and wars in the region, we could always depend on one or more of the camp's merchants to set aside an amount of rice, sugar, or oil, and one of my older brothers would go to fetch it for the family.

More importantly, the Palestinians in the Al-Hussein refugee camp had everything a Palestinian household needed. We could find any item from Palestine in the market, or if it was not available on the shelves, then in a week's time they were able to bring it in directly from Palestine. The camp was a reminder of Palestine but constituted in exile since many of the streets, store brands, and alleyways had names of cities, towns, and villages from historical Palestine affixed to them. They carried the hope and dream of returning one day, embedded in the collective act of naming them as a memory, preserving and resisting the multifaceted erasure. The camp was always bustling and overcrowded, with no sewage system and limited water supplies, which made it very challenging during the winter and, at times, facing massive floods after a heavy rain.

My early schooling and friendships were all formed around and with kids from the Al-Hussein camp. I went to Al-Ahnaf Ben Qais elementary school for boys, which was two blocks away from my home and one block away from the camp, where most of the kids came from. After Al-Ahnaf, I went to Al-Hussein middle school, which was just one block away from home and right across the street from the refugee camp bearing the same name. Most of my classmates, friends, teachers, and soccer buddies lived in the camp, and often we went together to the mosque for the daily prayers, which was just inside the camp and a mere one hundred yards away from the school. The soccer field on the other side of Al-Hussein secondary school was the daily meeting place for all the kids in the neighborhood, which extended the time spent in the classroom into many hours before and after school.

For high school, I went to Al-Hussein college, a ten-minute walk from home and located at the opposite entrance of the camp. Most of my high school classmates and teachers came from the camp. Our friendships were very close, forged inside the classroom but more importantly in playing endless games of soccer, basketball and handball. During my middle school and high school years, there was much unrest, including the protest movement inside the 1948 area of Palestine that culminated in Land Day,[3] the Lebanese Civil War during which Palestinians experienced the Sabra and Shatila Massacre,[4] and another episode of displacement and exile for Palestinians from Lebanon's refugee camps to Iraq, Sudan, Tunisia, and Yemen.

Palestinians constitute one of the largest and possibly oldest refugee group under the UN umbrella. When I was young, my proximity to the camp meant a constant engagement with everything political related to Palestine. Often, the protests began in the camp before arriving in the school yard to get everyone out of the classroom to join, which always meant the police and the army were not far away from the gathering. In the aftermath of the Sabra and Shatila Massacre, the protests went on for days, and the army was heavily deployed around the school with armored carriers stationed at the entrance of the school and the camp.

Similarly, on March 30, the annual anniversary of Land Day commemoration, the school was surrounded by armored carriers and a heavy army presence to prevent the students from protesting but to no avail. We always planned ahead for a protest at the midday lunch break and would run to the next-door school to get the students out for a march, with our few thousand protesters outnumbering the army and police. The protest and mobilization was organized and carried out despite having a number of teachers who actually were officers in the intelligence service, but we knew which students were on the payroll at the time and did not include them in any of our plans.

On July 17, 1974, the then-discredited at home US president Richard Nixon visited Jordan.[5] All of the school kids had to come out of school with their teachers to line the streets of Amman to greet him and wave the newly printed American flags as his motorcade passed. I was aware of the US support of Israel, the Vietnam War, the civil rights movement, and the Watergate scandal, which led me and my friends to plan to skip this orchestrated show as it was a real waste of time when compared to a fully engaged soccer game to be followed by *Kunafa* downtown. We lined up like everyone else in the school yard but managed to sneak away slowly as the line began to move away from the school and we moved into very familiar hiding places within our neighborhood. Let's say Nixon came but we conquered!

I remember very vividly that during the same year of Nixon's visit to Jordan, the October 29 Muhammad Ali versus George Foreman "The Rumble in the Jungle" boxing match occurred, which was my own distant connection to the champ, the greatest. The match was a much-awaited event for the neighborhood, and almost everyone crammed into the few houses that had a TV set to watch the fight. Every household had forty to fifty people packed in front of the small-screen TV waiting for the event to start and not wanting to miss the minute that Muhammad Ali entered the ring. Muhammad Ali was not Arab or Palestinian, but all of us on that day, and even before then, considered him as one of our own. He was a real hero that spoke about and identified with the pain and suffering inflicted on Black Americans, expressed solidarity with the "third world," and risked everything to give voice to the voiceless.

As the bout was about to start, the streets emptied and the

cafes were deserted since none had a TV at the time, and almost everyone found a place to watch, listen to the radio, and pray that Muhammad Ali would win another match for the world at a critical period in history. As the decisive knockout occurred in the eighth round, you could hear the cheers coming like a roar across town, and throngs of people came out in the street calling, "Ali, Ali, Ali," as if he was present among them. Kids ran out of the houses replaying the fight, pretending to be Ali, an occurrence that was repeated nonstop for days. Starting at age ten and going to school as kids, Muhammad Ali cutouts from magazines were ever-present, adorning the covers and the insides of our books and notebooks. Had social media been around at the time, Ali would have been the king of the medium, and his image and quotes would have been the most shared.

On the world stage, Muhammad Ali was the people's champ regardless of what anyone said or if the title was taken away by a government action. In so many different ways, Ali in the ring and at every turn represented the hopes, dreams, and aspirations of a world that was torn asunder by the Vietnam War, civil rights struggles in the US and Europe, anticolonial liberation movements in Africa and Asia, and, for us closer to home, the ongoing dispossession of the Palestinians. Muhammad Ali managed to transcend boxing and made the world his ring and managed to communicate to all people in a language they all understood: the language of love, justice, dignity, and wit, the like of which, possibly, will never be seen again.

Muhammad Ali was able to connect masterfully the fight for civil rights in America with transnational liberation struggles and anticolonial movements across the globe. For many, Ali's actions and words provided a window through which they were able to see America's racism and contradictions as well as the continued colonial imprint on the globe. Muhammad Ali was a child of segregation but refused to accept the limitations imposed by America's racial system. Ali proclaimed, "I am America. I am the part you won't recognize. But get used to me. Black, confident, cocky; my name, not yours; my religion, not yours; my goals, my own; get used to me."

The draft for the Vietnam War served as the stage that elevated Muhammad Ali to a global household name and transformed him from a beloved heavyweight champion of the world into America's most despised figure. Muhammad Ali's refusal to be drafted was a watershed moment for the US government and the antiwar movement. "I ain't got no quarrel with them Vietcong… No Vietcong ever called me n—," was Ali's response to the draft. Furthermore, in his opposition to the draft and the war, Ali connected his opposition to the racism at home: "Why should they ask me to put on a uniform and go 10,000 miles from home and drop bombs and bullets on brown people in Vietnam while so-called Negro people in Louisville are treated like dogs and denied simple human rights?" Ali stood high above everyone by giving up everything to stand for his principles and refused to join the war efforts in Vietnam. At the height of his career and with the opportunity to accept being drafted and possibly function as a recruitment poster child for a colonial war, Ali opted to go to jail, lose his title, and through it challenge the government and the country on the unjust nature of the war and the ongoing anti-Black racism.

Here, we see a connection between a president touring foreign lands to demonstrate leadership at home, the convergence of postcolonial elites and resistance during Nixon's visit, and the imprint of Ali's global defiance and local despots arraying their people with US flags in the streets as mere billboards for a crooked American president on the verge of impeachment, who was raining nonstop death on Vietnam and Cambodia. Nixon's Watergate plumbers reached all the way to Amman's streets and had us as school kids taking part in rehabilitating the image of a US president that was just a few months away from impeachment and resignation. The local and transitional are never far apart, and the distance between the streets of Amman, Jordan, Washington, DC, and the Congo is very far when examined only in miles traveled, but they are closely connected and intertwined in the political, economic, and postcolonial machinations. Growing up and living in the Arab region brings you closer and in constant contact to everything related to the US, Europe, the USSR, and Israel to the extent that we are, possibly, the only people that can name every US secretary of state, National Security Council advisor, and UN secretary general for the past seventy-five years because we have been subject to every colonial and postcolonial political, economic, and diplomatic deceit in the book.

My own consciousness around refugees, displacement, and controlling structures was formed at an early age in a complex relationship with the Al-Hussein refugee camp, with the ups and downs experienced by all Palestinians and a distant view of what is going on in America. I was fully aware of the circumstances that Palestinians faced, both in Jordan as refugees and in Palestine under occupation, and Nixon's visit was adding insult to an already injured and structurally erased Palestinian population but Ali's fight, stand, and solidarity made for the balance. On a positive side note, Ali's fight and watching it at the neighbors created the needed pressure for my family to get its first TV in the house in 1975, which made it possible to watch the 1976 Olympic Games at home.

The experience of Palestinian refugees and the subsequent immigration of many Palestinians to other parts of the world shaped and brought a deeper affinity to anyone who faced displacement from their homeland. More importantly, and after finishing high school, I immigrated to the US and followed in the footsteps of my own brother, who was already living in Concord, California, which opened a new chapter of entanglement to get a green card and citizenship. I will examine the Palestinian refugee and immigrant experience in detail later on in this book, which will help ground this work in the impacts of the colonial and postcolonial discourses.

The Palestinian experience is paradigmatic of the many displacements caused by the colonial period and the consequences that continue to unfold in the postcolonial era. In 1948, Palestinians became refugees dispersed across the world, facing the predicament of being a stateless people and subject to the whims of the international nation-state structure. The erasure of Palestine is the permanent predicament facing millions of Palestinians living in refugee camps, immigrants across the world in the diaspora and skilled professional hands spread across the globe. While not everyone who is currently on the move as a refugee or immigrant had an identical experience to that of the Palestinians, no two experiences are alike. Nevertheless, what human beings are facing in the current period, along with the massive flood of humanity of refugees and immigrants on the move, made this book project a must and a scholarly act of solidarity.

A second impetus for the book originates in my own work and activism around the Central American Solidarity Movement and the South African Anti-Apartheid Movement. In both of these struggles, I had close activist friends who were refugees, immigrants, and political exiles who made their way to the US from Belize, Chile, El Salvador, Guatemala, Haiti, Jamaica, Nicaragua, Nigeria, Puerto Rico, and South Africa. Furthermore, the Afghans, Chinese, Filipinos, Iranians, Koreans, and Mexicans were all part of the Progressive Coalition and formed a circle of close friends and colleagues during all my years at San Francisco State University (SFSU). Immigration, refugees, violence, racism and escape narratives were all around and part of any daily conversation and event at SFSU.

Critically, the student activists at SFSU navigated the hub of the local-global entanglements, and each of their narratives contextualized the long history of US interventions, support of death squads and economic imperatives connected to it. Interventions by the US in El Salvador and Nicaragua translated into a long line of refugees escaping a most destructive policy that started with the Monroe Doctrine[6] and continued throughout the Cold War years. In the case of South Africa, the US had long-standing relations with the apartheid regime and resisted any efforts directed at isolating and boycotting the racist government. In the 1980s, the US government introduced the policy of constructive engagement,[7] which sought to undermine the emerging international consensus directed at isolating South Africa's apartheid regime.

The engagement policy failed to change the apartheid regime, and the continued targeting of African National Congress activists inside and outside the country intensified. The Progressive Coalition at SFSU, which I led during my years on campus, had a constant engagement with Latin America's and South Africa's struggles, and both constituted an important part of our political platform. Local-global links meant that we had refugees and immigrants from these two regions that could provide firsthand experiences of what they went through just to make it out alive, arrive in the US and attend college. Across the Bay Area, Berkeley, Oakland, and San Francisco, one can find a thriving coalition of refugees, immigrants, and political activists from an array of countries bound together by a collective memory and a narrative of displacement, exile, and resistance. All the activists from the mentioned countries were engaged in each other's political mobilizations, sit-ins and for sure the many joyous celebrations.

This book is a small but important effort to bring context to the friends and coalition partners who managed to deepen my commitment to struggle for a better and more just future for all. The encounters, narratives, and the many events and protests we organized together provide an important Global South stitching of a different worldview born out of the colonial-postcolonial experience.

A third motivation to write this book came after teaching a summer study abroad course in France, which focused on the unfolding refugee and immigrant crisis. In particular, a 2016 visit to "Calais Jungle" was the inspiration that led to a series of articles that unpacked what was under way in Europe. With it came the urgent need to conceptualize a theoretical framework to the current crisis that goes beyond the proclivity to focus on the religious, racial and ethnic identities of the refugees and immigrants. During and after the visit, I began to formulate the theoretical framework that centered on the ongoing collapse of the postcolonial state in the post-Cold War period, which is the primary cause behind what we are witnessing. I will work to unpack this theoretical framework and trace its developments throughout the book's chapters.

The logistical and transportation point for individuals attempting to enter the United Kingdom is via the Port of Calais or the Channel Tunnel linking France to the United Kingdom. Many refugees and immigrants make their way from across Africa, Asia, and parts of Europe so as to get themselves illegally stowed away on lorries, ferries, cars, or trains to enter into the United Kingdom in search of safety and economic opportunity. For many, the journey into Calais begins in distant lands that are either facing ongoing civil and regional wars or a dislocation due to neoliberal globalized and hyperprivatized economic forces, which has caused the collapse of what was left of the few sustainable models of existence in the Global South.

"Calais Jungle" was the most shocking and life-altering experience for anyone who visited, witnessed, or interacted with the more than 8,143 refugees and immigrants who lived in makeshift tents without essential services, food, or support. At the time, the French government spent millions to construct a fence and install a 24/7 security system, including a heavy police presence and surveillance technology to prevent movement out of the camp and to limit the number of incoming refugees and immigrants. Furthermore, the French government provided only 2,000 meals per day to the 8,143 individuals inside the area. At the same time, volunteers from across Europe (illegally, if I may say) set up a logistical supply system to support and cover the needs of the camp. The camp's population was very diverse and covered the full spectrum of ethnic, racial, cultural, and religious communities from the postcolonial south.

Examining the crisis in France by taking students abroad was part of the larger academic and political discourses focusing on the unfolding challenge across Europe and on the southern US border, which was highly racialized. One can speak theoretically about refugees and immigration, but it is by witnessing what is going on in refugee-immigrant sites across France, as well as interacting with frontline service providers from various parts of Europe, that gives a different perspective altogether. I have been doing regular work and make a yearly visit to France focusing on the intersection of Islamophobia, racism, and antirefugee and anti-immigrant discourses in the country and other parts of Europe in the hope of crafting an intellectual response, but more so on developing coalitions to challenge the prevailing conditions. European entanglement with the refugee and immigrant crisis has not ended, and increasingly the continent had adopted a restrictive regime with closed borders.

During the 2016 summer program, we had a visit from Yousif, a Sudanese refugee living in Paris after a nearly four-month torturous journey. Yousif's story is reflective of many refugee-immigrant narratives coming to the US from Central and South America and provides a comparative lens to the experiences of those who the world has forgotten, erased, or criminalized. He shared his story, which started from the moment he left his home up until arriving in Paris. Yousif's story began with him and his younger brother in North Sudan, fleeing from the ranks of the military after refusing orders to shoot innocent people. After managing to cross into Ajdabiya, Libya, and move into the coastal Tripoli area, they connected with the second stage of the regularized human-trafficking network that transports commodified human cargo to the shores of Europe. Currently, Libya is in the throes of a prolonged civil war that was ushered in by the Arab Spring and the intervention of European (France, Italy, and the

United Kingdom), American, and Gulf States powers to prevent an emergence of a unified and independent stable state that is not beholden to expressed interests of global powers and their demand of unfettered access to the vast oil reserves in the country.

For Yousif, the journey through Libya with its ongoing civil war was the only open route and way to collect the payment required by the smugglers for spots on one of the boats departing daily from the chaotic and uncontrollable coast. The simple task of getting food became a difficult act of survival in a war setting—a war that neither Yousif nor his brother had anything to do with but simply were caught in the middle of during the long trek to Europe. The tragedy of leaving home was compounded for Yousif in Libya after losing his younger brother amid the fighting. Yousif can understand dying for a cause or a war that one has a vested role in—possibly defending a homeland, family, or society—but losing his brother in Libya was a devastating blow that will be with him for the rest of his life. If one can compare the circumstances of refugees and immigrants on the US's southern border and what they went through just to make it to the entry point, then we can begin to locate Yousif's story within the American context and possibly other regions as well.

The visit to France took place at the time of US national debate on the possible threat of admitting Syrian refugees into the country, which was a key theme that was used by then-candidate Donald Trump to stoke racial tensions to be followed by his attacks on Mexican immigrants. Syrian refugees were used as a vital tool to reframe the 2016 electoral campaign, and the successful racialization of targeted groups (Syrian and Mexican immigrants), which helped land Trump in the White House. The debate on refugees and immigrants has only intensified since then, and the Trump administration has made it a point to curtail both the legal and illegal processes of entry into the country.

Furthermore, the Trump administration committed itself to building a physical wall on the southern border to block the entry of Mexican and Latin American refugees and immigrants into the country. Building the wall and changing policy have led to refugees and immigrants facing massive violations of civil and human rights, including physically removing children and infants from their parents' arms in an effort to put pressure on, threaten, and dissuade others from making the journey to the border. The US's internal political debates and positioning for electoral campaigns translated into a multilayered and multipronged crisis that is still unfolding before the 2020 presidential elections.

Coming back to Yousif's narrative, the smugglers are running a thriving business as loads of people from across the Global South are making their way to the North African coast for an appointment with a hazardous journey across the Mediterranean Sea. According to Yousif, "It costs almost 700 euro and sometimes more. To get that much, people sell their homes, and some sell their kidneys or anything that can get them such an amount." In a similar fashion, smugglers in Mexico, Central America, and the US feast on human misery and use the existing political disarray, civil wars, intervention, and lack of leadership to commodify the crisis and make a handsome profit. The smugglers and smuggling networks are part and born out of the system rather than being the cause of it. Restrictive and xenophobic immigration policies give rise to the smuggling networks that commodify the human, and they become codependent and affirming of each other's approach.

More importantly, the relationship between the smugglers and local authorities is well structured, and the local police in many parts of the human-trafficking routes are paid to look the other way or provide logistical protection for a handsome fee, as well as engaging in sexual exploitation. In Yousif's case, the first part of the journey was to cross the desert in a 4×4 truck that was overloaded beyond capacity with the already-commodified human cargo. One can "add the desert, the thirst, the speed" to the trek, and after days of using off-road passageways, the smugglers arrived at the "delivery point at the Libyan border, Al Kufra district." Yousif recalled, "I remember that time clearly because we lost many people; there was no water (we drunk our pee); they left us for many days without any food or water."

Arriving in Al-Kufa was only the first leg in a long, expensive journey through various parts of Libya, witnessing and experiencing abuse, racism, and dehumanization at every turn. The humans on this long road and this journey are reduced to mere biological material and commodified in precisely the same way merchandise on a truck or cargo ship is conceptualized. Indeed, not all refugees or immigrants are fleeing war, and for sure, some are desperate to improve their economic conditions, considering the total collapse of the postcolonial order in the Global South and the destructive effects of the neoliberal economic order that has been set in place over the past three decades.

Fleeing war is easy to explain, but deciphering the compounded impacts of colonialism, postcolonialism, and the Cold War, which was anything but cold in the Global South, is a major challenge. The postcolonial era and the later period of the Cold War witnessed the introduction of neoliberal economic modalities, shock-and-awe debt-based funding, International Monetary Fund and World Bank structural adjustment programs, and debt for equity swaps to benefit banks and General Agreement on Tariffs and Trades and World Trade Organization policies—all of which require a PhD in multiple fields to begin to understand what happened in the Global South and why this massive flood of people are on the move to Europe and the US. The book is an effort to deal with the complexities of the colonial and postcolonial legacies, constant interventions, trade in oil and raw materials from the Global South, the impact of brain drain, and the utter destruction of people and the environment, which I feel is a discussion that is both timely and urgently needed.

The movement of commodified human cargo from the Global South to the North has been a feature of the modern world since the arrival of Europeans onto the shores of the Americas. America is often posited as a refugee-immigrant society, but this structurally is an erasure of the settler-colonial and postcolonial legacy, which brought about genocide of the Indigenous population and massive importation of African slaves to work the land. According to Huntington, America is defined as a white Anglo-Saxon Protestant Christian settler society, which means that African Americans, Native Americans, Latinos and other minorities are not part of his narrow conceptualization of the country.[8] I will spend time in a later chapter to address America's split personality and the constant torment directed at refugees and immigrants. The Americas experienced the largest movement of people in human history, both as Europeans colonized the lands and during the forceful importation of African slaves, which was done within the contexts of multiple genocides committed against the Indigenous population and Africans as well.

Making a distinction between refugees and economic immigrants is an easy way to flatten the argument and rationalize the building of walls of exclusion that end up preventing all types of human movement from the south to the north. Could anyone argue that refugees and economic immigrants from Afghanistan, Central African Republic, Chad, Egypt, Eritrea, Ethiopia, Iraq, Lebanon, Libya, Mali, Nigeria, Pakistan, Palestine, Somalia, Sudan, Syria, and Yemen don't have a right to seek a safe place to live and earn a living, considering the many years of colonial and postcolonial intervention by US and European powers? More critically, can we engage in any discussion or examination of the refugees and immigrants from Latin America without taking stock of years of US intervention, economic exploitation, and distortions of any normative pattern of development? Policies have their consequences!

My argument is the following: If any Western country sells weapons to the armies that are fighting whatever type of war or are engaged in, extending the US and European economic interests in the form of oil, natural resources, and market share, then their minimum responsibility is addressing the flood of human misery caused by it. Furthermore, if a country has been colonized in the past or bombed by European or American forces in the present, then the human flood fleeing from these conflicts belongs to the West, and the leaders who caused the flood of refugees in the first place must own the problem and its consequences. Human life and real people don't look or feel the same in a white paper written to extend wrongly headed and exploitative policies that are situated against the well-being of millions of people.

Yousif is part of the human flood that has paid the price and will continue to do so for highly racialized political and economic policies that have been under way for generations. Yousif is the direct outcome of the commodification of a large swath of Black, brown, and Asian humanity and transforming it into a mere rate of return on investment. Selling weapons and having a military-industrial economy has its consequences, which goes beyond the basic rate of return on investment. We must consider the flood of refugees and immigrants fleeing the Global South into cities and towns in the Global North as the moral rate of return for merchants of death that have pillaged cities and countries in pursuit of obscene profits!

In the past, it was guns for slaves, and now it is guns for natural resources and the transport of the commodified human being into the racialized cheap labor pipelines of the Global North and another cycle of disruption. The immigration (voluntary and involuntary) pipeline was opened in the pre- and post-1492 era, and since then has witnessed the massive disruption of every corner of the globe. Indeed, the modern era begins with the forced expulsion of Muslims and Jews from Spain, which included the Inquisition, a state-sponsored violent regime directed at the religious other. Europe's birth as a white Christian continent came about through the removal of the religious other, which was deemed to be impure and a cause of past calamities. Consequently, if the idea of Europe, as a distinct white Christian continent, to have any meaning in the 15ᵗʰ century, then this idea was only accomplished and maintained through the act of removing, eliminating, and total erasure of the Muslim and Jewish other at its inception and subsequently all the way up to the modern period.

What was perfected in Spain and Europe found a fertile ground in the New World and ushered in the age of colonization. Colonization meant the death and the structured erasure of cultures and societies the world over. Even in those areas where total erasure did not occur, the mental and psychological transfiguration is irreversible, with damage being transgenerational and transhistorical. The eyes that look at and experience the world are all shaped and framed by the colonial experience, including the populations of the colonial states themselves since their knowledge and contact with the world was made possible and epistemically framed through colonization. Thus, nothing has escaped the intrusion of the colonial and imperial epistemic effect, and it is glaring back in every corner of the globe. The problem is not the immigrant or refugee themselves, but what caused this human being to opt to jump on a boat not fit for sailing or to walk across the vast desert to a certain death—this is the real problem and the question that must be asked! The immigrants and refugees are the by-product of a system that produces a commodified and erased human being as a "natural" and "normative" outcome. This system and those engaged in it are the real culprits and agents of the ongoing misery and death.

Framing the refugee and immigrant problem around ethnic, cultural, racial, and religious differences is a distraction, which is intended to cast away the real causes behind this mass movement of people across the globe. Why are we seeing Afghan, Iraqi, Palestinian, and Syrian immigrants at the border gates of Europe?[9] Why are Libyans leaving their country in dinghy boats while their country is rich with oil? Who caused a disruption in El Salvador, Haiti, Honduras, and Venezuela and structurally forced people into migratory caravans? One can add questions about Mexican peasants' migration to the US and the disruption caused by the North American Free Trade Agreement (NAFTA), which triggered a massive displacement and dislocation of farmers who were dependent on subsistence farming for generations. Free movement of capital and goods but not people ended up sinking and commodifying the Mexican farmers and driving them up north to the US to flood the job market and put a downward pressure on wages and benefits for all. I will deal with the impacts of NAFTA, which I opposed at the time of its adoption and organized against it jointly with Mexican, Canadian, and US activists, but the election of President Bill Clinton led US labor unions to accept the most antilabor agreement to be signed into law.

The world has grown accustomed, numb, and indifferent to the plight of immigrants, asylum seekers, and refugees, which has no end in sight with the daily unfolding calamity becoming more acute. Death and drowning of the young and old on the shores of Europe, the US southern border, and across the vast coasts of the Indian and Atlantic Oceans are a stain on the collectivity of human consciousness, bringing disgrace to the last remaining vestiges of a long-gone civilization. What is astonishing is the mobilization of governmental resources to compound the problem rather than finding solutions to the crisis effecting 70.8 million human beings![10] The same individuals, forces, and governments that were vested in the colonial, postcolonial, and Cold War eras are the ones offering xenophobic arguments and building walls to escape responsibility for the damage they have reeked on the Global South.

Politicians and media promote racist, xenophobic, and Islamophobic narratives around the refugee and immigrant crisis while all along failing to provide a deeper examination of the predicament at hand. The immigrant-refugee questions of today are, at the core, another iteration of racism that is masquerading as a legitimate policy to address a real crisis. In many corners of Europe and the US, the rising tide of right-wing parties are using anti-immigrant sentiments to come back into respectability. Right-wing organizers and parties target immigrants and refugees by flooding society's airwaves with their racist venom[11] and use sophisticated analytics[12] to capture the social media spaces and stoke racial tension, anger, and resentment.

As I was almost two-thirds through writing the book, the murder of George Floyd occurred in Minneapolis, Minnesota, which made me want to add a specific chapter on anti-Black racism and the multifaceted erasures of the suffering of Black people in America. I had already written a short section on racism in the six features of colonization, but the murder and subsequent protest movement directed at defunding the police and the removal of Confederate statues, including those of Columbus, colonial figures, and slave traders, across the US and the world made for a seamless and already built bridge to expand upon. The chapter is expanding on the centrality of race and racism as the major analytical track for approaching the subject of postcolonialism and the immediate links to the current immigrant-refugee crisis.

At the outset, I caution the reader that the book is not about detailing the weaknesses or strengths of current immigration and refugee policies and procedures in the US, Europe, or any other parts of the world. Collectively, most if not all of the current approaches to the problem take the modern nation-state and UN state actors' perspective as the point of departure while failing to recognize that, precisely, the global state-centric structure is the cause of the unfolding problems across the globe. Here, the five permanent powers of the UN Security Council and the role they play is directly responsible for causing the immigrant-refugee crisis in the first place, which is due to their continued interventions and domination of all aspects of political, economic, and military decisions impacting millions of human beings across the globe.

In addition to the introduction and conclusion, I have five chapters forming a set of interconnected discourses focusing on the heavy imprint of colonization that continues to shape the postcolonial world. My own experiences, as a Palestinian, form the basis of the first chapter, and the direct link to settler colonialism. In the second chapter, "Colonization and the Modern World," I examine the six features of colonialism and how they shaped our contemporary political, economic, social, and religious discourses. The third chapter, "Chocolate and the Colonial Pact," traces the relationship between the colonial motherlands and the extracting of raw materials from the colonies in the Global South, which continues all the way up to the present. More critically, the chapter looks at France's domination and control of the Francophone Africa zone through a colonial pact that maintains the same type of control and domination in the postcolonial era. In chapter four, "Bouncers and Enforcers," I focus on the role played by the International Monetary Fund and World Bank as well as the onset of neoliberal economics and privatization schemes, which managed to extend the Global North's control of the economies and political discourses in the postcolonial Global South. "I can't breathe" is chapter five's theme that examines the murder of George Floyd but doing so while making the direct link to connected colonial histories and continuities; thus, locating the violence directed at Black communities within the longer trajectory that begins with the enslavement period and continues all the way up to the present.

Therefore, the book is not about how bad or critical the immigration-refugee crisis is in the US or Europe; rather, it reframes the discourse into the longer causalities and origins of the problem. Critically, I am not offering or pretending to offer any solutions in this work or how best to provide any type of services or support to the immigrants and refugees across the world, which is a badly needed undertaking. What I am offering here is a reframing of the crisis away from the momentary end stage or border problems, legal and otherwise, and centering the colonial and postcolonial analysis with a longer historical genesis for the modern world we all are inhabiting.

This book is intended to spark conversations and discussions that hopefully can give rise to a different mode of thinking on the refugee and immigrant crisis that is facing us all. I am hoping that readers will feel inspired to take action and bring forth projects and programs that can remedy the ongoing suffering and build a new world. Martin Luther King Jr. identified the cause of why things remain in the current state: "History will have to record that the greatest tragedy of this period of social transition was not the strident clamor of the bad people, but the appalling silence of the good people."[13] The immigrant or refugee who turned away at the border and shunned when they are living among us is indicative of our own human condition and accepting erasure of what ties us together as a humanity. If my work can lead anyone to become more involved in addressing any aspect of the crisis, be it in small or substantial ways, then I believe the book has accomplished its goal. I write to bring about social change and inspire action for a better future horizon. Writing is a social justice act that uplifts the stories and narratives of the marginalized, the nameless, and all those who face constant structural erasure.

Chapter One

Palestine and Settler Colonialism

In the introduction, I mentioned that one drive behind writing this book is being Palestinian and having lived next to and constantly passed through the Al-Hussein refugee camp in Amman, spending my early formative years with friends and classmates from the camp. I have already written a book on Palestine[14] that focuses on the settler colonial and political history of the dispossession of the Palestinians. But this book is more about the impact, or the creation, of the refugee and diaspora communities.

This first chapter deserves a multivolume treatment to really examine every aspect of the Palestinian experience of refugees, migrants, and immigrants in various settings since no two experiences are the same, and the rich material for the most part has been left unattended.

The majority of writings on Palestine have focused on the political dimension, which is understandable, but it has left an extensive aspect of the lives and experiences of Palestinians unengaged. A desired outcome of reading this chapter and other parts of the book is to encourage people to pursue further studies and generate new research and writings that can begin to contextualize the political and dispossession experiences of Palestinians. The discussion in this chapter will cover a wide set of topics and regions, which might be challenging for some to follow the various threads, but if anything, it points to the complexity and entanglements of the Palestinian cause within the global context.

Palestine's predicament in the twentieth and twenty-first centuries is directly connected to global powers' engagement, which caused the crisis in the first place. Critically, Palestinians navigate the colonial and postcolonial eras, receiving the refugee designation and the immigration and migration processes linked to it. The resultant diaspora and its consequences of structural brain drain; entanglement with UN institutions; and Arab and Muslim world political, economic, and social orders collectively make their circumstances inclusive and paradigmatic of the global crisis. Here, the uniqueness of the Palestinian situation can help develop another view to how the colonial and postcolonial is the most apt lens to examine what is under way across the world.

❧ Palestine, Palestinians and the International Community

As kids playing in the school yard, we would notice signs of UN and refugee status all around. For example, many kids in school wore clothes made from emptied UN flour, rice, and sugar sacks, usually shorts or sometimes shirts, which they dressed in on a regular basis. Likewise, it was not uncommon to use these same sacks to make underpants for kids inside and outside the camps. My own mother used the same sacks to fashion shorts for me and my brothers and design shopping bags to use for the groceries when heading to the Al-Hussein camp to shop. The UN was not only part of the Palestinians' political vocabulary for putting an international imprint on Zionism settler colonialism but was also a must-have fashion option.

The saying "necessity is the mother of invention" accurately describes the daily struggles and innovation of Palestinians and refugees in general, who are able to make do under the most challenging conditions. When I arrived in the US for higher education, many would talk about recycling and making sure to put bottles and papers in the provided bins, but growing up, the idea of wasting anything, small or large, was unthinkable. Even when it comes to how Palestinian refugee camps and status are managed is subject to a distinct separate structure.

Indeed, Palestinians occupy a unique and problematic status within the Office of the United Nations High Commissioner for Refugees (UNHCR) because they fall under the direct supervision of the United Nations Relief and Works Agency (UNRWA) for Palestine refugees. You might ask, what is unique about UNRWA? The agency is an outfit that comes out of, and is answerable to, the UN General Assembly, which was established in 1950 under Article 7(2) and 22 of the UN Charter. The UN mandate for UNRWA sets it up as a temporary agency, with the mandate needing to be renewed periodically and the funding being dependent on voluntary contributions, meaning Palestinian refugees exist at the mercy of donor states.[15] According to Lance Bartholomeusz,[16] UNRWA's "mandate is not conveniently stated in one place and must be derived from all relevant resolutions and requests," which means that "each year the General Assembly passes a series of resolutions germane to UNRWA; notably, resolutions entitled 'Operations of the United Nations Relief.'"[17]

Palestinians constitute possibly the longest and maybe the largest single group of people to become refugees in the post-World War II era.[18] The following UN refugee figures show 6.7 million Syrian refugees, which is the largest single group counted under the UNHCR.

In 2019, around 70.8 million forcibly displaced people were counted by the UNHCR, which is broken down to 41.3 million internally displaced, 25.9 million refugees, and 3.5 million asylum seekers. The data shows that three countries account for 57 percent of the refugee population—Syria has 6.7 million, Afghanistan has 2.7 million, and Sudan has 2.3 million—but the question that must be asked is what happened to the Palestinians and why are they not counted in the percentage as a fourth country? If we take the number of Palestinian refugees as 5.5 million, which is included in the blue section on the graph and added to the overall numbers, then the percentage would be 66.4 percent of all refugees come from four countries.

Palestinians and Palestine itself occupy a very precarious position within the international system; they are included through structural omission! Since Palestine is not a state, and its statehood and status are constantly contested by Israel and its allies, then Palestinians are subject to a separate regime when it comes to the refugee designation as well as all other elements pertaining to their rights—a crisis that continues up to the present (Why Palestine is not a state and Palestinians' rights are constantly under attack is directly connected to the colonial and postcolonial world order. Palestine was the last colony to be commissioned by Great Britain in the twentieth century, and this is still the key issue in the postcolonial twenty-fist century.)

Palestine sits at the crossroads of the colonial and postcolonial with all the vagaries of both eras crystalizing in daily practices that are inflected upon the Palestinians in all settings, not only in the West Bank and Gaza Strip. A Palestinian refugee is not a normal or clear-cut category since the actual place the refugee came from "no longer exists," or an even more pernicious statement that "it never existed," according to the Zionist narrative. So the person in reality is not a refugee but a person who left one place for another. The idea that there is no such thing as Palestine and that Palestinian refugees belong to an undefined or contested category is part of the problem in the articulation of international law. In this context, international law is the codification of the legal "rights" and "privileges" attained by the colonial powers during direct colonization, setting it as the measure and tool to regulate the postcolonial. How many Palestinian refugees are there in the world is one of the most explosive and often debated questions! How did the Palestinians become refugees, and why do they occupy such a highly contested space within the international system are other such questions.

In 2019, UNRWA put the number of Palestinian refugees at 5.5 million. It categorizes Palestinian refugees as "persons whose normal place of residence was Palestine during the period 1 June

1946 to 15 May 1948, and who lost both home and means of live-lihood as a result of the 1948 conflict."[19] Palestinians who lost their homes and land and were forced into exile from the arrival of the British on December 11, 1917, until May 15, 1948, are not included or registered by UNRWA. Critically, UNRWA's data is based on individuals "living in its area of operations who meet" the above narrowly crafted definition and "who are registered with the Agency and who need assistance. The descendants of Palestine refugees who are males, including adopted children, are also eligible for registration. When the Agency began operations in 1950, it was responding to the needs of about 750,000 Palestine refugees. Today, some 5 million Palestine refugees are eligible for UNRWA services."[20]

The actual number of Palestinian refugees is much higher than the figures provided by UNRWA and should include all those forced out or sent to exile by the British from 1917 to 1948; the 5.5 million already counted, a sizeable segment that was away from the country due to work or normal business affairs, and those who were refugees after May 15, 1948. Furthermore, Palestinians who were studying abroad during this period should be included within the refugee category. Including every Palestinian will re-sult in a full accounting of the impact of the British and Zionist settler colonization project on the indigenous population. Here, even as the UN worked to provide support, it actually allowed Israel and its allies to define who is and who is not a Palestinian refugee, thus aiding and abetting the dispossession of the indige-nous population.

Demographics is a central obsession of colonial enterprises and more pernicious in the settler colonial type. Demographics of Palestinian refugees is politicized, contested, and controlled by Israel, as the settler colonial power, that seeks to downplay and erase the issue altogether. Consequently, international actors work to mitigate the impact of the Palestinian refugees' right of return by making sure the demographic limits and definitions are upheld within the UN system. While positive and forceful stands from UN member states are evidenced in the past, nevertheless, the Security Council and the five permanent veto-wielding powers have constantly worked to weaken Palestinian claims, and more so in recent years.

Israeli-initiated ethnic cleansing and a violence campaign transformed the Palestinians into refugees and stateless people. During and in the aftermath of the 1948 Nakba, the Israeli army ethnically cleansed villages and towns, resulting in some 750,000 becoming refugees. In the aftermath of this forced expulsion, the UN General Assembly adopted Resolution 194, which stated in part, "refugees wishing to return to their homes and live at peace with their neighbors should be permitted to do so at the earliest practicable date, and that compensation should be paid for the property of those choosing not to return and for loss of or damage to property which, under principles of international law or equity, should be made good by the Governments or authorities responsible."[21] Needless to say, that Palestinian refugees, their children, and now grandchildren have not been able to return and are still living in refugee camps.

In his book *The Palestine Nakba: Decolonising History, Narrating the Subaltern, Reclaiming Memory*, Professor Nur Masalha maintains that "the Nakba is the turning point in the modern history of Palestine—that year over 500 villages and towns and a whole country and its people disappeared from international maps and dictionaries."[22] Also, Palestinian scholar Omar Dajani situates the meaning of the Nakba for Palestinians and its centrality in identity formation in the following way:

> The nakba is the experience that has perhaps most defined Palestinian history. For the Palestinian, it is not merely a political event—the establishment of the State of Israel on 78 percent of the territory of the Palestine Mandate, or even, primarily a humanitarian one—the creation of the modern

world's most enduring refugee problem. The nakba is of existential significance to Palestinians, representing both the shattering of the Palestinian community in Palestine and the consolidation of a shared national consciousness. In the words of Baruch Kimmerling and Joel Migdal, "Between the last month of 1947 and the first four and a half months of 1948, the Palestinian Arab community would cease to exist as a social and political entity." Hundreds of villages would be destroyed, urban life in Palestine's most populous Arab communities would disappear, and almost a million Palestinians would be rendered homeless and/or stateless. At the same time, the shared events of 1948… brought the Palestinians closer together in terms of their collective consciousness, even as they were physically dispersed all over the Middle East and beyond…Although it bears emphasizing that Palestinian political consciousness predated the nakba by several decades and many Palestinians' sense of connection to their towns and lands extends back many generations further, it seem clear that nothing forged Palestinian identify surely as the loss of Palestine.[23]

It is important to recognize that the Nakba is not a singular event that occurred in the past and is, as such, disconnected from contemporary developments impacting Palestinians inside and outside of Palestine. Palestinians are still experiencing and living the Nakba on a daily basis. In reality, the Nakba, as a multilayered and cross-generational traumatic experience, has not ended, and it continues to unfold daily in Palestine under occupation, as well as across the globe wherever Palestinians are living in the diaspora. The mere fact that the UNHCR has a different category for Palestinians and is not even including them correctly as being the largest or second-largest refugee group in the world, as well as running the refugee percentages accurately, is part of the problem. Palestinians are subject to erasure even when they are supposedly included by the international body that manages their calamity.

Coming back to the Nakba is an important undertaking to understand the full extent of what happened so as to locate the Palestinian refugee experience as the bridge and the crossroads between the colonial and postcolonial eras. On a personal level, my own mother lost her brother during the Nakba as he never returned to the family home in Jerusalem during the war period, and up to this day, no one knows what happened to him. How does one measure this loss and the inability to know what happened and to assess the emptiness felt at the time, as well as the loss for all the family members who have been denied the ability to experience and share life with him. Mourning and closure are difficult without knowing what happened and having a possible grave to visit for prayers. The stories of loss, separation, death, and flight are shared by every Palestinian family either directly impacted or having to respond to the massive influx of refugees streaming into cities and towns in what became known as the West Bank or the Gaza Strip.

My own father could not return to Palestine since he left and could not make it back to attend the funeral of his own father and then, after a period, the passing of his mother as well. On both occasions, my father received people at home in Amman to offer condolences, and up to the day of his passing, he never was able to make it back to Nablus to visit the graves of his own parents and to spend time in the city of his birth, where he spent his early childhood, worked, got married, and had seven children before moving to Jordan, where my brother and I were born.

One can make a direct connection between the Nakba and Palestinian circumstances inside and outside Palestine in such a way as to illustrate how the 1948 catastrophe unfolds daily in small and large ways. Consider that some Palestinians have had to endure multiple dispossessions and expulsions from their homelands and properties—first expelled in the 1948 Nakba, then again from the West Bank in 1967, Jordan in 1970, Lebanon in 1982, Kuwait in 1992, Iraq in 2003, and Syria in 2011 with no end in sight. I actually met a Palestinian in the US who was deemed a refugee seven times starting from 1948 until arriving to the Bay Area after the US invasion of Iraq in 2003. In each case, he had to start life anew with no possessions and only what he and his family could carry.

The specific events that caused each of the above episodes might be seen and considered as separate and distinct from the initial refugee episode. Nonetheless, the key and fundamental issue is that the creation of Israel and the expulsion of the indigenous Palestinians made the population into a stateless people. What the Nakba means for the Palestinians and how to view it correctly is important to Dr. Adel Samara for it emphasizes the ongoing ethnic cleansing that has not stopped since 1948.

> Ethnic cleansing takes place against a nation mainly once and for a certain period of time, but in the case of Palestinian ethnic cleansing it has been carried out till the present time. What they did and still do against us is different. They have never been satisfied with the 1948 occupation and they have been committing ethnic cleansing since then: on a daily basis in Jerusalem, confiscating land in the WB [West Bank], and making Gaza the largest jail in history. What they did and still do is a total destruction of our geography, social fabric, class structure, demography, economy, and even their culture they did not hesitate to steal.[24]

The Nakba is the price of birthing Zionist modernity, and Palestinians are living its consequences. For diehard Zionists, the price was worth it, and the expulsion of the Palestinians was further rationalized by a propaganda campaign. Taking stock of what happened to the Palestinians during the 1948 war—how they became refugees—is more critical and constitutes the first step in beginning to address the ongoing crisis affecting Palestine and the constant efforts to address the issue without digging deeper into how we got to where we are today.

Colonial projects are structured and sustained by violence, both the physical and mental type. Palestinians' experience with colonization has produced different categories and terms of violence, which they had to navigate for survival and to make daily life possible. Palestinians have experienced the status of being refugees, asylum seekers, legal and illegal immigrants, undocumented immigrants, migrants, foreign laborers, migratory temporary workers, and displaced and stateless persons. Immediately after being expelled from Palestine and becoming refugees in 1948, many Palestinians took the initiative to immigrate to Australia, Canada, Europe, Latin America, New Zealand, North America, and parts of Africa, while others sought entry into different countries through the political asylum door.

My own brothers, uncles, aunts, and cousins from my mother's and father's side chose to permanently immigrate or go to the Gulf as migrant workers in search of economic security. My nieces and their husbands have migrated recently from Amman to the Gulf, keeping up an almost similar tradition to Mexican migrant workers coming to the US. The fact that they have landed in professional positions should not veil the larger picture in this migratory process that is connected to the initial displacement of the Palestinians. What is significant is that even as refugees, Palestinians existed under differing structures within each host country, which provided for a complex set of entanglements that were possibly the primary reasons for the push to seek employment or immigration in other countries.

Palestinians who remained in historical Palestine, inside Israel's 1948 area, the West Bank, Gaza Strip, and Golan Heights lived under divergent circumstances. What united the Palestinians then and now is their experience with the 1948 Nakba and the transgenerational trauma and erasure. Palestinians who remained in the newly emerged State of Israel were given Israeli citizenship[25] and put under martial law from 1948 until 1966, while the state set up a separate classification system for the population. For Israel, and as a matter of state policy, there was no such category as Palestinians in the state, rather Arabs, Druze, and Bedouins, with each classified group subject to differing structures of erasure and exclusion within the state apparatus. "The Palestinians in Israel are occupied citizens, and the residents of the Occupied Territories are unrecognized citizens. Whether or not the legal line survives may be immaterial, however, as the effect is likely to be the same—the continuing subordination of the Palestinians."[26]

The absence of formal equality in Israeli basic law and the divergent classification for Palestinians were complemented by facially neutral discrimination. In Israeli society, the criterion of military service has been used as a pretext to discriminate against Palestinian citizens, even though they are prohibited from serving and are deemed by the state as an internal security threat. Military service is used by the Israeli government to influence housing and employment decisions, which adversely affects "the Arab" citizens of the state.

In crucial challenges to citizenship status, the Israeli Supreme Court has failed to protect the equal right to citizenship and constantly sides with the state discriminatory policies. In 2006 and 2012, the Israeli Supreme Court ruled in favor of a Knesset law, which prohibits the naturalization of spouses of Palestinian citizens if they are from the West Bank, Gaza Strip, or adjacent Arab countries. The court arguments used national security pretext for the ruling; however, it has in fact upheld the law's settler colonial demographic rationale and thus legitimated the depiction of the Palestinian minority as a demographic threat, a favorite discourse for many politicians and settlers in Israel.

After the 1948 war, Palestinians in the West Bank came under Jordanian jurisdiction and were granted citizenship and passports since the area was "legally" incorporated into Jordan.[27] At the time, Palestinian political leaders gathered in Gaza and took the step of declaring independence in 1948, but Jordan worked with West Bank dignitaries and, coupled with a back-channel communication with Zionist leaders, ensured that an independent state of Palestine was not born.[28] What happened to the Palestinians in 1948 is a multidimensional and layered tragedy, which includes the participation of all the major powers (Australia, Britain, Canada, France, Russia, the United States, and other European states), the Zionist movement, neighboring Arab states, and Palestinian elites or the prominent families that opted to strike their own narrow deals to the detriment of everyone else.[29]

Jordan's machination to prevent a Palestinian state from emerging did not translate into immediate limits imposed on Palestinian refugees in Jordan, which did occur at a later point. The granting of full citizenship to Palestinian refugees was a very important step that possibly, and from a long historical lens, provided the Palestinians the needed flexibility to build a bridge toward affirming Palestinian identity in the refugee camps and exile. Jordan, a state that had just recently come into existence and was sparsely populated with sizable nomadic tribes, benefited from the mass influx of Palestinian refugees, who were educated, skilled in business and farming, and well-travelled in the region. Over a short period of time, Jordan became a state with a sizable population, playing a central role in global affairs, not to mention receiving direct international aid for accepting and "settling" Palestinian refugees on its land.

For Palestinians, the Jordanian citizenship was the needed instrument to unshackle them and provide some avenues to keep Palestine's imposed erasure from being totally successful. Furthermore, Palestinians arriving in Jordan wasted little time in setting up their own businesses, filling the professional class ranks, and quickly opening academic institutions that, in a short period, became a destination for students from across the Arab and Muslim world. This does not imply or mean that successive Jordanian governments did not act to curtail and limit Palestinian political aspirations, which they did often in coordination with the Israeli, British, and American leadership.

The fact that Jordan was created as a buffer state and itself was part of British plans in the region does not imply that everything pertaining to Palestinians in Jordan was negative. The Jordanian citizenship and passport allowed freedom of movement, was the vehicle for many Palestinians to rebuild a solid financial foundation after the Nakba, and facilitated travel abroad for education and employment, which collectively benefited the community.

Certainly, the Jordanian government worked hard to curtail, and at times strangle, Palestinians' political, social, and cultural expressions, and more so after the emergence of the Palestine Liberation Organization (PLO). The Jordanian government considered Palestinian activism and organization a threat to the country, undermining the cohesion of the nascent national identity. Palestinian refugees constituted 65 to 70 percent of Jordan's population and created, at least in the early period and all the way up to the early 1980s, a fractured national identity when it came to what needed to be done for Palestine. The tensions in Jordan boiled over in the early 1970s, and a civil war erupted in the country, set off by the Popular Front for the Liberation of Palestine (PFLP) hijacking five planes and blowing them up in two separate locations in Jordan.[30] The PFLP action was the spark to a conflict that was already years in the making.

From the early 1950s, King Hussein wanted to maintain a balance between his behind-the-scenes relations with Israel and the public commitment to support the Palestinians' right of return and resistance. As the PLO began to gain standing in the refugee camps and a more revolutionary and assertive generation emerged, the ability of King Hussein to maintain this balance was coming under pressure. After the 1967 resounding defeat on the battlefield, Palestinians under the leadership of the PLO and supported by many began to take part in the War of Attrition, crossing into the newly occupied areas to conduct attacks. During the immediate aftermath of the 1967 war, the PLO launched raids from Egypt, Jordan, and Lebanon, which resulted in massive strikes by Israel.

It is certain that King Hussein did not want to enter into the 1967 war, and afterward wanted to stop the Palestinians from attacking Israel from Jordanian territory and sneaking into the West Bank through the border, which he wanted to keep calm. Here, one must know that King Hussein had maintained secret, cordial relations with Israel through the 1950s and 1960s. But he had to balance his interests in preserving peace with Israel against a restless and increasingly radicalized Palestinian and Jordanian population, which was threatening his throne.

Under the PLO leadership, Palestinian refugees felt empowered and began to take more assertive, and at times antagonistic, attitudes toward the Jordanian government and those who were connected to it. Certainly the Jordanian intelligence services had a hand in fomenting some of these emerging tensions, but the Palestinians were not without blame, as they began to operate a state within a state in the hope of using Jordan as a staging ground to liberate Palestine.

In summer 1970, tensions boiled over into an armed confrontation, coming close to involving both Syria and Israel.[31] Archives also provide evidence of discussions in the US on getting Israeli assistance in the conflict and the possibility of sending American troops to support King Hussein against the PLO.[32] For its part, Syria wanted to enter the fight on the side of the Palestinian factions connected to it, while Israel communicated with King Hussein, the US, and Saudi Arabia that they would be ready to defend and protect the kingdom's sovereignty if Syrian troops continued their move southward. Consequently, Syrian troops withdrew under threat from the Israeli air force bombardment if they continued moving southward, which gave the Jordanian military and special forces time to regroup and push to evict the PLO and all

Palestinian forces from the country.

The 1970 civil war in Jordan became known as the Black September and to a large extent accelerated the Lebanese civil war since most of the Palestinians who left Jordan ended up in Lebanon. Palestinian-Jordanian, or PLO-Jordanian, relations and conflicts are not the purpose of this book, which can't give it the needed attention. But the previous discussion is needed to provide some context to the later examinations of the circumstances confronting the refugees in the country.

I did not intend to leave the discussion on Palestinian refugees in Jordan on a negative note, implying that nothing else defined the relationship. Actually, much more can and should be said about the strong bonds and historical relations that were forged in the region over generations. Even speaking of forging relationships in this context is problematic since both Jordanians and Palestinians have inhabited and emerged from the same cultural, historical, and tribal lineages that were only cut off or separated by means of British and French colonial designs. All these areas are known in Arab history as Bilad al-Sham ("al-Sham" being the name given to Damascus, but it refers to everything to the north of the Arabian Peninsula). The British drew the borders that presently divide Jordan from Palestine and were done so arbitrarily and with the involvement of the World Zionist Organization, not the Palestinians or Jordanians themselves. Colonial legacies are present in the drawing of all the maps in the southern hemisphere, which managed to divide tribes and communities and embed the ongoing conflicts in these regions.

Consequently, and on the positive end of relations, Jordanian tribes and prominent families in Al-Salt, Irbid, Al-Karak, and Tafilah had long-standing education, marriage, business, religious, and cultural relations with all the cities and towns of Palestine, which fostered a deep solidarity reservoir. Without exception, all prominent families (Christian and Muslim) in Jordan's cities sent their kids to schools in Palestine before 1948 and even afterward because of the well-established and strongly developed academic infrastructure in the country going back centuries. Christian communities in Jordan were an extension of, and institutionally linked to, Palestine because most of the clergy either got trained in Palestine or spent a considerable number of years in the country before going back to their churches on the eastern side of the Jordan River. Before the arrival of the British and Zionists, one can hardly find a Jordanian family, tribe, or business enterprise that did not have long-standing relations with its counterpart in Palestine.

These were communities that lived, worked, worshiped, and built civilizations together. Colonization is a past crime that produces death and destruction in the present and, if not epistemically undone, will continue to torment humanity. Palestine, Jordan, Syria, and Lebanon are a single geographical, cultural, tribal, economic, and religious unit (ancient Jews that are not Zionist, Christian, and Muslim communities) with internal diversities and complexities born over generations of living, flourishing, and struggling together. The crime of colonization and colonial modernity is that it managed to epistemically seal the vistas of future horizons and possibilities that would have been correctly rooted in a collectively stitched past.

Today, we see Jordan, Syria, Lebanon, and Palestine, and we see ourselves through the colonial lens and the constructed other formed within ourselves. The Jordanian population across the country, like Palestinians, contributed to the Palestine struggle, offering blood and treasure for the resistance movement. Furthermore, Jordanian civilian volunteers and regular army personnel participated in the 1948 and 1967 resistance and war efforts, which created a bond at the popular and societal levels forged in the trenches. I view what happened in Jordan through the imprints of colonization, and the postcolonial era, which gave rise to it. This colonial imprint set in motion tidal waves of conflicts and contestations, while the excolonial powers that constructed this mess gaze from a distance waiting to seize the opportunity to come back as mediators, diplomatic heroes, business consultants, and, for sure, arms dealers to all parties to help in the "development" and regional "stability" process.

Another area that the 1948 Palestinian refugees moved to is Gaza, which is one of the oldest port cities in the region with the name appearing in old Egyptian and biblical texts. Following the 1948 Nakba, the Gaza Strip came under Egyptian rule, which kept it as a separate territory governed by Egypt but not part of it. At the time, Egypt wanted to maintain Palestine's territorial integrity while controlling the increasingly restless refugee population that was intending to return to their homes and lands across the border. Gaza's population, according to the 1922 British Mandate authorities' census, stood at 17,480 residents, consisting of 16,722 Muslims, 54 Jews, and 701 Christians. As of 2020, the Central Intelligence Agency World Factbook estimates Gaza's population to be around 1,918,221 inhabitants. In reality, around 90 percent of Gaza's current population are refugees that made their way to the narrow Strip in the aftermath of the 1948 Nakba and are included in the UNRWA's total figures.

The conditions of the Palestinian refugees who ended up in Gaza are the direst and compounded of all. For starters, Gaza's refugee population is stateless and lacks all formal travel documents to allow any and all to move from the area. Between 1948 and 1967, Gaza was under direct Egyptian rule, meaning the inhabitants were subject to the rules and regulations set in place by the Egyptian government. In the aftermath of the 1967 war, Gaza came under direct Israeli control and was subject to military occupation orders, not a civilian administration. The population was managed through a set of issued military orders, and a military tribunal system was set in place by the Israeli army to administer the Gaza Strip. Gaza's Palestinians are not able to travel and move outside of the Strip and can only do so through documents and a permit process that is highly regulated by the Israeli and Egyptian governments.

Gaza has experienced and witnessed the brunt of Israeli military brutality, and what the population has been put through constitutes war crimes. Immediately after the 1948 Nakba, Israel made it a point to inflict pain and torment on Gaza's refugee population in the hope that it would dissuade them from attempting to cross the border to return to their homes and lands and to give up resisting the newly built reality. For Gaza's population, the War of Attrition began immediately after the 1948 Nakba and witnessed successive Israeli air force bombing campaigns against the refugee population and in one of the most densely populated areas in the world. When Israel took over the Gaza Strip in 1967, it pursued a violent and repressive pacification campaign, which killed and imprisoned people and destroyed whatever vestiges of normal existence the Palestinian refugees were able to assemble while in exile.

In addition to the pacification campaign, the Israeli government issued building permits to settlers, who claimed some of the best agriculture lands and siphoned the underground water causing a collapse in the water table in the Gaza Strip. The violence on settlers was nonstop, protected by the military and the military court in case of any possible conflict. Because of this structured and protected settler violence, which took many shapes, it took only one more incident—an Israeli military jeep running over and killing four Palestinians in the Gaza Strip—to be the needed spark for the December 9, 1987, Intifadah (Uprising) to explode. The Intifadah brought a stark reality and an end to the Israeli dream of a successful pacification, putting an end to the Palestinian struggle through brute force, intelligence gathering with informants, and strategic settlements throughout to prevent continuity of territory and movement. Israel's control and system of governance collapsed and with it the idea that Palestinians could be wished out of existence unilaterally.

The birth of the Oslo process (to be discussed more later on) and the beginning of the negotiations to end the Israeli occupation were forced on the table by the Palestinians, not due to any grand gesture by Israel or its desire to arrive at a peace treaty. Gaza's Intifadah, which was joined by everyone in the West Bank, forced Israel into accepting the reality that Palestinians had put an end to and limits on its power and forced it to change the strategic math on the ground.

The signing of the Oslo Agreement in 1993 led to the creation of the Palestinian Authority and set in motion a peace process toward a final agreement on all the critical issues separating the two sides. On November 4, 1995, and after a campaign rally, Yigal Amir, an Israeli right-wing violent extremist, managed to assassinate the then prime minister Yitzhak Rabin because he signed the Oslo Agreement with the PLO. Some felt that Likud party leader Benjamin Netanyahu, who was a candidate for the prime minister position, fanned the flames of opposition to the Oslo Agreement, which ended with the assassination.[34] The events of 1995 followed the February 25, 1994, Baruch Goldstein's terrorist attack on the Ibrahim mosque al-Khalil (Hebron) during the predawn prayers in the month of Ramadan, killing twenty-nine worshippers and wounding one hundred and twenty-five others in an attempt to bring an end to the peace process.[35] Amir's assassination of Rabin followed by Netanyahu's winning of the Israeli election brought a complete stop to the Oslo process and an effort to reverse whatever modest steps had been taken in the past.

On September 28, 2000, in a provocative act, the Israeli Likud leader Ariel Sharon "visited" the Al-Aqsa mosque area protected by some one thousand military police personnel. Palestinians protested during the visit, and the next day, the whole West Bank and Gaza Strip erupted after the weekly Friday prayers into what became known as Al-Aqsa Intifadah. Israel's settlement building and increased confiscation of land from Palestinians, coupled with a dead-end negotiation cycle, contributed to the blowup of Al-Aqsa Intifadah, which lasted until 2005. Ending the Intifadah was followed by the Israeli unilateral disengagement from the

Gaza Strip and the withdrawal of settlements and troops from the area. Israeli withdrawal without negotiations or an agreement kept the Gaza Strip in a legal no-man's-land and effectively "free" in a fully occupied territory, or an open-air prison.

In 2006, the Bush administration's effort to wish away the erroneous claim of weapons of mass destruction behind the 2003 invasion of Iraq shifted to promoting democracy as the cause, and the Palestinian elections would be the test case for it.[36] Let's say that the planned election outcome never materialized, and Hamas, the Islamic resistance movement inside the Occupied Territories and Gaza, won almost two-thirds of the Palestinian parliament seats and the right to form a government and name a prime minister. As a way to contain the policy disaster, Egypt, European states, Israel, Jordan, the Palestinian Authority, Saudi Arabia, the United Arab Emirates, and the US all used their powers to isolate and pressure the newly elected Palestinian Hamas leaders to accept Oslo's terms and the signed agreement under its framework. This was asked of the Palestinians at a time when the Israeli leadership themselves had totally rejected the terms of the Oslo Agreement and continued to build settlements and confiscate lands in the Occupied Territories. Tensions between Fatah (the Palestinian Authority and the PLO's largest faction) and Hamas boiled over, which ended in the Gaza Strip being governed by a Hamas-led government while Fatah laid claim to the West Bank. Thus, the Palestinian body politic was fractured into two separate and antagonistic governing entities claiming legitimacy to represent and speak for the Palestinians.

In 2007, Israel, in cooperation with the US, Europe, the Palestinian Authority, and other Arab states, imposed a total land, naval, and air siege on Gaza, which limited the amount food, fuel, and medicine entering the Strip. The siege was followed by at least four major Israeli military assaults on the Gaza Strip, killing and maiming thousands and destroying the infrastructure, including hospitals, schools, homes, and private businesses. In 2014, the Israel government carried out a massive military attack on the Gaza Strip, code named "Protective Edge," which killed 2,205 Palestinians, 71 Israelis (including 66 soldiers) and one foreign national in Israel.[37] The war lasted fifty days and came to an end after a ceasefire was negotiated through Egypt's involvement on August 26, 2014.

After the war, Amnesty International issued a report charging Israel with actions that constituted a major breach of international law and committing war crimes.[38] "The report exposes a pattern of attacks on civilian homes by Israeli forces, which have shown a shocking disregard for the lives of Palestinian civilians, who were given no warning and had no chance to flee," said Philip Luther, Amnesty's director for the Middle East and North Africa.[39] It is important to quote part of Amnesty International's executive summary to drive the point home on what the Gaza Strip faced:

> There is overwhelming evidence that Israeli forces committed disproportionate, or otherwise indiscriminate, attacks which killed scores of civilians in their homes, on the streets and in vehicles and injured many more, including by repeatedly firing artillery and other imprecise explosive weapons in densely populated civilian areas during the attacks on Rafah between 1 and 4 August. In some cases, there are indications that they directly fired at and killed civilians, including some who were fleeing.

> Public statements made by Israeli army commanders and soldiers after the conflict provide compelling reasons to conclude that some attacks that killed civilians and destroyed homes and property may have been intentionally carried out and motivated by a desire for revenge, to teach a lesson to, or to punish the population of Rafah for the capture of Lieutenant Goldin.

There is consequently strong evidence that many such attacks in Rafah between 1 and 4 August were serious violations of international humanitarian law and constituted grave breaches of the Fourth Geneva Convention or other war crimes.

The UN Independent Commission of Inquiry on the 2014 Gaza Conflict examined the Israeli army attack on Rafah on 1 August and also raised serious concerns about the conformity of the Israeli army actions on that day with international law. The Commission investigated attacks it considered disproportionate or otherwise indiscriminate and found that in some cases they might amount to war crimes. The Commission also concluded that the Israeli army did not appear to have taken precautions to verify that targets of attacks were lawful military objectives and to choose the weapons which could avoid or minimize civilian casualties and destruction to civilian structures.

Israeli army commanders and officers can operate in confidence that they are unlikely to be held accountable for violations of international law due to the pervasive climate of impunity that has existed for decades. This is due, in large part, to the lack of independent, impartial and effective investigations. Despite the massive toll that Operation Protective Edge had on civilians in Gaza, almost one year after the conflict, military prosecutors have indicted only three soldiers for one incident of looting. A significant number of cases have been closed on the basis that no crimes were committed (this is the case in the majority of such decisions) or that there was insufficient evidence to indict.

With regard to Israeli army operations in Rafah between 1 and 4 August, the Israeli authorities have failed to conduct genuine, effective, and prompt investigations into any of the allegations of serious violations of international humanitarian law documented in this report, let alone prosecute individuals, including commanders and civilian superiors, suspected of committing or ordering related crimes under international law. They have failed to ensure that victims have effective access to justice, or to provide them with full and prompt reparation, including restitution, compensation, rehabilitation, satisfaction and guarantees of non-repetition. The events need to be independently and impartially investigated. Amnesty International's view is that no official body capable of conducting such investigations currently exists in Israel.

It is therefore calling on the Israeli authorities to co-operate fully with the ongoing preliminary examination by the Prosecutor of the International Criminal Court into the situation in the Occupied Palestinian Territories and any future investigations or prosecutions; to reform their domestic mechanisms for investigating allegations of violations of international humanitarian law to ensure that it is independent, effective, prompt and transparent; to allow human rights organizations access to Gaza to investigate suspected violations of international law by all parties to the conflict; and to immediately and fully lift the blockade imposed on Gaza since 2007.[40]

The Palestinian refugees in Gaza face a daunting task and exist under the most extreme political, social, economic, and medical circumstances that call for urgent attention. I can write a whole book on what Gaza faces and how the world has allowed a refugee population to be punished, bullied, and taunted by Israel and its military power, aided and supported by Western and increasingly some Arab states. The UN Charter, the Universal Declaration of Human Rights, the Fourth Geneva Convention, and a host of other international treaties are silenced when it comes to the Gaza Strip and the Palestinians in general.

Since March 2018, Palestinians in Gaza have been organizing a right of return march, which is focused on the border that separates them from their homes and lands, which Israel stole by declaring them to be absentee properties to be confiscated by the state. Crimes against humanity, war crimes, and ethnic cleansing actions don't have a statute of limitation, and the time to begin addressing their circumstances is as needed today as it should have been back in 1948. Palestinians in Gaza have no protection. The world community watches from a distance and the two million inside the Strip are subject to a total siege by Israel, a member of the UN, who is constantly testing weapons and killing civilians with no restraint. What makes this possible is that Israel is a settler colonial project that was foisted on the Palestinians and continues to be nurtured by the major powers!

Moving from the discussion on the Gaza Strip to focus on another group of Palestinian refugees who made it to Lebanon offers another dimension of the multifaceted crisis to explore. Palestinians, who escaped to Lebanon, ended up in refugee camps under UNRWA supervision but lived in the country without citizenship. Lebanon's postcolonial political, religious, and cultural fragmentation played a critical role in the status of Palestinians in-country and followed the ebb and flow of internal development. Palestinian refugees, who were predominantly Sunni Muslim, impacted the population's balance between Christian, Shia, Druze, and the Sunni Lebanese communities and challenged the confessional basis of the French-constructed political structure.

The weakness of the Lebanese central government allowed the newly arriving Palestinian refugees to set up their own autonomous political, economic, social, and military resistance infrastructure. Palestinians in Lebanon functioned as a state within a state, which created all types of legitimate concerns and tensions from all players inside the country. Palestinians, correctly, conceived of themselves as a refugee population that was in the middle of a liberation struggle to gain back their homeland, which was just a few miles away from their current camps. From the Lebanese perspective (not all internal forces' views were identical), the Palestinian refugees were a population that had disrupted the balance of a state that has just recently emerged from French colonization and taxed the limited resources of the country. Lebanese political, religious, and cultural factions felt and dealt with the impact differently, and each made its own cost-benefit analysis on the Palestinian cause and refugees. At the same time, one has to take into account the emergent Arab nationalist movement that has aligned itself strongly with the Palestinian refugees and the struggle for liberation.

From 1948 up to the present, Lebanon was the key arena for all regional and global players to settle their local and international disputes by engaging with the Palestinian cause and refugees. Lebanon's central government weakness and dependence on Arab and international funding meant that internal chaos and fragmentation was set by design, allowing all political players to strike their own funding deals and secure a foothold in this complex postcolonial state.

In the 1960s and 1970s, the PLO and its many factions were the uncontested power in Lebanon and acted as political brokers in the country. However, particularly following the 1970s Black September civil war in Jordan, Palestinian refugees and the PLO's leadership in Lebanon underestimated the forces arrayed against them internally and externally, and the wide-open political arena was an instrument to drive a dagger into the Palestinian cause and the strategies to gain the homeland back. The more Palestinians gained a foothold in Lebanon, the more resentment, antagonism, and enemies coalesced in opposition. By the mid-1970s, when the PLO was at the height of its power, the Lebanese civil war erupted, and by the time it concluded, the Palestinians were its biggest victims, with massacres, destruction, and a new stage of exile and a move to a new refuge.

The full extent of what happened to the Palestinians in Lebanon still needs to be researched and documented, as only some limited, yet valuable, work has been done on it. Palestinian refugees in Lebanon created a Palestinian state in exile, with a functioning political administration, media outfit, global financial investments, health care, and an educational and social services infrastructure, as well as a robust military research, development, and training program. However, the internal failures of leadership and external designs converged to destroy what was built with the blood and sweat of hundreds of thousands across the globe.

Refugees getting entangled in the internal political dynamics of host countries is not new, nor is the attention or often the demonization of their presence by figures seeking to climb into higher leadership positions. Palestinian refugees' role and entanglements in Lebanon is a unique affair, including all the internal and external players and interests that converged to make the country an arena for settling political accounts that had nothing to do with the Lebanese, the Palestinians, or the desire to assist in the liberation of Palestine for that matter.

As the exile of Palestinian refugees in Egypt, Jordan, Lebanon, and Syria dragged on, the door opened for them to become skilled and professional migrant workers in Algeria, Bahrain, Kuwait, Libya, Oman, Qatar, Saudi Arabia, and the United Arab Emirates. Others opted to immigrate to various regions in Australia, Canada, Central America, Europe, South America, and the United States, as well as the oil producing sub-Saharan African states. A darker side of the immigration process was the role played by the US and Western states in making it easier for Palestinians to get the needed immigration papers and visa approvals to both leave historical Palestine after the 1948 and 1967 wars and avoid recruitment in the refugee camps. Here, the context of facilitation by Western states was meant to ease the pressure on Israel, as demands of the right of return and political mobilization in support of Palestinians were becoming difficult to manage during the Cold War period and the emergence of the Non-Aligned Movement.

Educated Palestinian refugees were prized by the Gulf states, and an open-door recruitment policy was in effect. Indeed, the massive oil industry revenues flooded the Gulf countries and with it the desire to develop the infrastructure and provide education, health care, and services to their emerging urbanized societies. In a short span of time, Palestinian migrant workers became the backbone for building the institutional capacities across the Gulf by being the managers of the emerging enterprises and newly formed projects. From the early 1950s to the early 1990s, professional Palestinian migrant workers were everywhere in the Gulf and constituted the upper managerial ranks in the private and public sectors. Here, the presence of Palestinian workers and migrants in the Gulf provided much-needed financial remittances for their families and relatives in refugee camps in Jordan, Lebanon, Syria, the West Bank and Gaza Strip. The financial strength of the professional class in the Gulf provided the economic foundation and stability for the refugee camps, which helped propel education, development, and businesses in Jordan, Lebanon, the West Bank and Gaza Strip. Remittances from the Gulf and North Africa contributed to funding the higher educational pursuits of Palestinians in the refugee camps, and the support was in the form of numerous scholarships that sprung up to sponsor students to study abroad.

At the same time, the Cold War competition had also opened the gates for recruiting Palestinian refugees into the Eastern Bloc countries, and a large number made their way to universities in Bulgaria, China, Czechoslovakia, East Germany, Ethiopia, Hungary, Poland, Romania, and the Soviet Union. As a matter of fact, at the same time that I was applying to US colleges, I was awarded a full science scholarship by the USSR but opted to enter Yarmouk University in Jordan while waiting for responses from the

US universities. The decision not to take the USSR scholarship had more to do with the need to spend two years and possibly more learning Russian before I was able to start my actual studies. Jordan's second language is English, due to being part of the British colonial possession, which made pursuing a US education a better choice for me.

Palestinian refugees made their way to every corner of the world and carried with them the scars of conflict, the memories of their homeland, and the aspirations of one day returning to Palestine. The expulsion and forceful displacement from Palestine had transformed Palestinians into a global refugee population, who were not only displaced and residing in close proximity to their land but spread all over the world.

Examples of Palestinian refugees and global diaspora are too numerous to include in this chapter. However, two unique examples illustrate this development: the communities in Chile and those in the US. I will focus on Chile first then cover the Palestinians in the US.

The distance between Palestine and Chile is approximately 8,325 miles—not the farthest but it does give you an idea on how far Palestinians travelled to seek refuge and develop a diaspora community in the country. Precisely, Chile, as a choice destination, emerged in the late nineteenth and early part of the twentieth centuries because of the instability in the Ottoman territories, which intensified after the state introduced conscription laws, which included the Christian population in the Arab world. The Ottoman policy caused a flight out of Palestine, Lebanon, and Syria. Initially, the numbers were not that large, but it opened the door for Christian Palestinian migrations out and the start of small communities in South, Central and North America.

The arriving Palestinians and Lebanese had Ottoman travel papers and were derogatorily referred to as "Turks," a usage that was similar to Europe's negative deployment of the term to anyone arriving from the Ottoman territories, including those that happened to be Christians. Using "Turk," or racializing the term with a heavy dose of negativity, has had a long-standing history within European usage, and it was only after World War II that it receded into the background. The arrival of a mainly Christian Palestinian population did not alter being othered on the basis of a supposed "Turkish" identity, and it took a while for their integration into the Chilean society. In her article, Luna Patricia quotes Maurice Khamis, president of the Chilean-Palestinian community, stating that "Palestinians have lived in Chile for some five generations, arriving in the late 19th century in search of better economic opportunities when the territories in the Middle East were still under Ottoman rule."[41]

Immediately after World War I, Palestine came under British rule, which permitted Zionist settlers to arrive in Palestine, purchase land, and begin the process of building a settler colonial state. Palestinians resisted British rule from the start, but some began to read the writing on the wall and explored the already opened paths to immigrate to the US, Europe, and South America, with Chile becoming a major destination. Estimates of the Palestinian Chilean population range from four hundred thousand to upward of a half a million people in a country with eighteen million inhabitants. The community is 80 to 90 percent Christian, and many originated from the Jerusalem-area triangle of Bethlehem, Beit Jalla and Beir Sahour, as well as from Nazareth.

After the 1948 and 1967 wars, another group of Palestinians made their way to Chile and other parts of the world. Interestingly, even after both the Lebanese civil war and Iraq's invasion of Kuwait, which witnessed the expulsion of Palestinians in the aftermath, a number of those who stuck around in the Empty Quarter ended up making their way to Chile and countries in the region. Palestinian immigrants and refugees are present in Argentina, Bolivia, Brazil, Colombia, Ecuador, El Salvador, Guatemala, Honduras, Mexico, Nicaragua, Panama, Peru, and Venezuela, and increasingly are organized and connected within a regional framework of coordination.[42]

The Palestinian immigrants' narrative in Chile is similar to that of other arrivals in the US but less so in Europe with minor exceptions. Just like in the US, where early Arab and Muslim immigrants and refugees settled in the Eastern Seaboard and worked as street peddlers and handymen, the same is documented for those who made it to Chile and Latin America. Because of their heavy emphasis on education and focus on owning their own businesses, a trait they brought with them from Palestine, the Palestinians in Chile moved up in society and began to dominate or play a major role in the textile, banking, and finance industries, as well as having an extensive presence in all professional fields.

Their economic and professional strength has been translated into political power, with Palestinians comprising up to 10 percent of the Chilean legislature and having brought their influence on the recognition of Palestine's statehood in 2011. "The Palestinian community in Chile has a very long history, and the local community in Santiago is especially well established, so these elements alone mean that Palestinian Chileans stand out, not only in Chile, but also internationally," explains Siri Schwabe, an anthropologist from Stockholm University studying the Palestinian diaspora in Santiago.[43]

Economics, politics, and seats in the legislature are important indicators. Nevertheless, for the Chilestinians, or Palestinians of Chile, their pride and connection to Palestine is reflected in the expressed support for their own soccer team, Club Deportivo Palestino, which plays in the professional league and is based in Santiago, Chile. According to the records, the club was established in 1920, joined the Chilean first division in 1952, and won the championship for the first time in 1955. The club's jersey has the Palestinian flag colors, and it is a must-have for fans of the club or any Palestinian visitor to the country. It is not surprising to run into Palestinians in the US who actually migrated from Palestine to Chile or El Salvador before making their way to Arizona, California, or Texas during the 1980s civil wars in the region.

Palestinians living in the US provide yet another case of a diaspora community straddling the line between the refugee and immigrant status. Similar to the immigration link to Chile, Palestinian Christians from Palestine, Lebanon, and Syria made their way to the US and early on were assisted in the process by a network of missionary schools that sprung up in the region starting in the 1830s. What started with a trickle of students and few families pursuing higher education in the midnineteenth century became a steady flow of immigrants then refugees making their way to the US.

The political, economic, and social instability in the Ottoman territories led to the collapse of security conditions and regional competition for control with the central government. Tensions between the central Ottoman authority in Istanbul and the provinces made individual lives difficult, and demands for higher taxation as well as military conscription became untenable for the population. At the same time, the colonial powers pushed further to accelerate the dissolution and fragmentation of the Ottoman state, resulting in an outflow of immigrants seeking economic opportunity and better living conditions initially, followed by refugees after World War I.

Early arrivals settled on the Eastern Seaboard and worked as street peddlers, kitchen help, and in a host of other jobs. At a later point, the newly arriving Palestinians began to venture more into the Midwest as jobs became plentiful in the industrial and manufacturing regions. Thus, we can find Palestinian communities emerging in Chicago, Cleveland, Dearborn, Kansas, New Jersey, Toledo, and other areas throughout the East Coast and Midwest. The early communities were mostly Christians along with a number of Muslims making their way to the US after hearing the news about the economic success of their neighbors who made it "big" in America. Immigrant narratives tended to give a rosy picture of their circumstances, despite being dishwashers or street sellers, because they wanted their families back home to feel at ease and not worry about their state of survival thousands of miles away. The letters sent back home created the dream of coming to America, working for a few years, sending money home to improve the financial situation of the family, and then making it back as a success.

Muslims joined their Palestinian Christian neighbors in America, which accelerated in the 1930s after the 1936–39 revolt, and another sizable segment arrived following the 1948 and 1967 wars. Furthermore, Palestinians, Arabs, and Muslims benefited from the 1965 Immigration Reform Act, which opened the door for foreign student recruitment and admission to US universities. Here, the migration of Palestinians from the refugee camps in Jordan, Lebanon, and the West Bank and Gaza to the Gulf made it possible for them to sponsor the education of their own kids or their relatives' kids to study abroad in the US. It is common to see a Palestinian among the professional ranks in the US, be they engineers, doctors, computer scientists, or professors at American universities.

Palestinians in the US straddle the line between refugee and immigrant status due to the circumstances governing Palestine itself, the migrant worker status in the Gulf, regional conflicts, and the path they took to make it into the country. Prior to 1948, the majority of Palestinians who arrived came as immigrants seeking economic opportunities, while a smaller segment left Palestine due to the intensification of British oppression in the 1936–39 period. Those Palestinians arriving after the 1948 and 1967 wars were mostly refugees, who managed to land an immigration or refugee settlement visa to the US after spending time under Israeli occupation or in refugee camps across the region. Also, Palestinians arrived in the US after every conflict or war in the Middle East. Thus, the Lebanese civil war, Iraq's invasion of Kuwait, the US invasion of Iraq, Syria's civil war, the 2011 Egyptian Revolution, and Libya's ongoing civil war all resulted in another cycle of resettlement, refuge, and immigration for some Palestinians.

Palestinian refugees and migrant workers are present in every

Arab country and set at the intersection of local-global coloni-al-postcolonial relations with the superpowers involved. This fact has often translated into being at the forefront of all conflicts, even when those involved are not a party to it. Whenever Arab-Arab or internal civil war conflicts erupted, the Palestinians present in each of the states were called upon and put at the center of the clashes with devastating consequences. Palestinian refugees and the PLO leadership's heavy dependence on Arab, Muslim, and in-ternational funding sources placed all Palestinians as a bargain-ing chip in all emerging conflicts. Adding to the calamity is the PLO's propensity to get itself in the middle of fights that end up with disastrous consequences for Palestinians. Being a stateless and internationally dependent population, the Palestinian refu-gees and migrant workers are the easiest parts to blame and use as pawns in Arab-Arab conflicts all while dressing it up as a defense or steadfastness on behalf of Palestine.

Palestinians are found all over the US, and almost every major city has a functioning community. Estimates of the numbers vary, but it would not be a stretch to put it at 1.2 to 1.5 million Palestin-ians living in the US. The highest concentration can be found in Chicago and its suburbs, Illinois; in Dearborn, Michigan; in Los Angeles, Sacramento, San Diego, San Francisco, and Santa Clara, California; in Dallas and Houston, Texas; in Paterson and other cities in New Jersey; in Washington, D.C.; in Baltimore and the region, Maryland; in Tampa and other areas in Florida; in North and South Carolina; in Milwaukee, Wisconsin; in New York City, New York; in smaller communities in Phoenix, Arizona; in small areas of Las Vegas, Nevada; and in cities in Atlanta, Minnesota, Ohio, and Seattle. This list is not intended to be exhaustive or to cover every city and town in the US; however, it does point to the presence of Palestinians all across the country with a number of areas having a sizable and very much visible presence.

Because of the close relationship between the US and Israel, Palestinians in the US faced, and continue to face, high levels of surveillance and targeting. The history of such targeting extends all the way back to the 1960s and up to the present context of the Patriot Act and war on terrorism. Even before the events of September 11, 2001 (9/11), Palestinian activists and community organizers were subject to harassment and a well-designed federal strategy to entangle them in legal proceedings, an effort dating back to the Reagan administration.

One of the most famous and longest-running cases involved the arrest and prosecution of the LA 8, a group of seven Palestinians and a Kenyan charged at the time with supporting terrorism for no reason other than passing around copies of *al-Hadaf* magazine, the PFLP publication, in community gatherings. The case lasted from 1987 until 2007, a twenty-year ordeal that effectively criminalized advocacy for Palestine in the US and targeted Arab Americans based on constitutionally protected political activities.[44] Here, the targeting of activists working on Palestine predates 9/11 by decades, and cases are documented going back to the early1960s that witnessed the rise of the PLO around the globe. Tracing the history, targeting, and structural defamation of Palestinians and pro-Palestine activists in the US is an important subject for another time as it falls outside the scope of this book.[45]

No case represents the intrusion, criminalization, and targeting of Palestinians better than the government's systematic and successful targeting of Professor Sami Al-Arian. The targeting of Al-Arian began before 9/11 but takes shape and moves into legal action after the 9/11 terrorist attacks. More importantly, the case represents the intersectionality of the war on terrorism and the targeting of pro-Palestine activists and institutions in the US. It also led to imprisonments of the leadership and the shuttering of the Holy Land Foundation,[46] a critical humanitarian institution dedicated to providing relief for orphans and the poor inside the Palestinian Occupied Territories and refugee camps across the Middle East.

Professor Al-Arian's case provides a clear idea on how the

government utilized the catchall war on terrorism label to target Palestinian communities (other Arab and Muslim groups were included, but the majority of the cases targeted Palestinians) as a suspect class. The government's efforts provided a clear comparison to the COINTELPRO period, whereby Hoover's Federal Bureau of Investigation (FBI) agents sought to "expose, disrupt, misdirect, discredit, or otherwise neutralize" African American organizations and leaders, which is similar to what was, and is, under way in relations to Palestinians and pro-Palestine activists.

Professor Al-Arian's case dates back to the early 1990s when he was targeted by the government under then president Clinton's adopted Anti-Terrorism and Effective Death Penalty Act (AEDPA) of 1996 and suspected of supporting Palestinian organizations opposing Israeli occupation. Provisions in the AEDPA permitted law enforcement agencies to use "secret evidence" to arrest, prosecute, and possibly deport individuals without having committed a crime. What started in the 1990s during Clinton's era accelerated post-9/11, making it possible for the neoconservatives and pro-Israel advocates inside and close to Bush's administration to utilize the Patriot Act to go after Palestinian activists and charities providing support for needy families living under occupation and to criminalize groups by linking them to terrorism through fictitious "material support" claims. What developed is a new COINTELPRO strategy laser focused on Palestine's advocates and supporters, resulting in imprisonments for some, the Holy Land Foundation case, deportation for others like Professor Sami Al-Arian, and bogus entrapment instances for many others.[47]

Consequently, since the events of 9/11, the FBI and other security agencies have resorted to the recruitment of informants by means of enticement and, if necessary, threats of deportation or financial ruin to spy on Muslims in general but specifically on Palestinian communities. From the cases that have come to light, it is clear that vast sections of the Palestinian communities and their civic and religious institutions were the intended targets of the FBI's new type of COINTELPRO operations.

As a matter of fact, the then Bush administration's attorney general Alberto Gonzales stated, after a Lodi, California, terrorism indictment, "Since the terrorist attacks of September 11, 2001, the number one priority of the [Justice] Department has been to detect, disrupt and prevent terrorist attacks," which means using every tool available, including the recruitment and deployment of paid informants. For many, this is a legitimate use of national resources to possibly prevent another 9/11, and Palestinian communities, collectively, should be "ready to cooperate" with the authorities in conducting these much-needed operations. A more direct conclusion drawn from these operations is that the FBI and the Department of Justice considered Palestinian American communities as incubators of terrorism that must be monitored and, if needed, infiltrated to preemptively catch them before they plan an attack.[48]

The strategy was to create control structures to effectively silence the voices of Palestinians and intimidate them into supporting US interventions abroad while pressuring them to distance themselves from supporting Palestinians under occupation. Sitting at the intersectionality of Arabs, Muslims, and Palestinians, Sami Al-Arian was a well-known advocate for the Palestinians, a professor at the University of South Florida, a community builder, and a major public figure navigating the coercive governmental structures to create a political empowerment in Florida and nationally. What brought Al-Arian to the attention of the government was his success in creating a viable local political power base for the community and proactively speaking and organizing for Palestine nationally. Palestinian refugees and immigrants in the US experience the extension of Israeli security and surveillance apparatus in exile, and their relationship to their government is shaped and regulated by it.[49]

Palestinians in the US are still connected to every element of the Palestinian cause. The signed Oslo Agreement in 1993 included a multilateral track to help the negotiations and settlement of the Palestinian refugee problem, which included a large number of UN member states. In the multilateral track, the participating states' primary focus was again to work toward easing the pressure on Israel and facilitating all types of solutions, with the end result being settling the Palestinians away from their homeland.

Needless to say, the attempts at settling Palestinian refugees in the proposed manner stands in violation of UN Resolution 194, which called for the return of the refugees to Palestine and of their homes and lands immediately after the end of hostilities in 1948. Since the inception of the Zionist project, the "international community" has acted as a facilitator and deal broker to give birth to the State of Israel while all along steering the Palestinians to accept the unacceptable and agree to a political settlement that dispenses with their rights. Even the international community's support and funding for UNRWA is always contingent on extracting from the Palestinians political concessions that undermine their rights to sovereignty and self-determination.

In 2018, the Trump administration added insult to the proposed "peace plan" by defunding, or freezing, a US contribution of $200 million to UNRWA, a sum that accounts for one-third of the financial needs of Palestinian refugees. Trump wanted to force the Palestinians anew to let go of their right of return and reward Israel for its ethnic cleansing of 78 percent of historical Palestine and the forceful expulsion of 750,000 civilians. At the time, Trump's action followed the congressional bill HR 6451 from July 2018, which called for connecting UNRWA's funding to limiting the Palestinian refugee classification in such a way that "(1) the derivative refugee status may only be extended to the spouse or minor child of such a refugee; and (2) an alien who was firmly resettled in any country is not eligible to retain the refugee status."[50]

The US's action plan, in reality, is part of the racial and demographic hoops to jump through that are paradigmatic of settler colonial projects. If there are no Palestinian refugees and no right of return, then the apartheid "pure" Zionist state, Israel, would protect its borders, cities, and population from the possible racial, religious, cultural, and political "dissolution, defilement and encroachment" by the Palestinians. The Palestinian refugees are at the heart of the ongoing conflict, and wishing them away through denial of UNRWA funding will not begin disentangling the complexities involved in this issue.

Assuming that the removal of the refugee designation from five to six million Palestinians is accepted, then what are the next steps for their legal status in each country? Jordan, Lebanon, and Syria—which among them currently has most of the Palestinian refugees? A change in status must translate into transforming their legal designation in each of these three countries. While Jordan does give citizenship to Palestinian refugees living in the country (discussed earlier), this is not the case for Syria and Lebanon, and any change to the status will lead to far-reaching complications that can't be easily wished out of existence.

Coming closer to historical Palestine, the refugee population in Gaza and the West Bank has neither an interest in letting go of its right of return nor having a third country take responsibility for it. Egypt might be offered some financial incentives to help alleviate Israel's challenge with Gaza, but this will require granting citizenship to the population and incorporating the Gaza Strip into the country.

Chapter Two

Colonization and the Modern World

"I would cite you to the Apostle Paul and his clear and wise command in Romans 13 to obey the laws of the government because God has ordained them for the purpose of order," was then US attorney general Jeff Sessions' defense of Trump's "zero-tolerance" immigration policy, delivered at the Ashland Place United Methodist Church in Mobile, Alabama. Trump's immigration policy led to separating over two thousand children from their parents upon crossing the border illegally from Mexico. The use of religious text to justify a draconian policy is not new, and referencing Romans 13 is a favorite passage for law-and-order advocates. Forgetting the many other sections of the Bible, which extol the virtue of taking care of the stranger and the outsider, is politically expedient.

Religious and civic leaders across the spectrum spoke forcefully against the use of the Bible to justify the "zero-tolerance" policy, as well as a sizable majority of the American society, which led to Trump reversing course and issuing an executive order to end the practice of separating children from their parents at the border. The implementation of the executive order has been spotty at best, and the Department of Homeland Security continues to hold children away from their parents in detention. Indeed, the rationale behind the policy and the rising tide of antirefugee and anti-immigrant sentiments are at the heart of Trump's election victory in 2016, and many in his administration are hard-liners on the issue, which led to the family and children separation policy. This is not unique to the US as similar hard-line policies are being adopted across Europe by a new crop of right-wing politicians that are using and fanning the flames of anti-immigrant and antirefugee rhetoric and policies to win elections.

Separating families at the US-Mexico border, building "the wall," and erecting physical barriers across Europe is paradigmatic of the global anti-immigrant and antirefugee sentiments that have been stoked and intensified over the past thirty to forty years. Not since the end of World War II did the world witness such a total disregard for international legal principles, and the humanitarian crisis unfolding daily across the vast borders in Africa, Asia, Europe, the US, and on the high seas is being made worse by willful inaction. The United Nations estimates around 70.8 million human beings are currently on the move as refugees, immigrants, and asylum seekers or as internally displaced people, with the difference between the categories being increasingly blurred by the complexity of the problems contributing to the global crisis. Many of those on the move are seeking entry and a legal status that would allow them to resume a "normal" life pattern in a new land.

Leaving one's homeland is never an easy or preferred choice, and most of those on the move are doing so out of fear and necessity arising from local and regional wars, economic-social dislocation, and increasingly environmental and ecological collapse. The same countries that are building walls or physical barriers to keep the immigrants and refugees out are the ones that are primarily responsible for causing the crisis in the first place, a fact that can be traced to long-term and ongoing military and economic interventions, which ravaged the Global South beyond recognition. Moving to the North has been a response rather than the cause of the crisis because the primary force behind the movement of people is the economic and political interventions in the Global South.

Certainly, people's movement from one region to another is part of the human story that dates to the earliest period of recorded history, including references in religious texts. But the population shift that we are witnessing today is at a completely different scale, and the scope of it is directly connected to failed economic and political policies at a global level. Responding to the current crisis has been formulated on a very narrow basis and centered on addressing the symptoms rather than the multilayered causes that brought it to the fore at this point. European states' and the US's responses have boiled down to closing the borders and creating legal and physical barriers to prevent the arrival of refugees and immigrants from the Global South, despite the Global North being directly responsible for the policies that created this human crisis and tidal wave in the first place.

Moreover, the crisis produced populist politicians and political parties that were apt at stoking nationalist sentiment in opposition to the arrival of immigrants and refugees and using it win elections. Rather than finding a solution or addressing the causes of the crisis, the populist parties and politicians instrumentalize it to rally support among their base for their narrowly constructed economic and social agenda. Even though Europe and the US point to the flood of immigrants and refugees arriving at their borders, the bulk of displaced populations actually remains in the Global South.

In reality, the countries that have borne the brunt of recent Western interventions in the Middle East crisis are Ethiopia, Iran, Jordan, Lebanon, Pakistan, Turkey, and Uganda, and then marginally we get Germany, Greece, Italy, and the US. The US military and economic intervention in Latin America has produced a stream of immigrants and refugees. The discussion about immigration and the refugee crisis is used to obfuscate the nature of the problem and its origin, which can be easily traced to the prolonged colonial and interventionist policies that resulted in massive and ongoing disruptions and displacement in the Global South. How to understand the current immigrant and refugee crisis and what solutions we may undertake to address the root causes, rather than a band-aid approach to the symptoms, is of critical importance. In reality, the current crisis is a direct outcome of the colonial and postcolonial interventions in the Global South, which has become more acute with the end of the Cold War and the collapse of the bipolar world system.

Understanding the immigration-refugee crisis of today requires the researcher and reader to use a global lens to view events, policies, and economic actions across continents and historical periods in a connected web of entanglements and consequences. The propensity of politicians, media talking heads, and civil society in the Global North to narrowly focus on the tail end of the problem fails to account for the causes behind 70.8 million people being on the move.

In the next few pages, I offer a longer historical examination of the problem while situating the crisis within the scope of the collapse of the postcolonial political order and the end of the Cold War. I do put considerable emphasis on the colonial period because it is the era that produced the world we all inhabit. Nothing escapes the colonial epistemic—even the postcolonial era is formed by it and around it—a fact that often is taken for granted or completely erased from all political discourses.

❧ Immigration-Refugee Crisis: The Colonial and Postcolonial

Away from European and US borders, major immigration and refugee catastrophes are under way, but unfortunately, limited media and scholarly attention is focused on them, a consequence of the long history of colonization and a feature of the postcolonialism era. Mention Burma, Ethiopia, India, Nigeria, or South Africa, and the responses would not include immigrants, refugees, building barriers, and camps housing hundreds of thousands seeking safety and security. The largest number of immigrants and refugees are present in both Asia and Africa with millions living in refugee camps and seeking any type of international support that can bring about a change to their circumstances.

For example, Ethiopia currently has nearly nine hundred thousand refugees, who arrived in the country from Eritrea, Somalia, South Sudan, and Sudan. The refugee population in Ethiopia is not unique to the continent as the UNHCR data shows that Africa has either the largest or second-largest concentration of populations of concern (a UN term that has many different types of individuals included in it), with the Middle East being the other region with large numbers of refugees and immigrants living in camps or on the move in the region.

Populations of concern include people on the move from the Central African Republic; Nigeria, which has more than two million people who have been forcibly displaced, 1.87 million who have fled from the terrorist group Boko Haram's violence since 2014; and another two hundred thousand people have sought refuge in Cameroon, Chad, and Niger. On the African continent, Cameroon, Chad, the Democratic Republic of the Congo, Ethiopia, Kenya, Libya, Mali, Niger, Nigeria, Rwanda, Somalia, South Africa, Sudan, and Uganda are states that have large displaced immigrant and refugee populations that are living in camps or on the move away from their homelands and needing services from UNHCR.

In the Middle East, Turkey has one of the single-largest groups of refugees in the world with 3–3.5 million Syrians, who sought safety from the ongoing civil war. In addition, Turkey hosts another three hundred thousand Iraqi refugees that moved to the country after the US invasion of Iraq. In the same region, Jordan and Lebanon welcomed about one million Syrian refugees each into their countries while already having a large Palestinian refugee population living in camps since 1948. Here, European countries, Russia, the United Kingdom, and the US intervened in the civil war and participated in intensifying the unfolding crisis in the region, yet they refuse to take responsibility for their actions that resulted in the large Syrian and Iraqi refugee and immigrant populations.

The intervention and destruction of lands and society is not new; rather it is a major feature of the age of discovery and the colonial and postcolonial periods, which caused the uprooting of people across the globe and disruption of normative patterns of existence. Indeed, the issue is not the basic movement and migration of people from one area to another, since this is a basic fact of the human story, but the emergence of particular modes of modernity wedded to coloniality, militarism, capitalism, and imperial Christianity, which continue to be the primary disrupting factors in the world.

Premodern and precolonial people's migration and movement are well-documented in archaeology and history texts. Increasingly, DNA-based tracing can provide the evidence that early humans emerged out of Africa, then over thousands of years spread all over the world. Tracing the human journey around the world through DNA provides the scientific evidence of our common ancestry and the continuous movement of people from one region to another in search of food and security. The question at hand is, is the movement of human beings in the modern, colonial, and postcolonial periods distinctive from what occurred earlier? What has occurred in the most recent past in the Global South to cause the massive migration out and refugee crisis that is unfolding daily? Also, who is fanning the flames of racism, xenophobia, and demonization in the Global North, how are they doing it, and to what end? These are critical questions and others will arise as we discuss the unfolding crisis in this and following chapters.

At present, the immigration-refugee crisis is a direct consequence of the end of the Cold War, on the one hand, and the collapse of the postcolonial world order, on the other, which was maintained in a state of balance since post-World War II. However, right-wing politicians and the Global North media represent the crisis differently by the constant focus on racial, cultural, religious, and ethnic backgrounds of the immigrants and refugees, rather than by exploring the more complex causes behind the 70.8 million people being on the move.

The focus on the differences is directly connected to Bernard

Lewis's clash of civilizations[51] thesis, which was made popular by political scientist Samuel Huntington, who first wrote about it in a *Foreign Policy Journal* article and then made it into a book in 1996. The clash of civilizations thesis uses cultural differences as the basis for the supposed future conflicts, with the Sino-Islamic axis constituting the greatest challenge to Western civilization. Coming from a Cold War framing, Huntington's thesis and writing misses much of what is under way in the world and does not really engage with and interrogate what is occurring and changing in the Global South. While it claims to be a big picture, it is actually a very small racial lens despite protestation to the contrary. What is needed is both a Global South focus and a longer historical examination of the unfolding immigration-refugee crisis that makes the clash of civilizations thesis to be none other than an exercise in self-reflection and affirmations without anyone's involvement.

Recent events in South Africa have put the spotlight on the country as it attempts to institute new immigration, refugee, and asylum laws to limit and reshape its relations with African states and other countries around the world. In the context of southern Africa, states like Botswana, Lesotho, Malawi, Mozambique, and Swaziland, which are part of South Africa's periphery, have been part of the labor migration to fill the extensive mining jobs in the country for a long time. The mining industry in South Africa has a long and complex colonial history, which was one main factor behind European states' rush to penetrate and settle the region. European interests in the region date back to the era of exploration and the age of discovery, where the quest for new trade routes away from the existing ones that passed through Ottoman and Muslim territories took shape. South Africa's history is directly connected to European expansion into Africa, Asia, and the New World as the attempt to reshape trade routes and begin to dominate them energized the effort to colonize and take control of the region.

The "discovery"[52] of the Cape of Good Hope is a critical moment in history for it opened the door to colonize Africa and Asia and alter the existing world system. As a matter of fact, Bartolomeu Dias, a Portuguese navigator, was the first to reach the southern tip of Africa in 1488 and is credited for naming it the Cape of Good Hope. Four years after Dias made his way around the Cape of Good Hope, Columbus's expedition crossed the Atlantic Ocean in 1492, to usher in the New World system that is still unfolding today. The age of discovery was the start of the European colonial project, which took hold of the New World, then afterward unleashed its greed and power on Africa and the rest of the world.

Africa, as a whole, and South Africa in particular, faced the brunt of European settler colonialism and its immediate link to pernicious capitalism. Beginning in April 1652, the first European settlement took shape through the work and effort of the Dutch East India Company at Table Bay and with it the domination and expansion into southern Africa became possible. In South Africa, the Dutch East India Company took hold of vast lands and assigned them to Dutch settlers beginning in 1657, who in a short period began to import slaves from Angola; Java and the Dutch East Indies of Indonesia; Madagascar; Sri Lanka; and western Africa to work on these new farms. The Dutch East India Company set up the economic infrastructure in the region fused with the military, the slave trade, and the transnational markets.

When we think of enslaved people, the focus on the Americas and the transatlantic slave trade tend to disguise other elements of the European slave trade system, which was transnational in nature. A complete discussion on European slavery, settlements, and trade is incomplete without taking into account the various companies, institutions, and regions that were connected to it, not only those that were sent across the Atlantic. In the same way, the invasion of Iraq and the interventions in El Salvador and Venezuela are centered on fossil fuel, corporate economic interests, and military-industrial complex partnerships.

What makes South Africa a good jumping-off point to explore the collapse of the postcolonial world is its history and the multifaceted link to the colonial era, the pernicious imprint of capitalism, and the distinctive racial structure—the apartheid system—that continued to dominate societal affairs up until the end of the Cold War. South Africa is not your typical colonial outpost; rather it is the mother lode, the granddaddy of all outposts, and the springboard for European colonization of all of western Africa, southern Africa, Asia, and the disruption visited upon the populations of the globe.

From the fifteenth century all the way up to the last decade of the twentieth century, South Africans lived through and came out of a genocidal experience that transformed all aspects of society and continues to cast a profound shadow in the postcolonial era. If multinational corporate power is a contemporary concern, then the Dutch East India Company's trajectory on the world stage was actually as a private enterprise funding "exploration," establishing settlements, initiating and fighting wars, unseating rulers, shipping slaves across borders and oceans, governing territories near and far, and engaging in multiple genocides in Africa, Asia, and the Americas. The Dutch East India Company was the paradigmatic corporate enterprise fusing company and colonization or genocide on an industrial and global scale.

Colonization was not a single event covering one territory or concern but a multifaceted project that transformed beyond recognition everything it touched. Here, European colonization functioned around four main pillars: the company or commercial interest, the civilizational mission or the "white man's burden," Christianity, and the advancement of military technology making mass killing and violence at an industrial scale possible like never before. When Nelson Mandela walked out of prison on February 11, 1990, it marked not only his own freedom but the coming to an end of South Africa's colonization and the country's entry into the postcolonial era.

The European colonial project is distinctive from earlier periods of human movements across borders in search of livelihood and safety or of empires shifting populations regionally in the premodern imperial context and the quest for territorial expansion. I see the European colonial project through Palestinian eyes, looking back on history while at the same time experiencing, living, and witnessing a settler colonial project unfold in Palestine. Theory and system modeling are important to conceptualize and give form to ideas, to make the abstract accessible, but living and experiencing a colonial project provides a concreteness that goes beyond words and meaning. Palestinians' lived realties under the Zionist settler colonialism, a European-constructed project, informs and shapes what I write in this chapter, even though the specific examples mentioned are far away from Palestine. The European colonization project is different in six main ways than what the world has experienced before the modern period.

First, the European colonial project was global in nature, it covered every continent, and it touched the known and brought "the unknown" parts of the world into the newly developed colonial system. The colonial footprint marked every corner of the globe as the British, Dutch, French, German, Italian, Portuguese, and Spanish armies, companies, and Christian clergy marched across the globe, took hold of vast territories, pillaged what they touched, and demolished all existing barriers. Conquest or control for premodern imperial powers was of lands that were adjacent or across waterways within their own existing navigation routes, which can't be compared to what occurred in the colonial era. Indeed, the conquests in southern Africa, Australia, the New World, and New Zealand involved territories that are thousands of miles away from the colonial motherlands, which is a unique feature of this new era.

As the colonial expansion took hold in the late eighteenth, nineteenth, and early twentieth centuries, 85 percent of the world's surface was under one form of colonial rule or another, a fact that was never seen or experienced under the conquest of premodern powers. Diverse peoples, regions, and societies, those living on the 85 percent of the world's surface, entered the twentieth century experiencing and living a "reality" that was shaped and formed by the colonial epistemic. Often, a distinction is made between the age of discovery and the colonial era without actually coming to terms with how the difference is framed around Europeans' own views and demarcation of history rather than the actual developments, and outcomes for the impacted societies. For the purpose of this work, the arrival of Europeans to the New World is the starting point of the modern colonial era that opens the door for the emergence of the global empire.

I would like for us to consider the concept of time and the various relations and entanglements we have with it around the globe. One simple way to illustrate the global nature of the European colonial project is to think about how we mark time, the calendar we use, and the basic question we ask a person about their birthday, especially in the Global South! How we mark and measure time is not a neutral act. Marking time is a very difficult enterprise, and the use of the current calendar itself is informed by the colonial epistemic and is not a neutral act undertaken in a vacuum.

What year is it? Time itself, as marked today, is shaped by the colonial epistemic. The question about the current year is informed by the global nature of colonization and the total Eurocentric hegemonic imprint on the world. Is it the year 2020? According to what calendar, society, geography, and demarcation? When we say that European colonization is global and touches everything, including how we mark and record time itself and celebrate our own birthdays, this is precisely the point to drive home in understanding what is different in the colonial era. All calendars, and the epistemic systems of meaning they contain within, have been obliterated in the face of the Eurocentric Gregorian calendar, which interestingly enough was adopted in 1582, and over more than three hundred colonial years, it became the

hegemonic global system for marking time and, more importantly, narrating history.

All history is narrated through a Eurocentric colonial tunnel
that structurally and epistemically excludes all other demarcation
of time and the embedded systems of meaning. I very much appreciate Hamid Dabashi's framing of the situation: "The whole
world in one way or another is Europeanist. We have learned
Europe the hard way. We also get to write [about] Europe from
the shadow of Europe, for it stands too much in its own sun. My
writing on Europe is therefore neither from a position of power
nor from a position of weakness. As all other postcolonial think-
ers meditating the condition beyond postcoloniality, I too am
writing from inside Europe—for there is no outside Europe, anywhere, on this planet—for the sun never set on the union Jack."[53]

I am aware that we have other calendars and that different
cultures have ceremonies and festivals around them, but let's be
very clear that time, the economy, politics, meaning, and history
are marked through the global Eurocentric colonial lens. I am a
Palestinian that marks time by the Eurocentric colonial calendar
(1917, 1922, 1929, 1936–39, 1948, 1956, 1967, 1970, 1973, 1988,
1993, 2001, 2008, 2010, 2012, and 2014) and relates to the world
through its embedded meanings and consequences. European
colonization colonized time itself and all the meaning contained
within—a global phenomenon never before experienced in human history.

Second, the colonial era was distinctively racial and emerged
at the intersection of the line of demarcation between the human
and subhuman. Here, Ramon Grosfoguel's approach to the subject of racism is critical, which builds on Frantz Fanon's framing
of the problem of race. "Racism," for Grosfoguel, "is a global hierarchy of superiority and inferiority along the line of the human
that have been politically, culturally and economically produced
and reproduced for centuries by the institutions of the capitalist/
patriarchal western-centric/Christian-centric modern/colonial

world-system."[54] How to think of and define the concept of race has been an ongoing area of scholarly theorization and engagement, and Grosfoguel's work attempts to examine racism outside the color line. For Grosfoguel, the people "classified above the line of the human are recognized socially in their humanity as human beings and, thus, enjoy access to rights (human rights, civil rights, women's rights, and labor rights), material resources, and social recognition to their subjectivities, identities, epistemologies, and spiritualities. The people below the line of the human are considered subhuman or nonhuman; that is, their humanity is questioned and, as such, negated."[55]

I find Grosfoguel's distinction between the use of a workable definition of racism as a general concept and the fluidity of racial markers very useful in dealing with colonization, which in Grosfoguel's view "allows us to conceive of diverse forms of racism, evading the reductionisms of many existing definitions."[56] Furthermore, Grosfoguel accurately points out that "different colonial histories in diverse regions of the world, the hierarchy of superiority/inferiority along the lines of the human can be constructed through diverse racial markers. Racism can be marked by color, ethnicity, language, culture and/or religion."[57] I am using Grosfoguel's framing due to the complexity of the colonial and postcolonial period and how race and racial markers have been used to craft zones of inclusion and exclusion on its basis. The colonial epistemic is rooted and structured around race, and any examination of colonization is incomplete without it. Here, I am not dismissing other approaches to defining race, racialization, the significance of class, and the rise of capitalism; rather the "global hierarchy of superiority and inferiority" is a valuable analytical tool for understanding the colonial and postcolonial eras.

Europe's identity as both white and Christian was only made possible through crafting a racial other, removing it from the "continent" to assert the notion of purity of blood and race, and then affirming superiority on its basis. Even the idea of "Europe" as a white

Christian continent could not be sustained from the fourteenth to the twentieth century for the mere fact that sizable regions of what we call today Eastern Europe had a substantial Muslim population, and for a long period was ruled by the Ottomans, not to mention the presence of Africans and Jews in various territories. "The invention of Europe as a civilizational category," in Hamid Dabashi's view, "is tantamount to the inventing of 'the white people' as the normative measure of our humanity—and that invention must be reverse-engineered."[58] "Reverse-engineering" translates into asking, how did we arrive at a white Christian Europe?

Arriving at white and Christian involved the expulsion of Muslims and Jews from Spain and instituting a regime of terror under the Inquisition to arrive at "racial purity." If European areas inhabited by Christians are defined in those terms, then it would be somewhat accurate, but the adopted concept implied the existence of a racial purity and continuity, which was not valid then and certainly not now. Critically, the whole notion of racial purity is spurious at best, if not a total insult to logic, history, and human experience. For example, the genome of the United Kingdom's "Cheddar Man, who lived 10,000 years ago, suggests that he had blue eyes, dark skin and dark curly hair,"[59] which scientists maintain to be of Middle Eastern and African background.

The archaeologist at the British Natural History Museum, Tom Booth, who worked on the project, said, "It really shows up that these imaginary racial categories that we have are really very modern constructions, or very recent constructions, that really are not applicable to the past at all."[60] Another member of the Cheddar Man research team, Yoan Diekmann, a computational biologist at University College London, commented on the connection, which is often made by those asserting a link between Britishness and whiteness, as "not an immutable truth. It has always changed and will change."[61]

DNA evidence and research on British ancestry put to rest any notion of "purity" of race and blood and did so based on scientific evidence: "The results pointed to a Middle Eastern origin for Cheddar Man, suggesting that his ancestors would have left Africa, moved into the Middle East and later headed west into Europe, before eventually crossing the ancient land bridge called Doggerland which connected Britain to continental Europe. Today, about 10% of white British ancestry can be linked to this ancient population."[62] Race and racial categories are historically produced, socially constructed, and deployed as instruments for controlling, regulating, and excluding segments that are deemed subhuman and inferior.

Let's come back to the idea of race and Europe's deployment of racial difference on the basis of a religious marker, meaning Muslims and Jews were then the identified European other before Europe existed as an idea or separate geographical zone. Defining or putting Europe, the continent, into circulation as a distinct region with a white Christian identity was on the basis of constructing and identifying the other, the group(s) that does not belong and is an outsider to the aspired for purity of race, religion, and culture. Initially, Europe crafted the racial other by amplifying religious differences with Muslims and Jews then dressing it up on the basis of a pseudoscientific racial matrix and hierarchy. Here, the colonial and modern era formulating a racial theory or constructing race consciousness should not be again confused with the existence of otherization and forms of discrimination in earlier civilizations or communities. The modern colonial era begins with the massive expulsion of Muslims and Jews from the newly defined European continent, which becomes a foundational epistemic for every area or region that is touched by the colonial powers.

The speech of Jules François Camille Ferry, who twice served as France's prime minister, to the French Chamber of Deputies, on March 28, 1884, illustrates the racial dimension of colonialism: "Gentlemen, we must speak more loudly and more honestly! We must say openly that indeed the higher races have a right over the lower races...I repeat, that the superior races have a right because

they have a duty. They have the duty to civilize the inferior races....
In the history of earlier centuries these duties, gentlemen, have often been misunderstood; and certainly, when the Spanish soldiers and explorers introduced slavery into Central America, they did not fulfill their duty as men of a higher race....But, in our time, I maintain that European nations acquit themselves with generosity, with grandeur, and with sincerity of this superior civilizing duty."[63]

Colonization and racism went hand in hand and provided the rationale for the wholesale dispossession and the multiple genocides committed against people of the Global South. The French colonial projects in Africa, Asia, and the Caribbean used race as the primary tool to administer, pillage, and kill millions in the regions under their control. Race, a socially, politically, economically, and religiously constructed Eurocentric epistemic, is one of the main pillars that stabilizes the foundation of the modern colonial world and is the arbiter that defines and regulates all north-south global relations (including the south that inhabits within the confines of the north, and the north that inhabits within the south).

Critically, the rationale used to justify the racial project has shifted from theological or religion as the basis of difference to scientific or biological racism, and then in the late nineteenth and early twentieth centuries toward the crystallization of cultural racism to uphold the edifice of negation and otherization. I do maintain that the rise of Islamophobia has brought the racial justification discourse into full circle as those who use cultural racism are increasingly borrowing the discredited arguments from the Inquisition and Crusaders period.

The subject of race and colonialism is vast, and the previous paragraphs are intended to draw attention to the centrality of race and racism in the colonial project and the setting in place of a line of demarcation between the colonized and the colonizer, centering on the zone of being and unbeing. Furthermore, the discourse around race and racism is not geographically limited, as the internal colonial is ever present in the Global North just as the superior "white" is present as superior human colonizer in the Global South. Race is the defining category of the modern colonial era, which often is left unaddressed by solely focusing on class as a frame of analysis. Race informs all relations in society, dominates culture production, shapes literature and education, intrudes into scripture and religion, structures power, crafts the system by which resources are used and distributed, and defines human relations to land, water, and air itself. Can we overcome race, and is it possible without decolonizing every facet of the society and the humans that make it all colonially and destructively tick?

Third, the colonial era marshalled the fusing of newly developed modes of economic production and capitalism, technological innovation, and exploration that is dissimilar to any premodern period. Europe's age of discovery was propelled forward by innovation in maritime technologies, which included Hartman's astrolabe, the mariner's compass, the sextant, and better maps that made sea travel over long distances possible. The technological advancement in Europe occurred at the same time that China decided to withdraw from dominating the oceans with its massive fleet, a step that opened the door for the Spanish and Portuguese to become the uncontested seafaring powers in a short period.

On the Mediterranean front, the Ottoman had a strong presence, which was one of the primary motivations for exploring an alternative route to India to bypass Muslim-held territories and avoid paying taxes. Columbus's journey west to reach India was undertaken mere months after the expulsion of Muslim rulers from Granada, Spain, which opened up the next stage in the efforts to find alternative ways to avoid trading through Ottoman-held territories. Needless to say, Europe's bloody crusades and entanglements with the Muslim world provided the early foundation for the enlightenment through the transmission from the East of valuable scientific, philosophical, and cultural materials, which included maritime navigation technology as well. Between the legacy of the crusades and the wars in Spain, the search for alternative routes was part of a strategic effort to disrupt the old economic order and maintain a balancing act after the expulsion of the Europeans from the East.

Changes in trade routes brought different types of relations with the Old World economies, and the massive wealth brought from the New World propelled further innovations and modes of production. In a short period of time, the existing trade networks on the coasts of India, Asia, and West Africa came under Spanish and Portuguese control, followed by the British and the French at a later point. While West and northwest Europe were marginal to the Old World economic activities, the changes in trade routes in the fifteenth and sixteenth centuries and the domination of the seas through alterative paths away from Ottoman territories and their partners in the East and southeast Europe brought a change in power relations and status within Europe itself.

The total shift of trade away from the old economies and the emergence of a new region, the Americas, transformed western Europe into the center of a global empire, which was ready to dominate the world in ways never before seen or experienced. Wealth brought from the Americas, and new modes of economic production, gave rise to an accelerated stage for weapons and military technology, which was soon deployed to secure and expand the global imperial footprint. The emergence of the capitalist system, its imposition across the globe, and the onset of the industrial revolution propelled Great Britain and other European colonial powers into the imperial stratosphere and afforded them a controlling stranglehold on every part of the world. Regions that could not be subdued by brute military power had to contend with strangulation through disruption of trade and debt schemes that subverted sovereignty and independence, a process that continues to this day.

European powers needed the colonial system for economic and political purposes as France's Prime Minister Jules François Camille Ferry, in his speech before the French Chamber of Deputies, on March 28, 1884, expressed in clear terms: "The policy of colonial expansion is a political and economic system...that can be connected to three sets of ideas: economic ideas; the most far-reaching ideas of civilization; and ideas of a political and patriotic sort."[64] More critically, the prime minister provided the often missed connection between local French economic production and the needs for markets to sell or dump the finished products, or as he termed it "the need for outlets [for exports]."[65] The scope of the need is put in the context of the already adopted French policy, which the prime minister explains in relation to competition from Germany and protectionism of other industrialized states like the US:

Yes, what our major industries [textiles, etc.], irrevocably steered by the treaties of 18601 into exports, lack more and more are outlets. Why? Because next door Germany is setting up trade barriers; because across the ocean the United States of America have become protectionists, and extreme protectionists at that; because not only are these great markets...shrinking, becoming more and more difficult of access, but these great states are beginning to pour into our own markets products not seen there before. This is true not only for our agriculture, which has been so sorely tried...and for which competition is no longer limited to the circle of large European states....Today, as you know, competition, the law of supply and demand, freedom of trade, the effects of speculation, all radiate in a circle that reaches to the ends of the earth....That is a great complication, a great economic difficulty;...an extremely serious problem. It is so serious, gentlemen, so acute, that the least informed persons must already glimpse, foresee, and take precautions against the time when the great South American market that has, in a manner of speaking, belonged to us forever will be disputed and perhaps taken away from us by North American products. Nothing is more serious; there can be no graver social problem; and these matters are linked intimately to colonial policy.[66]

Ferry's speech points to the real reasons behind French colonial expansion and rallying domestic patriotic support for it. Furthermore, Ferry is providing the explicit link between colonial expansion, on the one hand, and racism, creating markets, industrialization, and military needs, on the other. At a later point in his speech, Ferry introduces another element, which I will discuss later, bringing Christianity, or as he framed it "spreading light," into the world, which can only be done through colonial action in this case. The economic, technological, and new modes of production that were central to the colonial project managed to reconfigure everything in the world, including humans themselves and their relationship to the human and the material at once.

Fourth, the onset of global settler colonialism made genocide of Indigenous populations a matter of policy and the critical ingredient used to empty vast lands, eliminate or transfer populations, and lay claim to their properties. In addition, the technological and industrial advancement in weapons manufacturing shortened the time needed to commit genocide and mass killing against Indigenous populations, rendering the existing defense structures useless. Consider the basic fact that the US has some 331 million people living in the country in 2020, but only 6.7 million Indigenous people, a mere 2.09 percent of the total, which means that 97.01 percent of the population are not indigenous to the land and have made their way either at the initial conquest or subsequent to it, all the way to the current period.

Entertaining the question of how many Indigenous peoples lived in North, Central, and South America is an unsettled scholarly subject that also creates all types of contestation. The larger the number of those present, the greater the genocide that was committed, while the opposite holds true, which means the scope of research is to determine how many Indigenous people have been and continue to be killed as a result of the European settler colonial project in the Americas. Estimates varies and are not conclusive due to the lack of any written records from the Indigenous population themselves. However, the lack of accurate numbers should not obfuscate the bigger point: the systematic and sustained genocide of the Indigenous populations in the Americas.

The Indigenous population was very peaceful and showed no hostilities at the time of the first encounter, as Columbus writes: "they are artless and generous with what they have, to such a degree as no one would believe but him who had seen it. Of anything they have, if it be asked for, they never say no, but do rather invite the person to accept it, and show as much lovingness as though they would give their hearts."[67] Indeed, the Indigenous people "would give their hearts" to anyone who asks for it, but settler colonialists in the Americas ripped out their hearts and everything connected to them, which ended in committing multiple genocides against generous and loving communities.

Colonialism, in particular the settler colonialism variety, unleashed one of the most successful and complete genocides in human history, with the end results being the total "replacement" of the Indigenous populations in Africa, Australia, parts of India, New Zealand, the western hemisphere, and significant pockets across the globe. Settler colonialism took the land and committed Indigenous populations to either immediate slaughter and death or slow genocide through transfer to reservations, which caused a disruption of the cultural, tribal, and communal basis of their societies.

The narrative of Bartolomé de las Casas, who participated in the conquest of Cuba as a young Catholic priest and documented the events in the Indies, describing then the treatment of the Indigenous population is illustrative: "Endless testimonies...prove the mild and pacific temperament of the natives...But our work was to exasperate, ravage, kill, mangle and destroy; small wonder, then, if they tried to kill one of us now and then....The admiral, it is true, was blind as those who came after him, and he was so anxious to please the King that he committed irreparable crimes against the Indians..."

In another section, de las Casas describes how the Spaniards "thought nothing of knifing Indians by tens and twenties and of cutting slices off them to test the sharpness of their blades...two of these so-called Christians met two Indian boys one day, each carrying a parrot; they took the parrots and for fun beheaded the boys."[68] The example is normative of the treatment of Indigenous populations and not an exception. The records and narratives of pain and suffering inflected on Indigenous people still calls for more systematic documentation and attention, and the scope of the work is still limited and lacks the needed attention and resources.

Genocide was also a feature of motherland-colonial possession, or a satellite type of colonization, which targeted populations that resisted or stood in the way of "civilization," "Christianization," and "progress." Consequently, the 85 percent of the globe that was colonized experienced systematic genocide, and a massive record of death and destruction was visited upon the southern hemisphere, which, at times, was transgenerational and in some areas continues unabated to the present. Just take a passing look at Africa's history, from north to south and east to west—every country, tribal group, and ethnic community came face to face with colonization and experienced genocide many times over. The European "scramble for Africa" has to be understood and translated to mean death of millions, destruction of a way of life, and stealing every last ounce of value in the society—a total genocide that continues to unfold even in the present.

The case of the Congo under King Leopold II of Belgium is illustrative of the genocidal norm of colonization rather than being an exception, with upward of eight million dead out of a population of sixteen million. British colonial genocide in India witnessed military, economic, and governing policies that resulted in fifteen million deaths in the Great Bengal Famine of 1770 and the Great Famine of 1876–78, which also seeds all the subsequent conflicts and killing in the region. Likewise, the French committed multiple genocides in Algeria, Haiti, North Africa, Vietnam, and most recently in its involvement in the Rwandan genocide.[69]

What is most pernicious in the colonization project is that the colonizing powers crafted the borders that shaped the postcolonial period. Here, the internal civil wars and regional conflicts witnessed in the postcolonial Global South were based on the ethnic, tribal, and religious divisions and structures put in place by colonial powers and instrumentalized to keep their domination by other instruments of power. The postcolonial intervention and the mechanisms of control and domination will be discussed in detail in a later chapter but needed to be mentioned here in the context of genocide.

Fifth, the genocidal campaigns against Indigenous populations in southern Africa, Australia, the New World, and New Zealand created the rationale and market for demand-driven slave markets, which also worked to firm up the social construction of race mentioned above. Slavery has been around since the earliest period of history, and this is not a discussion about the existence or lack thereof of such an institution. Indeed, human beings have had the propensity to enslave each other for a variety of reasons, and each civilization has had its share within this pernicious institution, including African societies. The argument about slavery in the New World is not about whether slavery occurred in the past and which civilization enslaved more than another, since this is already established factually beyond any doubt.

Modern colonization produced multiple genocides at an industrial scale and rapid rate never before seen in human history, which opened the door for the wholesale importation of commodified subjects, Black African enslaved individuals, to fill the needs created when Indigenous populations were put to a systematic genocide regime. Yes, the ancient Egyptians, Romans,

Greeks, Chinese, Ottomans, and Africans themselves had enslaved people, and the records are well established on this front, and no argument is put forth on my side on this specific question. The enslavement of the Black African population was a distinctive enterprise that had race or skin color as the defining characteristic for who may be admitted into the enslaved category. Another critical element was that it was demand driven versus circumstantial; that is, war captives or defeat of a tribe resulted in their transformation into slaves by the stronger tribe.

European conquest of the New World, which witnessed the committing of multiple genocides against the Indigenous population, disrupted the plan to farm and plant the new land, which created a massive appetite for importation of enslaved people from Africa and doing so on the basis of an already constructed racial epistemic. One can maintain that earlier societies had a robust slave market, which is correct, but what is different is the scale, the massive investment in this market, and all the participants across oceans and lands. The slave market was global, involved third-party investors, energized shipbuilding technology for transporting large amounts of human cargo, and linked politicians, landowners, bankers, and insurance and medical establishments in the thriving enterprise over a three hundred year period.

Another critical development directly connected to the colonization of the New World, and Africa and the enslavement of Africans, is the intensification of regional conflicts because it provided the needed "human cargo" to the coast. The more demand for enslaved people to be sent to the Americas, the more guns were exchanged with those bringing the human-commodified supplies. The more guns sold in the region, the more war captives, on both sides, got sold into the fully functioning and robust slave market. Guns for enslaved people was the currency of exchange, which made West and sub-Saharan Africa a focal point for conflicts and human misery driven by an evil and dehumanizing enterprise. The residue of kidnapping, fomenting, and intensifying regional wars to drive "commodified humans" to the coast deprived Africa of some twelve to thirty million of its best, strongest, and brightest people for generations, which still has its multilayered effects to the present.

Conflicts are not new to the world or to any society, but I do maintain that the European slave traders worked to foment and intensify regional, tribal, and religious conflicts so as to drive the needed supplies to a market that was on an upward demand trajectory. Colonization and enslavement went hand in hand and produced the racial and commodified world we are all inhabiting.

The slave institution and market were not incidental to colonization or the conquest of the New World. On his first journey back to Spain, Columbus took Indigenous captives as a gift: "They should be good servants....I, our Lord being pleased, will take hence, at the time of my departure, six natives for your Highnesses."[70] Columbus's first inclination in the New World was to view the population as a mother lode for future slaves, which was made clear in his diary: "Let us in the name of the Holy Trinity go on sending all the slaves that can be sold."[71] Prior to his 1492 journey, Columbus's first slave trade was from the New World to Spain across the Atlantic, with six slaves brought back in the first voyage, and then in the next trip, he brought back over one thousand, and two hundred died en route. The record of Columbus's first voyage is recorded:

> Gold in grain, as well as in dust—amber—cotton—branches and roots of aromatic, and medicinal plants—several animals, and forty parrots. He then drew the attention of the court to the six natives who were present; exhibited their dress, ornaments, arms and utensils; and added, that, notwithstanding their great ignorance, he had not observed any trace of idolatry amongst them; but on the contrary, that they all seemed to be convinced of the existence of a Supreme Being, who dwelt in Heaven, and that they

considered the Spaniards as descended from that celestial abode. They possessed; he said, much plain sense, docility, and inclination to adopt the Christian faith.[72]

In his new book, *The Other Slavery: The Uncovered Story of Indian Enslavement in America*, Professor Andrés Reséndez maintains: "We say that there have been 12.5 million Africans forcibly transported across the Atlantic as slaves into the New World. That is a very powerful thing to say. And I wanted to get a rough sense of how Indian slavery compared to that. So I came up with a figure of 2.5 to 5 million Native Americans enslaved throughout the Americas since Columbus to 1900."[73] The common point of departure in speaking of enslavement is to focus on the Africans taken into bondage, transported across the Atlantic, and held in the Americas to work in plantations and every other type of job, but the Indigenous population is never included in the discussion.

The enslavement of the Indigenous population and the multiple genocides created the demand for a labor force, but not any labor force: a cost-free and enslaved one is the best. Colonialism in the Americas brought about two of the largest human migration movements in history; one voluntary, the European settler colonialist; and the second involuntary or forced "migration" through the commodification and enslavement of between 12.5 million and 30 million Africans. In actuality, we will never come to know the exact number of African men, women, and children who were ripped from their homes and lands, moved to the coast, held possibly on Bunce Island in Sierra Leone, loaded on ships as cargo, transported while chained for months across the Atlantic, then arrived into ports up and down the Americas to be auctioned to the highest bidder.

The figures are not complete since they don't account for those who died on the continent resisting slave traders, the ones that died while in captivity, those who committed suicide, the many who died in the middle passage and were thrown off the sides of the ships, and the smuggling that took place outside the recognized system of importation. Furthermore, the enslavement period does not take into account those that were sent to other parts of the world through the same system. The evilness of slavery is still with us and constitutes the stitching that continues to bleed at the seams of modern life in America's inner cities for it has not yet been honestly accounted for, confronted, and remedied, and the same can be said in relation to Africa.

Sixth, the colonial era brought Christianity, as an imperial and colonially imposed religion, into circulation around the globe, acting as the colonial power's handmaiden to "theologically" justify and rationalize the massive violations of the moral and ethical underpinning of religion itself. Religion's entanglement, and at times open partnership, in pursuit of worldly power is a calamity that has confronted humanity throughout the ages and is not easy to deconstruct in a brief write-up. History provides amble evidence of religion's and religious people's pursuit and at times acquisition of power directly for themselves at the expense of the highest ideals they profess, and no community or group has escaped this basic fact. Some might argue that their religious history and experience is less intrusive or less partnered with power than another religion or group, which might be true on a comparative basis, but this misses the main point altogether as to the centrality and enticement of power in human history, which has captured the imagination and energies of many a religious person.

Power is not a determining factor on the veracity of a given religion or belief system; however, it has been often the case that acquisition of power and vanquishing others is seen or interpreted by religious people and those in power to mean that God is on their side. What is being said here is that God sanctioned their actions—the good, the bad, the ugly, and the in-between—which, in this case, makes God and religion mere instruments of worldly power and nothing else. The utilitarian deployment of religion in pursuit of power, empire, and colonialization is a serious crisis that continues to shape the status and position of religion and religious people in the contemporary period.

The colonial era witnessed Christianity embracing, supporting, and leading the way in pursuit of worldly power while cloaking genocide, forced conversions, pillaging, and total erasure of communities in the name of some high spiritual purpose. Christianity was in total partnership in the erasure of communities that lived thousands of years before coming into contact with the newly arriving European settlers. Colonialism, and settler colonialism in particular, was rationalized through manifest destiny, the "white man's burden" to civilize the "barbarians," and the doctrine of discovery in the New World, which provided religious cover for the wholesale dispossession and genocide of Indigenous and African populations. The fact that conquest and pillaging occurred is not the main issue since history provides sufficient evidence of it across generations and different settings; however, what is unique and critical for examination is the role that Christianity played, as a full partner, if not the actual beneficiary, in the colonial enterprise.

Christianity was the source of unquestionable authority and articulated this power in the notion of the divine rights of kings, a right bestowed by the church on each ruling monarchy in Europe in exchange for financial contributions. When it came to colonization, the pope blessed Columbus's endeavor and urged the conversion of Indigenous people to Catholicism and bringing them into the church's fold. The role Christianity played in the colonization of Africa, parts of Asia, Australia, and New Zealand is extensive, and each would need a multivolume book to provide a full accounting of it. In this section, I am only detailing the six distinctive features of the modern colonial period, not providing a detailed history of Christianity's role in this enterprise. For this sixth point on the list, I will provide a brief description of the Catholic Church's engagement in the conquest of and genocide in the New World.

Immediately after Columbus's return from the New World, Pope Alexander VI issued a May 4, 1493, papal bull granting official ownership of the territories, which had yet to be completely known to the Spanish crown of Ferdinand and Isabella. The pope declared:

> We of our own motion, and not at your solicitation, do give, concede, and assign for ever to you and your successors, all the islands, and main lands, discovered; and which may hereafter, be discovered, towards the west and south; whether they be situated towards India, or towards any other part whatsoever, and give you absolute power in them; drawing, however, and affixing a line from the arctic pole, viz. from the north, to the Antarctic pole, viz. to the south; which line must be distant from any one of the islands whatsoever, vulgarly called the Azores and Cape de Verde Islands, a hundred leagues towards the west and south; upon condition that no other Christian king, or prince, has actual possession of any of the islands and main lands found.[74]

The statement of Pope Alexander VI was sweeping and inclusive of territories "discovered" or to "be discovered" in the future without any considerations to the rights and claims of existing inhabitants, who did not matter and were not part of the pope's consideration. Indeed, Columbus's view on the value of the Indigenous population is very clear in the conclusion of his speech upon returning to Spain: "That God had reserved for the Spanish monarchs, not only all the treasures of the New World, but a still greater treasure of inestimable value, in the in finite number of souls destined to be brought over into the bosom of the Christian church."[75]

Building upon the sweeping powers and rights granted to the Spanish crown, the pope's declaration for all intents and purposes sealed the fate of Indigenous inhabitants of the Americas and provided the religious rationalization that put the genocide in motion. In the years that followed, the Spanish conquerors put in place a new set of rules, "the requirement," which was a demand that the Indigenous inhabitants must accept "the church as the ruler and superior of the whole world" or face persecution. The rules stated that if the Indigenous population did not immediately accept the requirement placed upon them, then, "We shall take you and your wives and your children, and shall make slaves of them, and as such shall sell and dispose of them as their Highnesses may command; and we shall take away your goods, and shall do all the harm and damage that we can."[76]

Consequently, the pope's authority and religious cover opened the door for the wholesale dispossession of the Indigenous population, multiple genocides across the Americas, and the transformation of the landscape into what continues to unfold to the present day. The Indigenous narrative from the moment of the arrival of settler colonialism speaks of massacres, cutting limbs, torture, rape, uprooting communities, the infamous Trail of Tears during forced relocation, killing buffalo herds, polluting waters and rivers, forced boarding schools under the church's supervision, and inflicting all types of diseases due to contact but also due to the total disregard of their humanity.

Colonization around the global was made possible and shaped by the coalescing of economic, military, and technological powers with Christianity, which managed to create and define the world we all inhabit. Another framing of colonization is to see how it was shaped around the three big C's—civilization, Christianity, and commerce—which were made possible and expanded through deploying the army and using modern military technology. All three forces worked hand in hand to give rise to and sustain the colonial modern world.

Thus, the immigration-refugee crisis that is the focus of this book is shaped and emerges out of the colonial and postcolonial periods, which opened the door for the mass movement of populations across oceans and continents. Here, the arrival of the Europeans as settler colonialists is a by-product of the colonial enterprise, which witnessed the migrations of large numbers out of Europe and into the colonies, followed by the forceful movement of Indigenous communities and enslaved Africans and disruptions of normal life patterns across the globe. The current immigration-refugee crisis has been in the making for the past five hundred years, and the world has reached a major tipping point in the post-Cold War era, which I will address further now.

Colonization made it possible for the European population to undertake the largest human migration process, which started in the early part of the sixteenth century and continues in different ways into the present. Who we call "illegal" today in America and Europe should be the actual description of those Europeans who made their way across the globe by force and genocide! We take it for granted that Australia, Canada, New Zealand, and the US have majority European populations, and in countless other regions of the world there exists a minority European ruling class that runs the government, economy, and security or has a protected and privileged status.

Pointing to the precolonial and premodern eras to draw comparisons and rationalize what took place is a faulty enterprise at best and a misleading and dubious scholarship at worst. The thrust of the argument of comparing the Chinese, Egyptian, Ottoman, Persian, and Roman empires is not intended to find the differences; indeed, if we are factual and honest, it emerges out of a certain worldview that attempts to flatten the surface and make a straight, direct line that implicates all earlier civilizations in the same mode of conduct that resulted in multiple genocides. Premodern and precolonial civilizations should be taken to task on their own merits and shortcomings, which I am sure we can find many elements to critique, including but not limited to killings in violations of their professed ideals, stealing and pillaging neighboring territories by conquest and military force, the existence of robust slave institutions connected to governance and economic production, and draconian laws targeting the demonized other.

The six distinct features highlighted above, of the colonial and modern eras, make the global developments stand alone as a unique occurrence and the most destructive period in the history of the world, which affected not only humans but land, the environment, and even in later stages the cosmos, with the race to colonize outer space.

Understanding what transpired in the modern colonial period is a precondition of taking stock of the developments that led to the postcolonial and the current state of collapse. Here, we are not making a straight line without detours, conflicts, and contradictions; on the contrary, one must reconcile oneself to the fact that the colonial period has produced complexities and entanglements that become points of departure on their own accord and productive in shaping the postcolonial period. Furthermore, at no time should the exposition of the colonial and postcolonial power dynamics and disparities lead to the conclusion that the Indigenous and colonized populations were ever, in the past and in the postcolonial period, passive in what they have collectively experienced. On the contrary, what has been constant throughout the colonized world is the never-ending resistance and struggle despite the overwhelming odds. People's struggle for liberation and popular movements brought an end to direct military colonization, which moved the Global South into the postcolonial period, a move that witnessed its share of difficulties and challenges due to the continuation of colonization by economic instruments of soft powers and frequent military interventions.

The twentieth century ushered in the shift from direct total control and military colonialism to postcolonialism, whereby the anticolonial movements forced the troops out of the countries, but the economic, political, and social structures remained intact. Across the globe, liberation movements' successes on the battlefields and in the streets, witnessing great mass mobilization and heavy sacrifices, were not translated into strong negotiations and mechanisms for extricating their societies from the jaws of colonial powers. Certainly, the twentieth century had two world wars with the death toll in the tens of millions, numerous civil wars, and Western interventions in the Global South and, likewise, witnessed monumental anticolonial struggles in Africa, Asia, the Caribbean, and Latin America, which took the lives of millions. However, what seems to escape writers' attention is that the colonized world emerged out of colonialization right into the Cold War contestations, which put them back into political, economic, and social disruptions and dependency, and a never-ending cycle of conflicts and war.

What we are witnessing today, in the movement of people from the Global South to the North, emerges as a direct result of the total disruption of normative patterns in societies and regions by colonial powers, which continues into the postcolonial period. In their quest to manage colonized societies, the colonial powers recruited members from these societies to travel to the imperial centers for the purposes of "education and training," thus creating the pipeline for immigration, brain drain, and cementing the colonial epistemic.

At a later point, the colonial powers began to bring unskilled and uneducated workers from the colonies to fill the lowest strata of blue-collar jobs in Europe and North America, which was cost effective on the financial front and allowed greater freedom for colonial citizens to pursue education, professional employment, and military service at all levels while not being disturbed to attend to the "small things" in life. The unskilled labor jobs of the colonial past are filled by immigrants and refugees today; the descriptive name might have changed but the functions carried out are the same, and the structural marginalization is embedded into the system.

Colonial disruption of the past gave way to modern-day military interventions, globalization, and structural dominations from the Global North, the net outcome of which is the "voluntary and involuntary" movement of people to the Global North. Here, I insist that any critique of colonialism must include the examination of the reinforced relationships and benefits drawn between the colonial citizenry and the ruling elites, which managed to secure their consent and participation in a global imperial structure that brings commodified humans to the postcolonial metropolis.

In cities across the Global North, the "imported" labor force lived at the margins of societies and were often set up for housing in areas at a distance from the financial and cultural centers, which effectively created the internal colonized south within the confines of Europe and North America. As cities and regions grew, what was at a distance became part of the expanding metropolis. Ethnic, racial, cultural, and religious enclaves emerged directly from policies designed around structural exclusion and maintaining the colonized subject in a special colonial setting despite the change in geographical location and the laws governing the new site. Often, policy-makers planned for labor movement from the colony to the center as a temporary employment opportunity with a foreseen or imagined return home for many if not all. Here, the total erasure of the colonized subject gets refined around legal and administrative structures that treat them as mere moveable objects lacking agency and independence of thought and action.

As the colonial period came to a close, the native bureaucracy administrators that kept the colonial system running sought refuge and evacuated with the troops to Europe. The US had a similar experience with its imperial interventions during and after the Cold War, in Angola, Cambodia, Costa Rica, Cuba, Haiti, Laos, Latin America, Liberia, Panama, the Philippines, and Vietnam, as well as recently in Afghanistan, Iraq, Libya, and Syria. On a side but important note, the US refugee designation for a person, or denial thereof, is a highly political matter and is connected to foreign policy objectives rather than the human needs of an impacted population. In the colonial, postcolonial, and Cold War years, each intervention, conflict, war, and evacuation translated into voluntary and involuntary movement of populations from the Global South into countries, cities, and towns in the Global North.

Today, the main driver for mass migration, refugees, asylum seekers, and other types of humans on the move from the Global South to Europe and North America is collapse of the political and economic structures in the postcolonial period. Precisely, the end of the Cold War ushered in a transformation of the global system and the consolidation around a unipolar superpower that accelerated neoliberal economic modalities and an intense privatization push for government-held assets and services. No longer existing under a bipolar structure, the elites in the Global South moved overnight to embrace the "New World Order" and connect directly to hyperdebt-financed "development" while signing on to "partnerships" in the age of free trade agreements.

The "New World Order" was nothing more than the Global North's interests dressed up in sexy open-market-economy development theories designed and intended to accomplish the opposite and an acceleration of raw materials extraction. Another dimension connected to the long colonial history, postcolonialism era, and Cold War rivalries is the destruction of the environment, pollution of rivers and seas, and disruption of habitats the world over, which caused further stress on the well-being of existing societies. Increasingly, the environmental crisis due to the above-mentioned causes will create another wave of climate refugees on the move with devastating consequences across the globe.

Colonization disrupted the Global South and opened the doors for continued movement of populations—those who moved voluntarily and those who were indentured and enslaved—across borders, oceans, and continents, which gave birth to the current world. Concurrent with the movement of people, the unleashing of European modern military technology and capitalist power and greed caused multiple and transhistorical genocides and traumas that continue into the twenty-first century. The postcolonial world is built on the colonial foundation, and the Global South is the site of erasure and the never-ending process centered on the commodification of the human and stealing of resources while dumping finished products into an engineered captive market.

The postcolonial state is the colonial one but managed by the "native elites," who are appointed to manage and "govern" the "independent states" for the benefit of the ex-colonial motherlands or Global North corporate interest that was connected to the colonial project from the inception. Precisely, it is colonization and postcolonial order that is the primary cause for the steady stream of refugees and immigrants crossing oceans, seas, rivers, and mountains in search of safety and a relative state of "normal" in a world that deemed them to be "abnormal" and "subhuman," if not in physical reality then for sure in policy.

Chapter Three

Chocolate and the Colonial Pact

Chocolate is such a delight and a sweet treat that everyone can easily fall in love with and get hooked on. Do you love chocolate? And in your opinion, what country has the best chocolate? I use these two questions in my class lectures on the postcolonial world and the ongoing immigration-refugee crisis and to examine the total absence of understanding of the current global economic system. Almost everyone raises their hand to answer yes to the first question, while the second generates well-known corporate brands and names of European countries, the US, and Canada. Rarely is an African, Asian, or Latin American state ever mentioned, except for a few times by Ethnic Studies majors and immigrant students of color who happen to come from the Global South and have a broader lens and experience.

My intent in asking these two simple questions is to jump into a conversation on the colonial structures that have laid claim to the sources of raw materials in the Global South while making sure to keep manufacturing and finished products in the Global North.[77] My own experience growing up with chocolate was seeing in the stores all the main brands—Mars, KitKat, and Snickers—among a long list of Western products that dominated the market then and know.

My interest in these two questions dates back to the 2014 Ebola virus outbreak in West Africa and seeing the following map that disturbingly framed aspects of the problem around the threat to the cocoa supply, 60 percent of which comes from countries that had the highest number of cases. The data for Ghana and the Ivory Coast (Côte d'Ivoire) lists the metric tons and percent of world total of cocoa produced with no reference to possible Ebola cases or any preparation for what is facing the region. Chocolate is far too important of a commodity to be impacted by a regional pandemic, especially for the countries that depend on cocoa imports from West Africa for their expensive and refined brands, which are unaffordable to those who toil daily in the plantations.[78]

Poignantly, none of the countries frequently mentioned by my students in response to my question grow or have any cocoa plants on their soil, yet they are the leading producers, distributors, and consumers of this valuable finished product. In some countries in the Global North, a high-end chocolate customer can sometimes pay ten or twenty dollars or more for a single piece of the refined, artisanal product, whereby someone in the Global South might not even get the chance to afford it or even see a picture of it.

Many grew up watching the movie *Charlie and the Chocolate Factory* and possibly loved the Willy Wonka character and cheered when Charlie Bucket won the golden ticket and more so when he ended up with the factory. However, in the real world, Willy Wonka would be living in the Global North, while Charlie Bucket, the poor boy in the movie, would be living away from home in a shack with other kids his age, working on a cocoa plantation. The Willy Wonka Candy Company would be located far away from Charlie, the raw materials, and the supply chain, and if a child like Charlie were to visit the factory, it would be a miracle and only after the intervention of some type of UN or human rights organization and the corporate public relations office using the opportunity for positive media coverage.

The movie is entertaining, and I am not writing to dissuade anyone from spending time with their kids watching it, but it does draw attention to an erasure that takes place on all fronts, including something as family friendly as *Charlie and the Chocolate Factory*. My intent is to expand our scope and examine the issues from a variety of lenses, including those that are constantly omitted.

The postcolonial nature of the chocolate industry is one such omitted lens. The cocoa market is not in the hands of the states that grow the plants in the first place or have the raw materials; rather the Global North has hegemonic control of every aspect of the supply chain, which leaves the farmers at the mercy of these global forces. Trade in raw materials for the Global South is not a natural occurrence; neither is it a response to market forces of supply and demand. Economic structures originating in the colonial era were maintained in the postcolonial period and incorporated into the neoliberal and globalized economic order, which is totally under the direct control of the Global North. The chocolate supply chain was formed and set in place in the colonial era, and the major players in Europe and the US militate against changes that might alter the basic framework of the relationship in the postcolonial.

Another wretched and distressing element rarely discussed when it comes to chocolate is the intensive use of almost two million child laborers to harvest and work in cocoa plantations across West Africa—the many nameless, faceless Charlie Buckets we never see, hear, or, in all honesty, stop to care about. The region accounts for two-thirds of the world's cocoa supplies, which is dependent on thousands upon thousands of child laborers toiling daily in hundreds of plantations. Kids as young as ten from across the region make their way to cocoa plantations primarily in the Ivory Coast (Côte d'Ivoire) to work long hours to harvest the beans that end up as chocolate bars and desserts in the Global North. Child labor in West Africa's cocoa plantations has been on the table for the chocolate industry at least since 2001, if not before, but the problem continues to fester.[79]

Criticism of the industry has been ongoing: "The companies have always done just enough so that if there were any media attention, they could say, 'Hey guys, this is what we're doing,'" said Antonie Fountain, managing director of the Voice Network, an umbrella group seeking to end child labor in the cocoa industry. "It's always been too little, too late. It still is."[80] The major chocolate companies had committed in 2001 to ending child labor within four years; almost twenty years after the pledge, they are still far from meeting their obligations. Fountain points to the reasons for not making any major headway in ending the problem: "We haven't eradicated child labor because no one has been forced to…What has been the consequence…for not meeting the goals? How many fines did they face? How many prison sentences? None. There has been zero consequence."[81] The *Washington Post* article quotes one farmer, who says, "I admit that it is a kind of slavery," while also recognizing that "they are still kids and they have the right to be educated today. But they bring them here to work, and it's the boss who takes the money."[82]

"The boss who takes the money" is the most critical part, which points to the global trade system and the embedded raw-material supply chain that was set in place during the colonial period and continues to the present. The small boss on the farm or in the region is devoured by a bigger one operating in the Global North with multibillion-dollar accounts at their fingertips that could make or break small farmers, and kids altogether. Labor movement—children, men, and women—across West Africa, Asia, the Middle East, Latin America, and the US is a reality that has its roots in the colonial formation of economic and political order in the Global South. Take any raw material in the world and examine it; what you will find is that Global North corporations control every aspect of the market and dictate the terms of the trade and the process through which these commodities enter the market. Child labor is present in every sector of the raw material economy in the Global South, and it is factored in when financial returns are considered by the boss. However, the local boss takes his cut while the bigger chunk goes to the big boss, who most likely lives in one of the major cities in the Global North and participates in all the normal affairs of the society without thinking twice about it.

Child labor is a reality across the Global South as families cooperate across generations to make a living and support all the things needed to keep life moving. In my own experience, I started to work at age eight by selling balloons during summer vacation in my neighborhood and by assisting the owner of a small grocery store up the stairs from our house. All my brothers worked during the summer and saved all their income to use for school supplies, clothes, and the things they needed that my dad and mom did not have the funds to cover. During the school year, I worked weekends at a café in a downtown movie theater, which was one way for me to cover my daily needs, buy essentials, and save money to purchase better quality soccer shoes.

I can't condemn or speak about child labor without putting in context the reality in the Global South, where the ideal of kids going to school, living a normal childhood, and playing with family and friends is something that sounds and looks good for a movie script but is very difficult to actualize considering the total dysfunctionality of the economy and political order. In my circle of friends at school, I recall everyone having a job connected to either their family's line of work or a neighborhood establishment like myself. My dad provided all the essential household needs— rent, food, electricity, major purchases—but we all worked to lessen the burden and cover what went beyond necessities. Thus, I have been working since age eight, all through my middle and high school years.

After high school, I moved to the US to attend university. I started working two weeks after landing at the San Francisco airport, as my brother, Suhail (may Allah bless his soul), landed me a job at the donut shop where he worked while going to school. A year after arriving in the US, we managed to open our own donut shop in the city of Antioch, California, and worked there with family throughout my college days. Aside from these two initial weeks in the US, I have worked throughout all my college years, paid my tuition, and graduated with a PhD from the University of

California, Berkeley, without any debt.

It is not easy to deal with this topic of entrepreneurial success without looking at the entanglements of so many issues all at once. The Bazians in Nablus were well-off at the start of the twentieth century and before the arrival of the British and Zionist colonization, with thriving businesses that included a wholesale enterprise and a soap factory, among other enterprises jointly owned by the extended family. British and Zionist settler colonization transformed Nablus's economy and disrupted the existing regional economies, the effects of which ended up in the small and mega narratives of each and every Palestinian.

Child labor, for Palestinians, is not divorced from the settler colonial history itself. Even today, child labor in Egypt, Jordan, and Palestine, just to name a few, is part of the daily realities of so many families and children; the postcolonial economy and the political corruption built from the colonial era and maintained over generations produce this outcome. Here, I am not advocating for the continuation of child labor or making my own experience a model to follow, but rather for an understanding of what takes place daily across the Global South and what is needed to change and transform it.

Coming back to the main point of the raw-material economic order, the Global South continues to supply the northern economies, which is the main key to maintaining the underdevelopment status in the postcolonial period. Indeed, chocolate is by no means the only raw material production employing children or causing regional disruptions, but it is the product that people least associate with abuse and corrupt profiteering. Take every single raw material extracted from the Global South and you will get horrific abuse, political corruption, civil unrest, outright murder of activists and labor organizers, pollution of everything and anything in sight, and slums built to house the "wretched of the earth" workers so as to facilitate the industrial scales of these operations.

All of us who might call ourselves "liberal or conscious" of the world are using computers, smartphones, electric cars, solar panels, and a host of other new technologies under the assumption that they are cleaner and better for the world and the environment. But we are, in all honesty, deluded and have developed the skill to compartmentalize our role from the destruction connected to everything connected to our daily consumptive life.

The "miracle" of the lithium battery, which powers the technological wizardry of our modern age, is dripping in the misery of Global South populations and Indigenous communities in particular. "Finding effective solutions to the climate crisis is an absolute imperative, and electric cars have an important role to play in this. But without radical changes, the batteries which power green vehicles will continue to be tainted by human rights abuses,"[83] said Kumi Naidoo, Amnesty International's Secretary General, on the occasion of publishing a report on the subject. "Every stage of the battery lifecycle, from mineral extraction to disposal, carries human rights and environmental risks."[84] Innovation and progress have always had an ugly and hidden underbelly that promoters and consumers chose to ignore even when it is sitting in plain eyesight. Who among us believes that the working conditions for the computer industry in China and India meet or provide labor and environmental protections and adhere to basic standards? Do we think of these issues when we all line up days ahead in tents outside the stores to get our hands on the new iPhone or Apple Watch so we will be seen as and deemed the most hip and coolest people around?

The fossil fuel industry needs a whole chapter if not a multivolume encyclopedia to document the exploitation, manipulation, cruelty, pollution, and wars that caused the death and destruction of millions of lives. Consider for a moment all the conflicts, coups, interventions, low-intensity warfare, death squads, and assassinations in the Middle East, Africa, and Latin America that centered on access to and control of oil and natural gas, which has taken the lives of millions and caused streams of immigrants and refugees to seek safety in the Global North.[85] Take any major raw material in the world, trace its origin, and you will find it mainly in the Global South. Then explore the extraction process, how it gets to the market, and you will find human rights violations, death, and destruction funded and managed by the Global North at every turn. It is a picture of sustained, sophisticated pillaging schemes, abuse, and destruction of the environment and the people who inhabit the area and has been under way for generations.

Critically, all of this exploitative raw material extraction is undertaken with the knowledge and participation of every segment of society in the Global North—the governments, corporations, bankers, insurance companies, media outlets, development outfits, religious institutions, and the not-for-profit industrial complex that acts as the emergency ICU for the structural dispossession of the Global South.

Walking into any major grocery store in the Global North, we are accustomed to finding all the vegetables, fruits, and items we desire and demanding they be available on the shelves 24/7, 365 days a year, no matter what season, condition, or calamity has befallen the world. The rainforest in the Amazon is burning[86] daily to open up space to graze cattle and grow fruits and a variety of other products in demand by US and European customers, including conservative, liberals, and all those in between with minor exceptions. Colonization is the ingredient that forged the raw-material supply pipeline and built the modern corporate edifice on a soil fertilized by the bodies, hopes, and dreams of the Global South. What is consumed, processed, manufactured, and sold in the Global North is literally soaked and dripping in the blood and sweat of faceless and nameless people who are locked into perpetual poverty by "civilized" design. Adding insult to injury, in the erasure of this humanity is the propensity of political figures, economic hit men, and media talking heads to use all types of lazy and racist rationales to explain away the obvious exploitation.

❧ South Africa, Racism, and Postcolonialism

Regional economic conditions in the contemporary period give the impression that the reasons behind what is under way is something specific to the cultural, tribal, or societal background of the area, rather than an outcome of long-term failure by colonial and postcolonial design. To contextualize the problem, let's return to the earlier discussion on South Africa as the last settler colonial project to come to an end in 1991. In the years since Mandela's freedom, serving as president and passing away, the country has been engulfed in ongoing internal violence, contestation, and political instability, which is directly connected to the long and painful colonial past in the region. The end of the apartheid regime was a critical turning point for the country, but undoing years of neglect, abuse, violence, and lack of investment will produce postcolonial contradictions, crisis, and tensions before long-term stability is achieved.

In South Africa, the political changes were swift, which was not the case on the economic, social, and regional immigration fronts. It will take a long time before the economic impacts of settler colonialism in South Africa are undone, and no one is sure that it will take place without a major breakdown of the society; the threat of a civil war is ever looming.

At present, South Africa is experiencing political protests centered on popular demands for greater economic opportunities, land reforms, labor rights, decolonization of curriculum, and immigrant and refugee rights. On the immigrant and refugee front, the public discourse has veered into extreme xenophobia, targeting Africans from outside South Africa. Indeed, rarely is South Africa brought up in regard to the immigration-refugee crisis, but the country has been a major destination for many people from the southern African region as well as refugees from the Central African Republic, Ethiopia, Somalia, and Sudan, to name a few.[87]

The violence engulfing South Africa brought to the fore the precarious conditions affecting immigrants and refugees across the globe and that the country is not immune nor an exception to the worldwide crisis. Immigrant numbers in South Africa vary from two to five million, including both legal and illegal arrivals, with most making their way to the country in search of jobs and better living conditions. At a time when unemployment in South Africa is hovering around 24 to 26 percent, the worsening economic conditions, coupled with the perception that foreigners are taking away jobs and opportunities, fuel the anti-immigrant and antirefugee campaign.

However, the focus on South Africa's violence, which has already claimed many lives and caused the flight of many immigrants and refugees, misses the broader issues at play in Africa, Latin America, Middle East, Southeast and West Asia, and other parts of the world. The problem, and indeed, the crisis, should be understood in relation to the collapse of the postcolonial state and the failure of neoliberal and globalized economic programs in providing a sustainable development model. This caused regional disruption and the massive influx of immigrants and refugees from the Global South to the ex-colonial motherlands and the Global North. What are the real causes behind the massive flow of immigrants and refugees into Europe, the Gulf states, India, Israel, Japan, South Africa, Turkey, and the US? The flow of immigrants from southern African states into South Africa, the last settler colonial project in Africa, is paradigmatic of the crisis and the collapse of the postcolonial order coming at the end of the Cold War, which, when taken together, calls for a deeper historical examination of the problem at hand.

Certainly, the driving force behind this massive immigration and refugee movement is economic dislocation, political instability, and wars in the postcolonial states. The massive waves of immigrants and refugees are emerging from the collapsing postcolonial states in the Global South, which, in economic terms, operated as satellite units connected to the ex-colonial motherlands and advanced economies in the North by providing raw materials and captive markets. Raw materials shipped to the Global North are turned into finished products for at-home consumption and exported back to captive markets in the Global South.

West Africa's cocoa plantation and fossil fuel paradigms are normative and not the exception in this postcolonial economic order. In the modern era, the industrial Global North incentivized a raw-material-based economic order and bribed or bombed its way into hospitable markets for its finished products in the postcolonial Global South, which maintained the order that was set in the colonial period. In this context, the postcolonial economic order was determined by the colonial economy and was maintained intact during the quest for independence and subject to the established colonial antecedents.

Instead of thinking of the immigration-refugee crisis as a disconnected problem and pursuing a state-by-state analysis, a much more robust understanding emerges once a longer historical trajectory is considered with the colonial discourse at the center. The postcolonial state economy was the colonial economy minus colonial troops and administrators. At the moment of independence, the colonial powers managed to stitch together their economic rights and interests within each colonized state in the Global South. The next step was to cement these "rights" through using colonially drafted, framed, and codified international law, which was written to maintain and legitimize colonial thievery and pillaging at the expense of Indigenous populations.

The national flag and stamp, along with the presidential guards and plane, in the Global South were the trappings of independence, while the economy and the livelihoods of the people were the domain of the colonizers, even in the postcolonial period. Examine the economies of most postcolonial states in the Global South (including South Africa), and you will find that their raw material reserves are owned and operated by the Global North and the markets are totally dominated by the multinational corporations. The best-case scenario for some Global South states can be found in a multinational corporation from the north locating a manufacturing base and providing cheap employment opportunities, but at the expense of the environment and local production possibility. The postcolonial state remained rooted in providing raw materials, a captive market for finished products for the ex-colonial north, while making sure to stamp out and destroy any local competition.

Consequently, the distorted economic foundation of the postcolonial state in the Global South is tearing at the seams with the immigration-refugee crisis being the immediate visible outcome, but the stench of death and destruction drives people out toward safety. The colonies never arrived at economic independence, only the perception of one.

☙ France and the Postcolonial Pact

A good example of the postcolonial pact is France's continued economic domination of its ex-African colonies and institutions in each state. In debates focusing on the immigrant-refugee crisis facing Europe, Luigi Di Maio, Italy's Deputy Prime Minister, blamed France for the current state of affairs in Africa and the flood of people escaping the continent, stating: "If today we still have people leaving Africa, it is due to several European countries, first of all France, that didn't finish colonizing Africa."[88] What Di Maio was referencing is France's work to manipulate "the economies of 14 African countries[89] that use the CFA franc, a currency underwritten by the French Treasury and pegged to the Euro."[90] He then added: "If France didn't have its African colonies, because that's what they should be called, it would be the 15th largest world economy. Instead it's among the first, exactly because of what it is doing in Africa."[91] In the post-World War II period, the control of independent African states was carried out "through political, security, economic and cultural ties," which allowed France to "maintain a tight stranglehold in Francophone[92] Africa," and "both to serve its interests and retain a last bastion of imperial prestige."[93]

France's control of the economies of what is known as the Francophone Africa zone is so pervasive that the terms "independent" and "states" for this region are a true misnomer when used in the same sentence. Immediately after the end of direct colonization, the French instituted a colonial pact with its "ex-colonies," which mandated the "requirement of these countries to use a common currency (the CFA franc) that is controlled directly from the French central bank in Paris."[94] In simple terms, the "14 African countries do not have an independent monetary policy. They do not hold the right to determine details of how much currency to release into their economy or to revalue their currency at will. All decisions pertaining to monetary policy are controlled from Paris. The 14 countries are also obliged to deposit 65% of their foreign reserves into the French central bank. In addition, the 14 countries cannot access this money at will; rather they have to seek France's permission to do it. In fact, if they need more than 20% of this 65%, they must take it as a loan from France at the prevailing market rate and secured by their existing deposits."[95]

Currency control and monetary policy are the core of each modern nation-state's ability to govern independently and determine what is best for its citizens, a basic right that is not present in the Francophone Africa zone. One can see that it is in France's interest to extend loans to the fourteen Francophone states since they are making money from engaging in a sophisticated postcolonial financial tool of control and manipulation. France determines monetary policy and controls the funds of each of the governments, which also allows it to play a major role in the flow of import and export into the fourteen states and determine the domestic political outcome for each state.

In her *New York Times* article, Megan Specia references the book written by Senegalese development economist Ndongo Samba Sylla, who maintained "that the CFA franc allows France to continue what he called its monetary imperialism in Africa. The same guarantee that stabilizes the currency has also limited growth…because the value of the CFA franc is fixed against the euro, rather than being determined by international markets."[96] In Sylla's view, "The CFA franc is the last colonial currency in activity,"[97] which allows France to control the economies and political decisions of the Francophone Africa zone. The most glaring aspect of the zone's currency and foreign exchange reserves, for Sylla, is the interest spread between deposits and loans, which gives African countries "a lower interest rate—0.75 percent—than France's own inflation rate, which stands at around 1.6 percent." According to Sylla, this spread means, "It is as if these African nations are paying French banks to hold their money."[98] The control goes beyond rate spread and includes the requirement for the fourteen African nations to maintain a 50 percent deposit of their foreign exchange reserves in an "operating account" in the French Treasury, which between 1993 and 2006 was set between 65 and 100 percent at the time of independence.[99]

Estimates on the financial impacts vary, but what is certain is that the fourteen African countries provide a constant capital flow into the French Treasury, which then can be loaned out at a higher rate, even to the same countries that deposited the funds in the first place. Accurately, former French president Jacques Chirac commented in 2008 that "without Africa, France will slide down into the rank of a third world power."[100] Chirac's predecessor François Mitterrand prophesied in 1957 that "without Africa, France will have no history in the 21st century."[101]

France's economy and political standing is made possible by its constant domination and control of the Francophone African states and their massive reserves. Often, the argument in favor of this French arrangement posits the attempt to confront corruption in postcolonial states and the need to have some mechanism to prevent the possible disruption inside each of these states. However, this brings another issue to the front, which is the relationship between ruling elites in the postcolonial south and the ex-colonial powers.

❧ Postcolonial Elites and Political Domination

The postcolonial financial picture is muddied by a colonially con-structed elite that was ready to continue the mode of economic operation they were educated under, accepting it to be the uni-versal norm. If France (the same applies to the US, the United Kingdom, and other Global North countries) is concerned about corruption, which it should be as it is always a highly worthy proposition, a fundamental question must be asked: who educat-ed these people who then set up these corrupt structures in the colonies in the first place?

Indeed, the elite and the ruling circles were nursed on corrup-tion during the colonial period and, likewise, were kept on the take (bribed) in the postcolonial period or during independence. Many who came into leadership positions were first educated in the colonial north, employed during the colonial period by Glob-al North corporations, and, once in positions of power, repro-duced the same colonial patterns learned and internalized over generations. France, the United Kingdom, and the US need look no further than their own "educational and training" programs that produced the needed elites to implement postcolonial, neo-liberal, military strongmen and globalized economic plans at the expense of each country's interest and populations needs.

Not to imply lack of diversity in leadership in the Global South, as there is and were efforts to challenge and transform the societies, but the use of military coups, interventions, assassina-tions, and a host of other tools of the jackals made sure the sta-tus quo remind intact.[102] This strategy can be clearly illustrated in France's action in Guinea after demands for independence in 1958, where the French government and military "unleashed its fury destroying schools, nurseries, public administration build-ings, cars, books, medicine, research institute instruments, trac-tors; animals were killed and food in warehouses was burned or poisoned. This was meant to send a message to other colonies that the consequences for rejecting France would be high."[103] Even

121

more recently, the French intervention in Libya and economic interests behind the effort was rooted in attempts to maintain the postcolonial order.

No, Africa is not full of corruption, it has been made as such by the colonial powers and is maintained by an economic and political structure that rewards corruption to avoid accountability for France's robbing the fourteen countries anew. The Global North is not interested in nor seeks anitcorruption from political actors; rather, it wants elites to do its bidding and maintain the flow of raw materials, open their markets to finished products, link their currency and all their trade to the dollar or euro, deposit their reserves in Western banks, and open up every part of their economy to multinational corporations. What the Global South elite gets in return is the ability to funnel the bribes into Western banks, deposit the commissions earned for betraying their own country and society to offshore and off-the-book accounts, secure "retirement" homes and vacation spots in Europe or the US, and, more importantly, provide special security forces, independent contractors, and on-hand jackals to eliminate domestic opposition.

There is an important link between corruption and postcolonial control. French control of the assets and foreign reserves of the fourteen African countries creates the needed incentives for France to recruit and keep in power corrupt "leaders" since it prevents change from taking place. A handpicked or recruited leader is much cheaper, in the final analysis, than returning control of deposits to an independent and self-assertive political elite. Paying off the leader, his family, and the circle of military officers is much cheaper and cost effective than returning 100 percent of the deposits and giving back the properties and assets stolen over generations and control to the fourteen countries. In other words, what will they do with all of it since they don't know the value of what they have and will end up destroying what "we," the colonial and sophisticated Global North, have built for them in the first place!

In reality, the French colonial attitude is still present by insisting that they built infrastructure in the colonies that "saved" lives, which is the same argument that the US makes in relation to Afghanistan, Iraq, and Latin America. Behind every project or development program in the Global South is a massive gas-guzzling engine that structurally siphons resources into the Global North. In each case, the French, European, and American banks and corporations facilitate the payment of the bribes, setting up the secret bank accounts for these handpicked "leaders," and use the payments as the needed leverage to continue to extract colonial economic and political terms from each of the countries.

Let's stop to ask a basic question on corruption: Are the banks and governments in Europe so ill-equipped to ascertain the illegal nature of large sums of deposits made in the name of African, Asian, Latin American, and Middle Eastern leaders, and their families, who happened to be poor or middle class mere months before taking office? How is it possible that a person whose government salary is in the hundreds of thousands can amass billions in deposits in European and American banks? It is all part of a cost-benefit analysis for European and American decision-makers, banks, and corporate institutions; you pay some to the corrupt few so that you may own the whole country, the people, and everything that is of value for generations.

So, if Zaire's President Mobutu Sese Seko can stash away billions over thirty years, then the question is, how much did the governments, corporations, and banks who facilitated this in Europe and the US make over the same period? The corruption we set up in the Global South pays out in the millions or billions, but our corruption is measured by the countries we own and trade in a big political chessboard where you take Egypt, I keep Libya, and let's split the difference over Iraq!

❧ Postcolonial Corruption and the Cold War

The economic domination and elite's corruption dynamics were further complicated during the Cold War as postcolonial states got recruited to fight the wars on behalf of the Global North—the US versus the USSR. President Mobutu Sese Seko of Zaire (currently of the Democratic Republic of the Congo), among many others across the Global South that embraced the Cold War, played a key role for the US and the West in the Angolan war and brought further instability and disruptions to the postcolonial states. Here, recently "independent states" entered into a new cycle of violence, both internal and regional, that obstructed the possibility for real development and the earnest desire to break away from the ex-colonial powers, which now constituted around the East-West conflict zones.

The Cold War was anything but cold in the Global South, and millions of postcolonial subjects died in the armed conflicts as frontline dark bodies and pawns for the two superpowers. A by-product of the Cold War in the Global South, and once coupled with the role of the military in the colonial period, is the elevation of military power and violence as the main tools for administering society, which made the fusion of corruption and military power seamless. The Cold War further distorted the emergent postcolonial state and introduced yet another level of dependence, internal conflicts, and manipulations.

It is important to emphasize that the military power's centrality and violence in the postcolonial state was born out of the colonial period, and in sub-Saharan Africa, it can be traced to the emergence of the slave trade in the region. We must recall that the slaves-for-guns strategy was facilitated by European powers to increase and intensify the regional wars in East and sub-Saharan Africa in order to boost the supply of enslaved people to the transatlantic market. In his paper, "Guns-For-Slaves: The 18th Century British Slave Trade in Africa," University of Michigan economics professor Warren C. Whatley observed: "I find that the supply function shifted out over time in a systematic way, primarily because British gunpowder exports to Africa had a multiplier effect. Gunpowder was not only exchanged for slaves; it was also used to capture slaves."[104]

Gunpowder supply was instrumental in fomenting regional conflicts, which produced more slaves to the coast. In this context, European slave traders sold gunpowder and weapons to all parties in East and sub-Saharan Africa, which intensified the wars among them with the end result being commodified humans and slaves (i.e., war captives from each side were brought to the coast and sold for more guns to fight another round, resulting in more slaves being brought to the coast).

Guns for slaves of old is transformed into military hardware, tanks, planes, and special training to the postcolonial state to protect the colonially constructed economic interests and the handpicked and nurtured local elites. We can add to the list the extensive use of mercenaries, or as they are euphemistically called "private contractors," that are deployed outside the confines of international and domestic laws (as if law has prevented Europe or the US from invading and destroying states in the Global South). The national military in the postcolonial state is anything but national; rather, its primary function is to protect the colonially trained elites who managed the postcolonial economic interests of the Global North and were ready to burn down cities and towns in the process if threatened. France's postcolonial order in Africa is perfectly summed up in the following passage that details the scope of control:

> After World War II, the colonial pact maintained the French control over the economies of the African states; it took possession of their foreign currency reserves; it controlled the strategic raw materials of the country; it stationed troops in the country with the right of free passage; it demanded that all military equipment be acquired from France; it took over the training of the African police and army; it required that French businesses be allowed to maintain monopoly enterprises in key areas (water, electricity, ports, transport, ener-

gy, etc.). France not only set limits on the imports of a range of items from outside the franc zone but also set minimum quantities of imports from France. These treaties are still in forceandoperational.[105]

Indeed, not to leave things to the local military, France used "covert action and dozens of military interventions" and coups to make sure that the conditions are maintained according to its expressed interests.[106] The same applies to the US and its constant use of interventions, covert operations, and coups to maintain its total control in Latin America, the Middle East, and other parts of the world. The relationship between local elites using power and France using its own military muscle to reconstitute its postcolonial order is dependent on whether control can be maintained by the existing handpicked elites or not.

Thus, France "has intervened in sub-Saharan Africa on five different occasions in the recent years, in addition to using intelligence and surveillance operations and countless semi-permanent military campaigns. Most recently, France launched Operation Barkhane, an ongoing counter-terrorism initiative spanning five countries in Africa's Sahel region and involving more than 3,000 personnel."[107] In reality, the constant interventions in the Global South by the US and European powers is intended to maintain the postcolonial states in an infant stage of economic, political, and social development, which necessitates further "training programs" that are calculated to produce the opposite of the much-needed state maturity.[108]

❧ "Economic Hit Man" and Postcolonial Development

Another dimension of the postcolonial economy and the state is the preoccupation of the elites with wanting to imitate and replicate modes of development and progress present in the Global North—the location of "civilization" itself, racial superiority, and the imagined perfected ideal. This imitative approach further cements the existing colonial links in the postcolonial era and centralizes the role of the colonizing state in all ongoing internal and external affairs. Ex-colonial powers, the US, and the trendy and sophisticated development gurus hired by banks, governments, and corporations from the Global North recommend such strategies because they lead to strengthening the postcolonial levers of control and put Western companies in the driver's seat, not to forget the loans involved in undertaking many of these dead-end or dependency-producing initiatives.

Opting for an imitative project leads to heavy dependence on the expertise of the ex-colonial motherland "professionals" and the readiness to follow economic prescription on how it should be done, as well as the nurtured eagerness to seek "partnerships" for the postcolonial state development projects with the big and successful corporate brands from Europe and the US. By opening the door (assuming it was closed) once again to the colonial, superior Global North master to enter into the picture, the postcolonial state returned willingly into the colonial structure and was ready to pay everything it had and take the needed international loans and debt to finance it.

In the colonial period, the colonizers had to bring to the colonizing mission an army, officers, administrators, spent blood, and treasure to control and dominate the colony, and then begin to extract benefits and raw materials while facing constant resistance. However, the postcolonial era witnessed the ex-colonizer "expert" being invited and flown in first class on the national airlines; received with pomp and circumstance; put up in five-star hotels or the state palace; served as a king by the independent and exotic natives; given free and unlimited time to pontificate his superiority on national TV, radio, and in newspapers; and then handed handsome contracts and payments as an advisor or consultant to the country's own structured dispossession and disasters in the making.

After the "expert" finished their dispossession of the postcolonial state in the Global South, they return home to a new job, possibly as a professor of development, economics, or area studies; or at a government agency or think tank; or as a media expert or some other gig that allows them to speak from a position of "authority," adding to this would be pure gold if they knew a few words or the language of the colonized natives so as to, yet again, inspire a new crop of colonial managers in the postcolonial era.

In reality, the consultant, advisor, expert, or more accurately "the economic hit man"[109] worked to entangle the postcolonial states in debt, dependency, and a failure-by-design approach. The colonial powers used armies and brute force to rob and pillage their way into the Global South, but in the postcolonial era, businessmen dressed in suits, flying on planes, and driving luxury cars did the dispossession with the stroke of a pen while sipping wine and eating caviar in five-star hotels. Debt and loans are the magic elixir sold by the experts to help bring about development and progress in the Global South, while all along it was a scam that put the subprime mortgage and derivative players to shame. The scheme was protected by the International Monetary Fund, the World Bank, and a host of other international organizations, which made sure that the robbery was legal and sanctioned by colonial legalism framed within international law. And in the case that a country is unable to repay, then a debt-for-equity swap is introduced as a remedy—the most sophisticated plan to "legally" rob a nation and present it as a rescue plan!

France's control of foreign exchange reserved for the fourteen postcolonial African states and facilitating loans and debt acquisition was an intentional scheme that enabled successive French governments to intervene and determine the affairs of each of these states. Debt financing for postcolonial states was an instrument used to nullify the effects of ending direct colonial control, and the Global North was able to lay greater control over the Global South. Recent data shows that "developing country debt payments increased by 85% between 2010 and 2018,"[110] which means that the poverty-stricken populations in the Global South are the source of wealth and upkeep for the Global North, the trickle-up economic model.

In the past, the colonial power had to use its own resources to extract the colonized resources, but in the postcolonial states the responsibility was shifted to the local population and elites to do the work and pay for it. Debt and loans served as tools to maintain the colonial in the postcolonial while making sure that the elites in the south are incentivized to play along with bribes and commissions deposited into secret Swiss,[111] British,[112] German, French, Italian, and American bank accounts, which often are managed by the same banks or subsidiaries of the financial institutions originating the loans in the first place.[113] Often the loaned funds never left the safes of the banks that extended the loans in the first place since they also prescribed the companies that were hired to undertake the imitative development project; likewise, the companies were directly or partly owned subsidiaries of the banks making the loans.[114]

Not to be seen as ignoring or leaving out the native expert, a local interlocutor was available to assist in formulating the proposal, making sure the "local" view was present for the projects to be financed. The native expert, who most likely studied and graduated from Oxford, Sorbonne, Harvard, or NYU, was schooled in how best to lead the inferior Global South out of its supposed backwardness by increasing its dependence on and imitation of the Global North's success model. Projects that might be a great fit for London, Paris, or New York are pitched for states in the postcolonial south with debt financing and a list of big US and European corporations waiting to devour the funds before they even arrive.[115]

The native expert's role is to map the tribal landscape, understand religious divisions, navigate the local elites, and know who must be invited to tour the Global North and, as well, is open to sexual exploitation,[116] drugs, and luxury corruption schemes.[117]

Entangling the elite in corruption schemes is good for business and will land the deal 100 percent of the time. Often with the help of the native expert, the Global North corporations, banks, and governments are in total control of any contract negotiations, and all sides sitting at the table are paid and compromised to sign the deal that will most adversely impact the local economy. This is not an open market economy or capitalism at play but the most sophisticated mafia-like shakedown and robbery scheme planned, produced, and executed with laser precision. If elites refuse to sign, then the plane accident is not far behind to bring about a swift change of leadership or a military coup led by an officer that was recruited as an asset during training programs in Europe or the US some years back.

❧ Postcolonial Regional Conflicts and Distractions

The constant local and regional conflicts and bloodletting in postcolonial states, shaped, produced, and nurtured in the colonial womb, are often misleadingly described in religious, tribal, and ethnic terms. For beginners, the postcolonial borders are the same colonial borders that were shaped by competing European colonizing interests and crafted around local tribal, religious, and ethnic fault lines to maximize penetration, control, and domination.[118] The tribal, ethnic, religious, and cultural postcolonial borders were shaped by the colonial powers to maximize internal rivalries and create the conditions for constant conflicts so as to manufacture the needed rationale to meddle in and control each country's affairs in the postindependence period.

In reality, the drawing of borders was done with the idea of keeping the colonized society fragmented and constantly in need of military and civil intervention by the ex-colonial motherland. While the colonial military power was expelled from the country, however, and through this process, the structure that was set in place made sure to keep the colonizers hanging around in the windows, in the driveways, and on the roofs, and for sure cooking the postcolonial meal that is filled with raw material extraction and dispossession of the natives in the "civilized" postcolonial kitchen.

The majority-minority power relations in the postcolonial states were crafted in the colonial period through a divide-and-rule scheme and often with the specific goal of maintaining the colonizers' interests by design. On the one hand, an empowered group, a minority, or a small handpicked colonized elite from the majority, who is constantly threatened because most of the existing leadership lacked the popular mandate and legitimacy from the population, is translated into an enduring reason for intervention in the military, economic, and political affairs of these states. The right to rule was achieved through the schemes already discussed and maintained through brute force and military power, training, and expertise provided by the ex-colonial power for the purpose of preserving and protecting the Global North's economic and strategic interests.[119]

Wherever you find a majority-minority conflict, whether religious, tribal, cultural, linguistic, economic, or political in the Global South, look for the colonial footprints first before attempting to consider any dumbed down analysis of the causalities. In addition, ask the question about the nature of the economic market in the region, the type of natural resources extracted, and the multinational corporations' interests before searching the religious text, tribal history, or past cultural differences among the people dying and being maimed in the process.[120] Colonial merchants of death are at work in the postcolonial world and are apt to use all existing fault lines to maximize their returns on investments. Currently, religious differences and tensions between local groups is the most successful tool to rationalize intervention and authorize wholesale transformations of societies.

Existing fault lines in postcolonial states have a long history and are present across the world. Some may assert that we cannot accuse the Global North of initiating or creating them in the first place. Agreed, the existing fault lines have been in place for a long time, but what makes them flare-up and intensify is the critical question. The colonial powers have achieved mastery at the divide-and-rule game, and nothing was deemed sacred within the colonially framed set of end-justifies-the-means approaches, including humans and their relation to God.[121]

The colonial powers used three primary strategies to achieve their goals: "The first involves colonization—the settlement of large numbers of Europeans among the subject peoples, as in southern Africa and Algeria. The second consists of co-opting the native elite through assimilation or bribery; there are many examples of this in Africa and the West Indies. The third strategy is 'divide and rule,' a policy that has played a crucial part in ensuring the stability—indeed, the viability—of nearly every major colonial system."[122] Here, the "divide-and-rule" strategy, according to Richard Morrock, "may be defined as the conscious effort of an imperialist power to create and/or turn to its own advantage the ethnic, linguistic, cultural, tribal, or religious differences within the population of a subjugated colony."[123]

Much of what we see in current conflicts between different groups in the postcolonial Global South has been stoked to the surface so as to serve short- and long-term colonial and imperialist interests. Sitting at the root of all these ethnic, tribal, and religious conflicts is a new articulation and mobilization into policy of the long discredited notion of the "white man's burden" of the colonial era, which did not shift much with deploying a racist rationale for interventions, exploiting historical differences to intensify existing conflicts, and using it to achieve greater control of resources.

Think about the Shia-Sunni tensions in Iraq that get mobilized by the US in an effort to divide and rule, while all along access and control of oil and providing regional security for Israel were the reasons behind the invasion. Every news reporter in post-Iraq invasion asks, what about the Shia-Sunni divisions, the history of conflicts between the two sects, and why do they hate each other? Then they immediately jump on how the US is attempting to solve the problem, bring peace, and get "democracy" established in the country. The white man's burden new lease on life: democracy through the barrel of the gun, or "democratize or die," as my colleague at UC Berkeley Professor Ramon Grosfoguel aptly puts it.

Indeed, the link between colonial discourses and racism is ontological, with each one being the progeny of the other as a two-headed monster sharing a disfigured heart and body. Today's world is framed and organized around the colonial epistemic and nothing escapes its hegemonic reach. The term "globalization," the current invasive and exploitative type, is nothing more than the continuation of the colonial regime under a more improved control-and-command structure with the highest value being cost savings and efficiencies.

❧ Postcolonialism and Immigration-Refugee Crisis

How is the immigration-refugee crisis today linked to colonialism and postcolonialism in the first place? Indeed, this is an important question I will turn to next while keeping the earlier discussions in mind. Earlier we discussed how the colonial and postcolonial project was vested in capturing and maintaining access to raw materials, dominating markets, and controlling trade with the use of violence coupled with internal and external control structures. In order to develop a concrete argument on the link between the collapse of the postcolonial state and the immigration-refugee crisis, I will have to go back and trace key factors that shaped the colonial project itself, with particular emphasis on the forceful movement of Indigenous populations across the globe.

Certainly, the modern colonial project included the forceful and "involuntary" movement of millions of people across borders and continents, which resulted in the current configuration across the globe. This fact is illustrated by going back to 1492 as an important demarcation in the ushering in of the modern colonial project. Central to the colonial project's success was, first, the expulsion and removal of Jews and Muslims from the Iberian Peninsula, which was needed to allow for white and Christian Europe to emerge into being. Prior to this period, the idea of Europe as a continent that is separate, white, and Christian had no meaning or reality. Thus, Europe had to be ideologically invented and brought to life through the theological otherizing and removal of Jews and Muslims from the continent. Purity of race and blood was constructed and refined in relation to the "opposite" other: namely, the Muslim and Jew (mostly of North African and sub-Saharan African background).

The expulsion did not end in 1492; rather, it continued with the Inquisition and the issuing of various Black codes that culminated almost one hundred years afterward in the forced removal from Spain of all those who initially were converted to Christianity but continued to practice some elements of Judaism or Islam in secret. If racism is understood to be the governability of the bodies and spaces of targeted communities, then the Inquisition, as a state-run system, was vested in total control and regulating the public and private sphere of Muslims and Jews. Indeed, it was the panopticon of total control, and before the concept was even invented, Europe had constructed a regime to control every element of life for the targeted communities.

On April 9, 1609, King Philip III of Spain issued a decree that called for the total removal of the Moriscos, the descendants of Muslims, who a century earlier were forcefully converted to Christianity, as a precondition to being allowed to remain in the Iberian Peninsula. Aside from focusing on the religious identity of those expelled, the bigger picture had to do with Europe constructing its identity through this process and then setting in motion the very pernicious and racially hierarchical modern world. In this context, modernity was constructed on the basis of race, expulsion, and exploitation, whereby existing religious differences were racialized to become the basis of separation and exclusion. Critically, the Inquisition used a state and church sanctioned regime of terror and torture, which ironically included the use of waterboarding,[124] a tool that became a favorite of the Bush administration during the Iraq and Afghanistan invasions. What was the racial imaginary and stream of thought relative to Muslims that introduced waterboarding as an appropriate torture regime by the Bush administration remains unanswered!

Modern European colonialism's first targets were internal subjects, the Jews and Muslims alike. Europe's ideological and epistemic walls were constructed around a supposed Muslim and Jewish threat or the possible defilement of the Christian-only demarcated geographic space, which must be purified and cleansed so as to serve its "sacred" purpose. If we understand racism to mean controlling and governing the bodies and space of the targeted racial group, then Muslims and Jews were subject to a state-run racialization project. At the same time, and just a few months after the forceful expulsion of Muslims and Jews from Spain, the most destructive and successful genocidal settler colonial racial project was unleashed on the Indigenous populations of the Americas. Often the treatment of these two monumental events as separate and belonging to different episteme is shortsighted, since the basis of otherization, subhumanness, and racial difference was articulated in Europe before Columbus's journey across the Atlantic.[125] This was a continuation (more violent and genocidal) rather than a break from the recent past in Spain.

The multiple genocides in the Americas were made possible by a series of European ideological shifts, technological developments, and persecutions that calumniated first in expulsion, then with attempts to search for an alternative route to India, away from Muslim-held territories that ended with Columbus crossing the Atlantic. More critically, the alternative route was an attempt to disrupt and bypass existing trade patterns that had been operational for centuries with Europeans' focus on dominating and controlling the market for themselves. Furthermore, the competition between northern, southern, and eastern European powers was, likewise, focused on trade and domination of markets. Those southern and eastern European powers who were part of the existing trade system in the Mediterranean lost out to the northern and western European powers with far-reaching effects lasting centuries.

One may legitimately ask, what does all of this have to do with immigration, refugees, and the massive influx from the Global South at present? This is an important question that still needs further historical contextualization leading up to the present circumstances and waves of humans coming from the Global South. Genocides against the Indigenous populations in the Americas necessitated the importation of a "labor force" to work the massive lands seized by European settlers. In the Americas, the lands were systematically and industrially depopulated by disease, death, and destruction visited upon the Indigenous population. A "labor force" it was, but not by choice; rather it was the massive importation of enslaved people from Africa that supplied the need for the new colonies.

Importation of enslaved people to the New World was a type of involuntary immigration (this term gives little justice to what was or is done to the enslaved people and their descendants) that disrupted regional economies in West Africa while accelerating and intensifying conflicts at the local level to produce the needed commodified subjects to be shipped to the colonies in the Americas. European settler colonialism in the Americas was a global project and emerged out of an interconnected set of events in Europe, Africa, and the new colonies in the West. This project was further connected to the expulsion of the Jews, Muslims, and Moriscos from Spain; multiple genocides of Indigenous populations; and importation of enslaved people that led to the disruption of West and sub-Saharan African regions, altering trade routes and reconfiguring capital and industrial markets across the globe. Every part of the globe was and continues to be affected by the events that unfolded since 1492, with no end in sight.

Indeed, the settler colonial moment of arrival in the Americas was ushered in with forceful dislocation that has never been accounted for and is yet to be fully documented or undone, let alone stopped. Colonialism set in motion involuntary human movement from all parts of the globe, which is totally different from anything experienced in the past, and once coupled with the introduction of racial classification, it made for the most devastating consequences. We are living, breathing, and experiencing the world that was created by Columbus's journey across the Atlantic, and efforts at altering the trajectory have been futile up to this point.

Settler colonialism in the New World left the door wide open for the forced and involuntary human movement across borders and continents. The nonsettler type of colonialism likewise introduced forced human movement across the Global South, starting with removing Indigenous populations from regions rich in natural resources and handing them to northern companies to exploit and pillage. The removed populations were then recruited to work at times on their own stolen lands or in other regions and became a steady source of cheap and migratory labor that was disconnected from its land, history, and tradition.

Movement of people on a regional level within the Global South brought to the surface at times historical tensions and conflicts among Indigenous groups in various areas. This facilitated the divide-and-rule colonial tactic and put the colonial powers in the driver's seat to supposedly mediate between the various groups but all along keeping an eye toward neutralizing internal resistance and making it easier for the colonialists to control all resources and power.

In time, the colonized populations who were left landless, stateless, and unemployed got recruited into the colonial military and bureaucracy, then shipped to distant lands to enforce the colonial structure against other colonized subjects or to defend the territories of the colonial motherland itself. In this, we have the beginning of the labor relationship between the colonized and the colonizer that down the line would lead to importation of this same workforce to the colonial motherlands and major cities in the North. Furthermore, the "native expert" or "native informant" was taken to the colonial motherland to be "educated," and similarly, it opened doors for voluntary structured immigration from the colonized Global South to the North. Initially, the numbers were rather small but in due time increased to include most, if not all, members of the elite ruling class from the colonies, who were educated and sent back to manage native populations and oversee the economy for the colonizers.

The practice of voluntary movement of the colonized subjects from the Global South to the North, and then back to the South, initiated a process that continues until the present day. More to the point is the critical role played by the colonial Global North powers in shaping and constructing meaning and ideas about the colonized person's self through the colonial lens and not independent of it.

Furthermore, the movement out of the Global South unleashed the endemic brain drain crisis since the best and brightest are inducted into the colonial machinery of the Global North and are incentivized to stay in close proximity to the colonial center. They are relocated to the Global North, and while some become very critical and produce masterful contributions, nevertheless, the structural damage to the South is irreversible. Indeed, for some, the success of the few is introduced as proof of the veracity of the colonial "civilizational" project itself.

⮞ Media Framing and Brain Drain

An important factor in the brain drain and immigration-refugee crisis is media framing and production concerning the conditions in the Global North and the desire to arrive at the pinnacle of "human progress" and "paradise" on earth. Here, the Global North becomes the location where the imagined good life and possible perfection of the human condition is located, which is precisely what colonial racial conditioning desires to achieve, helping in consolidating white racial superiority in the Global South. The media becomes an avenue for transplanting this notion in the colonial subjects' subconscious, driving them to seek arrival at the shining white northern colonial city upon the hill. Media and image production are not separate or distinct from the colonial epistemic, which emerges and is represented in popular culture, literature, paintings, songs, and movies of all kinds as a canvas to blot more whiteness onto its existing colonial white supremacy.

The colonial project moved slaves to the Americas, imported and used colonized populations as foot soldiers around the world, trained low-level bureaucrats to administer various colonies, recruited elites for the purpose of education and administration of the Global South, and finally brought a massive illiterate and uneducated menial labor force to clean the houses, cook the food, dig the trenches, pave the roads, work the farms, and collect the garbage in cities and towns in the heart of the colonial motherland. What made these populations available for such forced movement and immigration was an essential element of the colonial project itself and shaped the postcolonial dynamic that is being experienced up to this point. The racists and the nationalists who ask why these immigrants and refugees are here, meaning in the Global North, never stop for a minute to reflect on colonial history and interventions that created the crisis in the first place. Indeed, we are here because you were there as a colonial and postcolonial power!

Colonization begins with land and the natural resources contained therein, but the Indigenous populations were dispensable and transferable. Controlling the raw materials was made possible by the forceful removal of populations from their ancestral lands, and in the process, the colonizer gained access to and eventually owned the land and everything on it, including the people themselves. Thinking of land and its centrality to daily life, just take a minute to reflect on the following list of items that are connected to it: housing, agriculture, natural resources, groundwater, roads and transportation, all types of pipelines, electricity generation, energy, silicon, gold, silver, minerals, precious stones, sport activities, advertisement space, and defense industries to name the obvious few, but many more could be added. The takeover of the land was central to the colonial project and continued to shape the postcolonial since the stolen lands were never returned and continue to be dominated by the Global North.

Indeed, removing colonized populations from the land created surplus labor or more likely manufactured conditions that made individuals focus solely on seeking employment to fulfill basic human needs of food and shelter. Possessing land for Indigenous populations translates to self-sufficiency in food as well as sustainable living from what can be grown and consumed locally from the owned land (be it individual or collective ownership). Colonization was focused on severing the Indigenous populations' land relationship and replacing it with a colonial economy focused on achieving total dependency on colonially supplied and market-controlled products. Since the colonizer already took possession of the best lands and the most lucrative resources, the ability to control the livelihood of the colonized populations was the instrument deployed to engender cooperation and malleability to colonial demands.

Forceful removal from the land had far-reaching consequences and disrupted the existing tribal, social, political, economic, and religious balance in the colonized regions. A by-product of forceful removal and population movement away from ancestral lands is the intensification of conflicts among the various local groups. As each group is moved or separated from its own land, they begin to struggle to keep more of the shrinking territory and resources at the expense of another group facing similar circumstances. This conflict had the further benefit for the colonial power of fragmenting existing societies at the micro level, thus increasing the ability to control and manipulate local politics and select those who were ready to sell their souls and communities to the highest bidder.

Death, murder, destruction, and genocide are constitutive and productive in the colonial project with devastating results across the globe. Whenever violence is witnessed in the Global South, focus not on the immediate identity of the foot soldiers fighting for survival on the plantation but look for those near and far who situated, nurtured, benefited, and administered the colonially constructed plantation with murderous viciousness.

The loss of land disrupted local economies built over centuries and destroyed existing supply and demand patterns to be replaced by major colonial companies and corporations vested in driving maximum profits to investors in the Global North. Furthermore, the local economy was to be kept at a low level of development, producing raw materials to feed the industrialized colonial motherland's economy, which then turned around finished and more expensive products to sell in the Global North and South. The raw material economies in the colonies were structurally kept at an underdeveloped stage so as to maintain employment, manufacturing, and innovation in the Global North.

Forceful removal from land, displacement, intense local conflicts, and other factors already discussed created a transhistorical dependency and structural disruption in the Global South, the end result being immigrants and refugees seeking better and safe living conditions. The immigration-refugee relocation door was opened and used by the colonial powers to drive the material and political benefits from the Global South, which continued unabated in the postcolonial period with minor changes.

The end of the Cold War brought new dynamics and an end to the balance of power era, which brought about an accelerated push toward privatization and a market-driven and neoliberal economic order. In the US, the signing of the North American Free Trade Agreement (NAFTA) caused massive displacement of Mexican farmers, resulting in American agri-business takeover of vast tracts of land while manufacturing shifted jobs to Mexico. The signing of NAFTA was followed by other US bilateral agreements in Latin America, which caused yet more displacement and disruptions. Similar privatization and neoliberal economic and political patterns took shape in Africa and the Middle East, thus transforming and distorting the already distorted postcolonial states.

Each state and region has its own unique features and differences, but what brought them all together was the failed economic and political models, which became far more acute once coupled with military interventions and destruction of democratic and grassroots institutions in the process. Military interventions since the 1990s, and pernicious capitalist penetration in a unipolar world system followed by the massive financial crisis in 2008, brought about the collapse of the postcolonial state, and with it the massive flow of immigrants and refugees.

Global South postcolonial elites embraced neoliberal economic models and hyperprivatization schemes, which were layered on top of the postcolonial raw-material and natural-resource extraction structure. The "new" system accelerated the displacement of farmers, reduced the economic well-being of the average worker, wiped out the middle class, and put each country at the whims and powers of global markets. It was sufficient that the elite was well-paid and taken care of with deposits and bribes in offshore accounts and fancy shopping trips to Paris, London, and Milan, but all was at the expense of what little was left in the treasuries of the postcolonial state. A clear example would be the developments that led to the events of the Arab Spring, which should be read through the lens of postcolonial economies ruled by Western propped-up dictators that shifted in a short period into a neoliberal economic model, hyperprivatization, and open market schemes for the benefit of a small ruling circle that got caught in a rapid funding crisis in the post-2008 financial market collapse.

Raw materials, like cocoa from West Africa, minerals from the Global South, oil from the Middle East, and agriculture and cattle raising from Latin America are the primary causes of Western interventions and the stoking of regional tensions. Every military intervention, trade agreement, and economic destabilization leads to displacement of the poor, the middle class, and those at the margins in the Global South. As the economic opportunities shrink and violence escalates beyond control, then the only path out is immigration or refugee status in neighboring countries, followed by a journey to Europe, the US, or Canada. Immigrants and refugees follow a well-travelled path that was paved during the colonial period and continues to function all the way up to the collapse of the postcolonial state. What made the crisis more acute is that the collapse occurred in a number of states and regions at the same time, which made it a global phenomenon and not limited to one state or even a cluster of states in a continent.

In addition, the collapse in the Global South emerged at the same time as the economies and social welfare state came undone due to successive years of budget cuts and tax cuts for the rich at the expense of the middle class and poor, as well as the adoption of trickle-down economic models and structural adjustment programs. We have arrived at a point where the populations of both the Global North and South are marginalized and are pitted against each other by domestic and international powerful forces. Stoking anti-immigrant and antirefugee sentiments obfuscate the economic and political crisis in the Global North, while the ruling elites in the Global South exploit their own populations for the benefit of multinational corporations, and in return, they are permitted to maintain their seats of power and hefty deposits in a Western bank account.

Chapter Four

Bouncers and Enforcers

At the beginning of the twentieth century, almost 85 percent of the world's land surface was subject to either direct colonization or some form of protected status. Africa and Asia were the private dominion of European colonial powers with millions living and existing under the boots of pernicious colonial control relegating them to servitude, bondage, and treatment as mere "beasts" of burden. At the time, a traveler making the journey from Africa's north to the south, then from east to west, would find that all territories were colonial possessions of the British, Dutch, French, German, Italian, Portuguese, and Spanish, with only a few areas experiencing any type of independence, self-determination, or freedom. The western hemisphere was under US domination and subject to the Monroe Doctrine.

Movement of raw materials, rendering of services, and cheap labor were the tasks assigned to populations in the colonies by European powers. The pillaging of the southern hemisphere was systematic, structured, and total, leaving nothing untouched in the process—animate or inanimate. In 2018, when the world commemorated the 100th anniversary of the end of World War I, we were reminded of the hundreds of thousands of troops recruited from the colonies to fight imperial wars and who sacrificed themselves to protect and defend one European colonial power from another. This, at a time when the colonial man or woman was not considered equal to a European or even considered fully human. The colonized subject was used as a fighting force and, at the same time, brought to inhabit the human zoo[126] spaces within the European capitals, to be publicly gazed upon and touched as the uncivilized and subhuman.

The end of World War I did not bring peace to the Global South or end the colonial project itself; rather, it was granted further legitimacy under the newly formed League of Nations and the paternalistically crafted mandate authority[127] to extend the control of European colonial powers. As a matter of fact, under the League of Nations supervision the colonial footprint was expanded, and vast swaths of land in the Arab world were brought directly into French[128] and British[129] possession. The region currently named the Middle East was born, its borders drawn, and the Palestinian dispossession occurred through the facilitation or direction of colonial powers during this period. Likewise, Africa and Asia witnessed further entrenchment of the colonial project and forced a voluntary movement of populations across the globe, as well as intense demands for raw materials and labor to rebuild Europe.

One way to view the dispossession of the Palestinians is to think of it as a process of forced removal of Jews from Europe and Arabs from Palestine, which was facilitated by colonial logic, Eurocentric power, racism, and British strategic planning to protect its trade and colonies. The forced removal of Jews from Europe came on the heels of an intense period of anti-Semitism in Eastern Europe, England, and France, with the Dreyfus Affair[130] being a paradigmatic representation of the time and making Zionism a logical solution to escape the continent's intensification of anti-Semitism, bigotry, and racism. England, for its part, along with other European powers, acted purely from a strategic and racist consideration in supporting the creation of a Zionist state. On the one hand, it was seen as a buffer to protect British colonial possessions in Egypt and trade routes, and on the other, it removed from an anti-Semitic perspective the "undesirable Jews" from Europe. In this context, the dislocation of both Jews and

Palestinians and setting them on a collision course against one another to serve a larger colonial project is at the heart of what was set up in the newly colonized region and emerges out of the depths of a Eurocentric, millenarian Christian and white supremacist worldview.

World War II witnessed similar and equally massive forced movement of human beings, with the Holocaust representing Hitler's horrific and genocidal "Final Solution" to Europe's permanent and persistent other: the Jew. As such, the Holocaust represents a European norm if one locates the centrality of racism directed at Jews for being Jews and going back even to the period before the expulsion and, indeed, to the Inquisition. The actual World War I[131] and World War II[132] efforts included moving colonial subjects from the colonies and into the battlefields to fight and defend European powers from each other, with hundreds of thousands dying a nameless and faceless death since they belonged to the realm of nonbeing and the subhuman. The movement continued after the war with many from the Global South brought into the North to rebuild destroyed cities and economies while having to contend with constant otherization, racism, and xenophobia.[133]

The anticolonial liberation struggles took shape in the 1950s and throughout the 1960s with most of the countries in the Global South gaining the right to political self-rule but not economic or epistemic self-determination and independence. Certainly, the new countries declared independence, had a new flag, a national stamp, ruling assemblies, and all the trappings of imagined power, but the economy and the resources remained in colonial hands or in the hands of the carefully selected and nurtured elites, who acted as middlemen and managers of the colonial subcontract. In this regard, the newly minted postcolonial independent states acted more like a franchise when it came to wealth distribution and relations with the European ex-colonial powers.

The colonial powers left behind a whole set of constraints and control levers that were intended to keep the raw materials flowing northward while continuing to find ways to expand the levels of structural dependency. The General Agreement on Tariffs and Trade (GATT), the World Bank, and the International Monetary Fund (IMF) became instruments of both stabilization of the post-World War II world economy and maintaining the existing trade order between the Global North and South (which I will deal with in more detail later on in the chapter).

ᴥ Petrodollars and Floating Dollars

Toward the end of the anticolonial struggles, two major economic shifts occurred that impacted the Global South: the oil crisis during the 1973 Middle East war and the US quitting the gold standard and opting for a floating dollar. The 1970s oil crisis created much bigger and deeper economic problems for the postcolonial and newly independent states by unleashing a massive global inflation crisis that devalued currency, raw materials, and other segments of the economy.

In addition, the rising cost of oil made it impossible to carry on normal economic activities and caused governments to increase or institute massive subsidies for fuel, electricity, food commodities, health care, and education. Some of these subsidies existed prior to the oil crisis; nevertheless, the level of price support and government expenditures increased so as to keep the lid on possible protests and prevent the internal political opposition from exploiting the economic weakness to push for radical change. At the same time that the oil crisis hit the global market, the US Federal Reserve ended the dollar link to the gold standard, making it a floating currency, which led to massive circulation of dollars in the market, and the banks moved to unload as much as they could on the global market and in the Global South, in particular.

The debt crisis was the direct outcome of the petrodollar phenomena, the floating dollar, and the role played by banking institutions in the Global North in fomenting the global debt crisis as a way to unload the massive liquidity deposited by oil-producing countries, petroleum companies, and the US Treasury's nonstop printing of dollars. As oil prices shot up and with it a massive increase in deposits coming from oil-producing countries, the banking institutions in the Global North were faced with a major crisis, needing to pay out more interest on deposits with no end in sight, so the easy way out was to send it to the Global South. Banks make money when they sell loans and have others pay the interest to the bank, rather than the other way around. When you deposit your money into your account, the bank enters it as a liability on their books, and it can be changed into an asset once it is loaned out to others, with this process repeated many times over.

The banking industry went into overdrive and set in motion one of the most aggressive global loan sales initiatives to unload billions of deposits and transform them into revenue-generating loans. The postcolonial "third world" was a primary target for unloading these deposits. Loading up the newly independent postcolonial states with billions of dollars' worth of debt meant achieving deeper levels of economic control. When coupled with the already corrupted elites, this made for dismantling any prospects of freedom, dignity, and a future with fair and just economic opportunities. Debt salespersons were sent across the Global South to search for loan opportunities and to look for funding big-ticket items and projects that could unload massive amounts of petrodollars in the quickest way possible.[134]

No attention was paid to the viability of the funded project or whether the country had even the capacity to undertake such a project since the sole driving force behind all of it was to unload the cash and make it someone else's responsibility to pay the interest on it. The colonized elites were overjoyed with the flood of cash coming their way and were more than happy to play along since it meant a bigger and fatter commission or, at times, outright theft of all but a few dollars spent on decorative and ceremonial projects. Often, the same banks that made the loans in the first place assisted these colonized elites to funnel the money back into secret accounts in Swiss or other Global North financial institutions[135] while taking a cut for services rendered.

The debt crisis of the 1970s and 1980s transformed the postcolonial state into an effective financial prisoner to the banking and financial institutions of the Global North and with it the loss of control over its decision-making capacity. Consequently, the recently independent postcolonial state lost all control and was placed under direct receivership of the Global North financial system. The strategy called for sending to the south none other than the IMF and the World Bank, the bouncers and economic enforcers for the global financial system, who made sure that the debt was being paid while all other internal services and subsidies were cut to the bone. The IMF and the World Bank acted to protect Global North banking interests at the expense of the postcolonial South. The IMF-mandated structural adjustment programs were the tools used in the postcolonial period to achieve maximum dependency and control over economies of the Global South.

❧ The IMF and the World Bank: Bouncers of the Financial System

Having sold loans to impoverished countries, which facilitated wealth transfer for the elites who signed the documents, the banking industry then sent its well-dressed henchmen and global bouncers, the IMF and the World Bank, to break the metaphorical legs of the population and extract payments by any means necessary. The structural adjustment programs[136] called for increased export of raw materials to bring hard currency to pay for the debt; liberalization and privatization of the economy; reduction or total removal of government regulations that prevent foreign control or ownership of assets; currency devaluation[137] while "recommending" connecting it to the dollar; encouraging foreign investment in mines, raw materials, agribusiness, and tourism;[138] and topping it off by cutting governmental support for education,[139] health care,[140] price support for food staples (such as wheat, corn, rice, and beans),[141] and social services.[142] Collectively, these adjustment policies worked to further ruin what little was left of the ability of postcolonial populations to sustain a livelihood and a dignified life.

The increased export of raw materials by the Global South created a flood of commodities in the market, thus collapsing prices and reducing the hoped-for foreign currency returns. In his article, "Third World Debt: Anatomy of Genocide," F. F. Clairmonte precisely describes the outcome of the structural adjustment programs: "What we are witnessing at a far more critical level of the international business cycle is that the third world is literally being driven to market larger and larger volumes of commodities on the global market in return for higher priced goods and services imports. Which means that larger and larger amounts of their collapsing export earnings must reimburse an unending spiral of bigger debt interest and amortization payments. In short, a prescription for accelerated genocide."[143]

The policy recommendation was intended to help the Global North by reducing raw material costs for the manufacturing base while increasing the rate of exports directed to the postcolonial South. Indeed, Clairmonte observed that "larger and larger volumes of primary commodities at lower and lower prices were thrown on the market in a desperate bid to maintain their export purchasing power. This was translated into near zero levels of inflation for the developed capitalist economies as one of its inevitable by-products."[144] Furthermore, the privatization and liberalization policies made it possible for the multinational corporation to devour what little was left outside of their control by buying out and disrupting any small and incipient economic base in the Global South. These plans should be correctly named destructive adjustment programs that manage to reassert a deeper colonial control in the postcolonial period, which likewise, results in another massive wave of immigration and dislocation from the south.

Instead of reducing dependency, the IMF[145] and the World

Bank deepened the crisis and effectively became the real power in countries that were put under these adjustment programs. In short, "debt-equity swaps" and other IMF and World Bank instruments were "not only destabilizing and inflationary, but a weapon for deepening third world indebtedness by demanding a preferential exchange rate which is the crux of debt-equity swaps transactions."[146] The context on the impact is made clear by Emily Sikazwe, then Zambian director of the antipoverty group Women for Change, who expressed her frustration on the IMF's and the World Bank's policies in her country, stating, "What would they [the World Bank and the IMF] say if we took them to the World Court in The Hague and accused them of genocide?"[147]

Dependency on the Global North affected every part of the economy with the sole focus directed at paying the debt and enabling the global banking institutions to transfer wealth again from the Global South to the Global North.[148] What started during the colonial period reached its pinnacle in these adjustment programs as postcolonial independent countries were tasked with implementing sweeping policies that, again, delivered each country's economy and society to the ex-colonial motherlands without any questions being asked.

◈ Colonial Elites and Adjustment Programs

The colonially trained elites were complicit during the whole process of the adjustment programs and got paid handsomely by getting the country into debt, managing the privatization, and using might and power to keep the population in line.[149] Protests and popular mobilizations in the South were expected and prepared for jointly with the IMF and the World Bank as a way to break the backbone of any movement that might challenge or alter the recommended policies. The corrupted, colonially nurtured and paid for elites deployed maximum force and power to crush the opposition, which was part of the policy and not an unplanned for anomaly in the implementation phase.[150] The protests and violence were used to extract even deeper concessions from the elites and then to commit whatever remaining resources to bolster the military, which was supplied, trained, and designed to protect the Global North's economic interests at the expense of populations in the South.[151]

Employing maximum violence, ordering targeted assassinations, and sending activists and intellectuals into exile crushed the opposition and enabled the Global North corporations and financial institutions to purchase further assets at much lower and discounted prices. The Global North banks were all "aware of the desirability of having a repressive totalitarian social order to stimulate and consolidate the growth of such transactions."[152] The bankers and colonial motherland policy-makers came up with even more insidious plans to shake the pockets of the post-colonial South by introducing what is known as a debt-for-equity swap framework.[153] A debt-for-equity swap amounted to one of the most sophisticated and civilized international methods of thievery produced, directed, and acted on the world stage by faceless and nameless suits sitting in offices and country clubs in the Global North.[154]

It should be called "death-for-equity swap" for it squeezed the last drops of hope and life out of populations by robbing them of their property during daylight hours on national TV and for all to watch. Each country that owed money and was indebted to the banks because of loans taken out and signed for by presidents, ministers, and elites in the Global South was forced to surrender its assets. The debt-for-equity swap deals were worked out and planned by governments and banks in the North, whereby states in the South had to give up their gold mines, rainforests, natural resources, water and telephone companies, and vast agricultural lands to pay back the bad and "unperforming" loans. The debt crisis that was written, produced, advertised, and executed by the Global North in the 1980s set the stage for the intensification of poverty, economic failure, and political instability, which brought further entrenchment of the elite and more pernicious neoliberal plans and privatization schemes.

The debt-for-equity swap was the final nail in the coffin, if any was needed, to completely recolonize the Global South anew, but in this case, the focus was on tangible and fixed assets without having to deal with anything else. In the earlier period, the colonial troops had to be on the ground along with military equipment, staff running prisons, the administration, et cetera. But the new-and-improved revolutionary colonial project in the postcolonial structure removed any costs for control and domination and shifted it to the local managers, who are paid a contractual fee to oppress and sell their country and soul to corporations and banks in the Global North and to the ex-colonial motherlands. Postcolonial states and the global financial structure made it possible for the Global South to actually subsidize its own dispossession. As ownership of the assets were moved to the Global North, then all internal economic activities became even more regulated by the needs and demands of multinational corporations running the global market.

ᴥ The Cold War, Deregulations, and Trade

The 1980s witnessed the reemergence of Cold War warriors and a renewed focus on defeating the Soviet Union, undoing the Iranian revolution, and reversing any miniscule political changes in Africa, Asia, and Latin America. Ronald Reagan's election and reelection for a second term in the US, coupled with the Conservative Party's return to power in the United Kingdom under Margaret Thatcher, brought about neoliberal economics modality[155] with an emphasis on privatization, economic expansion, trade expansion, and market deregulations. Add to this a massive military expenditure and nuclear weapons buildup in an effort to win the Cold War while at the same time increasing intervention and attempted domination of the Global South. What was unique in this period is that the deregulation efforts were at once internal to the US and global.

On the internal front, hard-line conservatives and Cold War warriors worked diligently and maliciously to reverse the civil rights and anti-Vietnam War movements' gains made by the poor, middle class, and communities of color in the Global North.[156] The conservative governments were successful in achieving the rollbacks through formulating something akin to internal structural adjustment programs directed at reducing or removing support for social welfare programs,[157] education, health care, and environmental protection while facilitating distorted privatization and deregulation schemes for the economy and pushing for accelerated military buildup.[158] The strategy on the external front included continuing IMF and World Bank adjustment programs; pushing for accelerated privatization; sponsoring bilateral and multilateral, ruinous "free trade" agreements; and unleashing a muscular interventionist foreign policy to further disrupt the postcolonial state in the Global South.

The Cold War euphemism describing the period obscures the burning fires, death, and destruction visited upon the Global South across Africa, Asia, Latin America, and the Middle East. Reagan's and Thatcher's elections emboldened the hard-line conservatives in Washington, DC, and London, who fanned out across the world to reclaim "lost" terrain and moved to support and prop up yet again discredited and despotic elites in the Global South as long as they committed themselves to the Cold War efforts. "Low-intensity warfare" was the operable term used to describe the unleashed new strategy intended to disrupt and overturn any and all regimes that refused to come under Reagan's newly reinvigorated Pax Americana. The shift from Carter's focus on human rights to confronting communism and the Soviet Union translated into confronting terrorism, or as Elliott Abrams put it, "By taking a strong stand against the Soviet Union, we are dealing with the human rights problem wholesale rather than retail."[159]

Putting the new postcolonial strategy into action involved supporting regional wars in Asia, Africa, Latin America, and the

Middle East with massive military expenditure[160] and recruitment of both regular and irregular forces across the Global South. The countries that experienced one aspect or another of the strategy include Afghanistan, Algeria, Angola, Chad, Chile, Colombia, El Salvador, Eritrea, Grenada, Haiti, Iran, Iraq, Lebanon, Liberia, Mozambique, Nicaragua, Nigeria, Panama, Peru, Somalia, South Africa, Sudan, Venezuela, Yemen, and Zaire.[161]

Fighting and defeating what Reagan called the "evil empire" translated to using postcolonial subjects and territories to bleed the Soviet superpower of its resources and topple leaders and governments allied with it in the Global South. In this case, both the US-led NATO alliance and the USSR-led Warsaw Pact engaged in protracted "low-intensity warfare" across the globe; consequently, in the surge of conflicts, brown, Black, and Asian postcolonial bodies ascribed with subhumanness were piling up, once again merely nameless, faceless, disposable biological substances sacrificed for a higher purpose: saving the Western white Christian capitalist economic world system. It was not the Cold War warriors from the Global North that died in these battlefields; rather, the postcolonial subjects were once again made the pawns, easily moveable and disposable, used for settling accounts and dividing the world. While the Russian invasion of Afghanistan was costly both in blood and treasure for the Soviet Union, it was, nevertheless, an unconventional anomaly to use troops from the Global North to fight during this period.

Cold War warriors used existing cleavages and contradictions that were already magnified, sharpened, and intensified during the colonial period to shape Eastern-Western bloc discourses and fight the wars in the Global South. The proxy wars managed to destroy what little had been built since or saved from the colonial period, which in a short time led to further economic, political, and social destabilization. Each conflict in the Global South caused another flood of refugees and immigrants to make their way to the North in perpetual search of peace, security, and basic livelihood.[162] As local economies in the South collapsed and more resources were syphoned off to build up and equip militaries fighting "low-intensity warfare" against internal or external fomented threats, the human waves of refugees escaping the carnage ended up in cities and towns in the Global North.[163]

For Washington, DC; London; Paris; and Moscow, the Cold War was conducted in conferences, extended strategy sessions, and war games using the "low-intensity war" and "local assets" euphemisms to conceal pernicious and murderous policies. Some of the nefarious instruments implemented in the Global South with devastating results during this period include the use of death squads, assassinations, torture, placing mines in harbors, Central Intelligence Agency (CIA) training programs, disruption of trade, tampering with currency exchanges, manipulating agricultural policies,[164] attacking religious figures and institutions, flooding the markets with oil or wheat, and threatening and firing workers.[165] It is important to keep in mind that these strategies and policies employed in regional wars came on the heels of the debt crisis and the imposed structural adjustment programs by the IMF and the World Bank.

The debt crisis, structural adjustment programs, and "low-intensity warfare" brought the Global South into a worse condition than that of the direct colonial period. All internal cohesion was destroyed, social structures were fragmented, and even the distorted sense of nationalism was not sufficient to counter this strategy. Neighbors turned against neighbors, young men and mere children with guns were unleashed on populations across the Global South, and controlled chaos was implemented to bring societies and states to their knees to accept the new world order.

The colonized elites received assistance to move wealth and family members outside the country while continuing to manage the war efforts. This accommodation for the elites sets in motion another massive wealth transfer from the Global South as well as a cycle of brain drain since those with education and skills found ways to escape the turmoil and become refugees and immigrants in the North. Now cities in the Global North are home to a plethora of refugees and immigrant populations that escaped the wars and settled, or were made to settle, in countries that were either directly or indirectly involved in fomenting the conflicts in the first place.

❧ The Cold War and Imperial Religion

The global East-West conflict, or capitalism versus communism, witnessed an expanded role for religion, using it to implement imperial policies across the globe. Religion is a powerful force capable of unlocking great potential; however, in imperial hands, it can have devastating consequences. No stone, holy or profane, was left unturned and untouched during the Cold War as each power assembled its own set of assets and resources onto global battlefields. Marx's statement that religion is "the opium of the masses" has relevance in this period and must be understood in its proper context since the concept fits into his overall theory and critique of society. The practiced religion is shaped by the text as much as the material, economic, political, racial, and social conditions present in society.

Confronting communism in the Global South meant the mobilization of religious institutions across the world to counter the "ungodly" empire. Religion was an instrument brought to bear against the "ungodly" communist and in the service of the capitalist empire.[166] "God" and religion were cast as a procapitalist, open-market economy and free enterprise, which must be guaranteed by joining the global "holy crusade" against the evil empire.[167] Consequently, the emergence of modern religious fundamentalism can be traced to this period, and leaders within the Jewish, Christian, Muslim, Hindu, and Buddhist traditions were brought into the imperial court and given the stage to shape the needed countercommunist responses.

The critique here is not a defense of communism under the Soviet Union, which operated a state-centralized capitalist enterprise; rather, the aim is to elucidate how distorted religious traditions become a function of, and partner to, an empire with the centrality of the exploitative military-industrial complex within it. Religion, used as a tool by the empire, is a powerful mobilizer if the right people are involved, appropriate resources are made available, and selected texts are deployed; the desired results can translate into making individuals and societies support oppression and war in the name of a god.

Any religious text is considerably malleable and open to varied interpretation depending on the methods, authority, and accountability of those making the argument for its deployment in the postcolonial period. Certainly, religious figures played an important role in resisting and defeating colonialism. However, the postcolonial period witnessed the perversion and corruption of religious thought initially through the nationalist project itself, which operated with a reductionist and antagonistic vision toward religion, and then by its recruitment into the countercommunist global war efforts. The fundamentalist religious literature emerged from and followed the existing material conditions produced by the forces acting upon it, with the results translating into a fatal alliance that left millions of nameless and faceless commodified religious people dead on the battlefields. As a result, religion was implicated in the profane and became a worldly problem.

Religion in the Global South was transformed initially during the colonial period to produce a negative indigenous and mirror-opposite epistemic of the modern, rational, industrious, and progressive colonizer.[168] In order to achieve this desired outcome, colonial powers set out to promote a fossilized, restrictive, and undynamic aspect of religious traditions in the Global South while frustrating and prosecuting those who resisted or refused to stand aside. Colonial modernity needed a traditional backward "other" to illustrate its wizardry and mastery over human and material, which could not occur if the indigenous and tested practices remained intact. Furthermore, colonial powers wanted to wrest control of the ethical and moral underpinnings of the society that existing religious traditions and leaders wielded, which hindered colonial domination and thievery. The colonizers made sure to work diligently to sever the existing social relationships governed by indigenous religious traditions and structurally worked to erode the status and authority of the anticolonial and spiritually grounded leadership.[169]

The empire transformed "prophetic" figures into capitalist and materially grounded salespersons for a distorted and exploitative globalization. Militarism and war were sanctified by imperial religious figures that worked as handmaidens to rally laities across the Global South into the battlefields while offering assurances that fighting in the Cold War was for a lofty spiritual purpose. The role of the Catholic Church[170] in Latin America was closer to US policy in the region than the emergence of liberation theology in response to it. The US intervention in Latin America against leftist or democratically elected governments was assisted by a religious establishment that was ready to strike a deal to extend its economic, political, and social interests at the expense of the populations. As such, liberation theology and the theologians who worked to reeducate the laity about the purpose of religion in society, in the process, managed to challenge power and militarism. Liberation theology emerged in direct response to, and a push against, imperial religion, which was allied with power and engaged in illegal and criminal wars.

Similarly, the role of Muslim-majority states, groups, and organizations in the Afghan, Yemen, and Iran-Iraq wars was critical as global recruitment and crafting a jihadi prototype got under way to retaliate against the Russians for their part in Vietnam and against the Shia for the Iranian revolution. Tariq Amin-Khan maintains that "the pivotal role of client postcolonial states" emerging and sinking their "roots in Muslim-majority societies of Asia and Africa" was a direct outcome of "the Cold War's commencement in 1947."[171] In his view, Muslim-majority "states—

such as Suharto's Indonesia, Sadat's Egypt and Zia ul Haq's Pakistan—began to collaborate with the followers of political Islam, in step with the USA's imperial aims of the cold war era to fight 'godless' communist."[172] At the same time, the success of the 1979 Iranian Shia revolution brought state-framed Sunni Islam into a dual engagement with Western powers, an external fight against the godless communist and an internal religious fight to confront the Shai in Iran.

In addition, fighting communism and Shias meant fashioning an extremist and militant Sunni fundamentalist willing to sacrifice himself while fighting against Shia Iranians as well as the godless Russians. The trail for these operations leads to postcolonial states and the readiness to partake in shaping an imperial religion that is accommodating to power and works to integrate itself into the global economy. Shaping the Islam versus Islam conflict or confronting communism with Islam had far-reaching consequences, of which the results are visible daily with extremist groups that—unleashed during the Cold War era—are currently subcontracting their services or possibly acting on their own across the Global South.[173]

Likewise, the Israeli invasion of Lebanon and war efforts against the PLO, Iraq, Syria, and Libya should be viewed from an imperial lens, considering the use of religion as an instrument of power in the postcolonial period. Israel is a settler colonial state that worked to integrate itself into the postcolonial political, economic, and strategic structure by offering its unique set of security-training and intelligence-gathering capacities. Israel rendered its services in Latin America[174] through training the Contra's death squads,[175] in Africa by training and equipping Zaire's Special Forces, through weapons sales to apartheid South Africa,[176] and, for the West, intelligence-gathering efforts against the USSR.

Furthermore, Israel pre- and post-9/11 provided police and security trainings to police departments, FBI officers, and numerous agencies in the US and Europe, which was rooted in an Islamophobic and racist framing.[177] In return for these services, Israel demanded, and continues to expect, constant opposition to Palestinian aspirations. Contrary to popular opinion, Muslim postcolonial states and Israel often cooperated, shared information, and assisted each other (Morocco, Jordan, Syria, and Gulf states), as expected, by being partners in imperial religious discourses.

The 1980s brought about many changes and the reemergence of a triumphant extreme right wing that unfolded its militant policies with fire and fury around the world. Gone were the gains made by the civil rights and human rights movements across the globe. A period filled with secret wars, death squads, and massacres captivated the news cycle and brought many a dreamer into the imperial court seeking false gods, glory, and power. A renewed nuclear arms race shifted resources away from societies' real priorities and into a bottomless pit of conflict and confrontation that devoured everything in its path. Increased military expenditures resulted in cutting funding for everything else as well as falling into debt to finance unnecessary and expensive military equipment and interventions across the globe. More military spending meant more cuts in social programs; thus, more debt was generated in creating and sharpening the internal colonial model.

As a way to remedy the limited availability of funding in the US, Reagan's team began to facilitate the smuggling of drugs into the country so as to fund wars in Latin America and Afghanistan. The drug trade devastated communities of color in the US as well as causing disruption of sustainable agriculture in the Global South, which once again caused dislocation and migration away from zones of conflict and drug trading. Cold War warriors operated with an "ends justify the means" epistemic, which translated into death and mayhem abroad while pushing debt, cuts to social welfare programs, deregulation, drugs, and destruction of lives at home.[178] The flood of immigrants from the Global South was a by-product of these policies and not independent of it; however, no one wants to take responsibility for what transpired since the defeat of the USSR. Felling communism was far too important an endeavor to worry about the lives of the "little people" in the Global South or the people of the South living in cities and towns in the Global North. The collateral damage of ordinary, nameless, faceless, often impoverished, and mostly powerless lives was a price the Cold War armchair warriors were willing to pay.

At San Francisco State University, you could see and experience the outcome of US interventions in the makeup of the faculty, staff, and student population, which reflected every country and region that had "low-intensity warfare" and a long line of immigrants and refugees. The consequences of the empire's footprint filled the halls and plaza of every campus and inner cities across the US, thus promoting the internal colonial apparatus and heightened surveillance, repression structure, infiltrations, and spying on local activists to prevent solidarities from forming or demonize them once established.[179]

❧ Neoliberal Economic Order and Free Trade

Earlier, I discussed the role played by banks, the IMF, the World Bank, and elites in the Global North and South in shaping the continued dependency in the postcolonial period. The next stage of this structured control and manipulation in the postcolonial state took a sharp trajectory after the end of the Cold War and the triumphant march into neoliberal market economies, free trade, and privatization, which was assisted by concluding the last Uruguay Round of GATT negotiations in 1993. It is in this context and with the introduction of the World Trade Organization (WTO) that the new and highly abusive globalization trend was set in motion, which continues to unfold today.

In the post-Cold War period, the US emerged as the sole remaining superpower without any counterpower to offset this unipolar development. The Soviet Union's collapse meant that only one world system remained intact—the unrestrained capitalism. Eastern bloc countries, as well as Russia itself, embraced capitalism and sought and received admission into the sacred halls of the World Bank and the IMF. As expected, countries across the world lined up to join the victor of the Cold War, and as a result, the emerging capitalists opened their economies for foreign investments and the opportunity for wealth accumulation, a global rush for super asset sales and entry into the "free" market. On a global level, the free trade engine set in motion years earlier by Ronald Reagan was humming across the globe, intent on removing restrictions and regulations that might impact or hinder multinational corporations' access to world markets, raw materials, and economies.

The world trade system's governing body, the GATT, was set up in 1947 by twenty-three countries as a multilateral trade institution with the specific task of abolishing quotas and reducing, if not totally removing, tariff duties. The agreement was signed in Geneva and went into effect on January 1, 1948, but at the time it was considered an interim accord that would be incorporated into a United Nations structure once finalized. Needless to say, the United Nations did not develop such a structure, and GATT continued to govern and regulate the international trade system. From its inception, GATT was designed to look after and protect the Global North's trade interests at the expense of the postcolonial South as well as the Communist bloc during the Cold War.

Trade liberalization and the removal of quotas and tariffs sound appealing and might indicate the pursuit and foundation of an equal playing field in the global markets; unfortunately, such equality or opportunity has never been the case and was less likely for the Global South in the postcolonial period. GATT's inception was to cement the new global economic, political, and social order post-World War II and constitute a controlling agency to project into the future and make permanent the market advantages of the Global North over the postcolonial South. How to keep the embedded disadvantages and give them a legal imprint was at the heart of GATT[180] and its many rounds of negotiations; any evidence to the contrary was just for public relations purposes.

It was through GATT that differentiated sets of rules were put in place to regulate the market and to make it supposedly more "advantageous" for the Global South to export raw materials while complicating and instituting tariffs on finished and processed products from the same countries. It is in this way, and through the sophisticated GATT international mechanisms, that the Global South was incentivized not to develop a fully integrated economic system away from raw materials and into finished products. By keeping trade favorable for raw materials, it was possible to disrupt any incipient economic plans in the postcolonial South.

When a country trades in raw materials, the economy remains rudimentary, comprising two or three stages from field or mines to the Global North markets. Thus, the structure connects the local farmer or small mining operations to big corporate manufacturing interests in the North, and through various schemes, including, at times, military coups d'état, the raw material supply chain is kept intact. Developing a local processing economy would translate to creating money circulation in the market, increasing employment vertically and horizontally, incentivizing innovations, and fostering internal dependency between various parts of the society, which is something that colonialism worked hard to disrupt and prevent and continue in the postcolonial era. The raw material economy that was promoted and protected by GATT—and continues with the WTO—went a long way to disrupting future horizons of a truly independent and dynamic economy in the Global South and in the process provided a long imperial stick to beat into submission the postcolonial subject.

In addition to the raw material trade mechanism is the regulating of payment systems for international trade through establishing the basket of hard currencies (US, British, Swiss, German, Japanese, and also the French-designed currency for the Francophone countries), through which commercial transactions can be commissioned between states. Through the hard currency system, it was much easier to control and regulate trade with the Global South and have constant leverage over their economies. At the same time, one must account for the basic fact that transacting in these currencies implies, by necessity, the need to purchase and constitute reserves of these five currencies (the euro replaced a number of these currencies, but the basic principle still applies), which, if understood correctly, is one way that the Global South subsidizes the North, by constantly needing to invest in these floating currencies.

More critically, the basket of five hard currencies represented the new world order and with it the implied or promoted stability and constant growth that can produce returns on investments. This perceived or, at times, real stability, if measured against the Global South rate of return, created the potential for economic turmoil in the postcolonial state, forcing those countries to invest in the five hard currencies, treasury bonds, and various commercial instruments connected to each or, at times, all. Consequently, the structure of global trade under GATT was the exact instrument that led to total control of the postcolonial South economies and structured dependency via the policies and machinations of the Global North.

Since the 2008 economic crisis, it has become common knowledge that the banking institutions in Europe and the US have constantly and regularly manipulated the benchmark interest rate index of the London InterBank Offered Rate and currency exchange rates so as to increase their profits. The stranglehold through these exchange mechanisms and hard currency requirements is a disturbing reality that rarely receives the much-needed scrutiny it deserves, though it is an important economic profit-making and controlling tool.

In her dystopian young-adult novel series *The Hunger Games* (2008), and the films that have been made from the books, Suzanne Collins describes a postapocalyptic, fractured North America in which the peoples from the various regions must pay tribute as punishment for rising up to protest and change an abusive system of exploitative government. *The Hunger Games* describes the existence—what they have cannot really be called a life—of a people who are not fortunate enough to live in the Capitol. In these outer districts, the residents are imprisoned, controlled, monitored, and sometimes starved if they step out of line. Each year, two children from each district are selected to participate in a fight to the death against each other. There is no opportunity to refuse to fight as the arena in which the games are held is a controlled environment, and the players and the elements within can be and are manipulated. It may be useful to think of the scenario of *The Hunger Games* when considering the consequences of the implementation of the North American Free Trade Agreement (NAFTA) (and other trade agreements) as described in the next section.

❧ NAFTA and the Hunger Games

On December 15, 1993, after seven years of negotiations, the Uruguay Round of GATT was concluded with an agreement between 117 countries, in which they pledged to reduce trade barriers and further decrease tariffs. The agreement called for a "substantial reduction of tariffs and other trade barriers and the elimination of preferences, on a reciprocal and mutually advantageous basis," between signatory states. Officially named the Final Act Embodying the Results of the Uruguay Round of Multilateral Trade Negotiations, the agreement was signed on April 15, 1994, and subsequently ratified by the US Congress on December 1, 1994, and became law on January 1, 1995.

If the term "Final Act" conveys anything, it is indeed that reality was transformed into the theater of the absurd since free trade for the Global South has always meant structured dispossession and civilized robbery. Trade liberalization and reducing tariffs, according to its proponents, would bring forth the hoped-for better life and create wealth and prosperity across the globe. It was a cheap elixir sold to jubilant crowds that were ready to climb onto the fast-moving, triumphant American bandwagon and try to get rich quickly. The signed treaty introduced the WTO, which was empowered to implement the agreement and oversee all elements related to global trade.

What Reagan started in the US with deregulations, privatization, and procorporation policies became the new sacred text for the market under the WTO's promised worldly salvation through free trade. The democrats in the US joined the trade liberalization and procorporation bandwagon with the election of Bill Clinton, who moved the party to the right so as to appeal to Reagan democrats in an effort to recapture the White House. Clinton's shift to the right was a crafty strategy developed through the Democratic Leadership Council (DLC), a private outside group to the Democratic Central Committee and founded with the intended goal of reshaping the party away from its traditional base and onto a new-and-improved probusiness and deregulation footing.[181] The motto "if you can't beat them then join them" was Clinton's and DLC participants' strategy to unload the party's political left, social programs, and Latino and African American interests.

Clinton—and his surrogates—during the campaign made sure to present themselves as being tough on Blacks by instigating a confrontation with Rev. Jesse Jackson at the Rainbow Coalition Conference. The Clinton campaign, through his speech in the convention, took on the African American poet and activist Sister Souljah by selectively using her remarks concerning the Rodney King beating and Los Angeles uprising and comparing her to David Duke.[182] Certainly, "being tough on Blacks" was an important message for Clinton in order to appeal to Reagan democrats and soccer moms and get them to send him to the White House, which they did. And with Clinton's election, a new republican-light Democratic Party was born.

The shift to the right was undertaken on the backs of African

Americans and Latinos, who are likewise attacked under an anti-immigration campaign that included democratic leaders. Ending the social welfare state was the sacred mantra for the newly emerging democrats in republican skin, and deregulation, free trade, and privatization were the way forward internally in the US and Europe. Those of the working and poorer classes were often told either directly or through implication, "You are poor because you are not lifting yourself up by your bootstraps, and if only you believe in free enterprise and trade, privatization, and deregulation, then you will become rich."

The move to deregulate the financial markets went hand in hand with reducing government support for the poor and middle class as well as privatizing everything imaginable including prisons. In retrospect, the internal program can be viewed as a sophisticated structural adjustment program whereby corporations get to devour the economy while the poor and middle class get to pay for it through reduction in support for education, health care, and social programs, as well as a tax-rate break for the rich, or trickle-down economics.

The link between the local and global, or the internal and external, postcolonial became clearer during this period. Clinton's first act after being elected was to fast-track the signing of NAFTA with Mexico and Canada, which was, effectively, antilabor, anti-small business, antifamily-owned farms, and antienvironment, yet enormously benefited multinational corporations.[183] NAFTA opened the door for movement of capital and goods between the three countries, but not people or labor forces. The economies of the US and Canada are broadly comparable, and there is no substantial motive for mass migration from either country; however, this was not the case for Mexico. The Mexican economy was far behind both other countries and, as such, would have needed considerable investment and support to bring it up to par with the US and Canada.

For Mexico, NAFTA translated into a massive movement of

capital from the US to take over small family farms and transform them into an enormous agribusiness to supply US markets. The agribusiness moved to Mexico to escape and bypass increasing environmental regulations in the US that limited the use of pesticides, as well as minimum wage increases and overall labor costs.[184] In addition to the agribusiness, the manufacturing business began to relocate its assembly plants and the toxic aspects of its operations to the Mexican side of the border, which provided a cheap and captive labor market and no environmental regulations to limit or negatively impact production.

While NAFTA did mention raising the environmental standards in the three countries, no monitoring or enforcement agency within NAFTA itself was put in place to make sure that policies were implemented. Greed was the only environmental standard operating at the corporate level, and enforcement of any standard was easily bypassed by means of the always readily available subcontracting remedy, which was put into masterful play on the Mexican side of the border. The emergence of the maquiladoras, the factories in Mexico set up by American corporate interests, imported raw materials and produced goods for export to the US and other markets but with little or no oversight. NAFTA made the maquiladoras into a successful model to be emulated while pointing to the slight improvement in income levels for workers hired in these abusive enterprises.

Moving the production and manufacturing to Mexico opened the multinational corporations' eyes to the limitless possibilities of reducing labor costs, escaping environmental regulations, and reducing their tax bills. NAFTA in Mexico proved to be a successful and profitable corporate model for moving production outside the US and drastically increasing profit margins. In the light of the corporate success in Mexico, the US began to negotiate bilateral free trade agreements with various Latin and South American countries as well as continuing to push for global access through the WTO so as to cement the new-and-improved free market economy.

NAFTA's untold story is the direct link to the displacement of thousands of peasants and family subsistence farmers who had for generations cultivated public lands and were granted communal titles through the Mexican constitution. One key demand made by the US and Canada was for a change in land rights in Mexico, which President Carlos Salinas de Gortari moved to modify. The change in Article 27 of Mexico's constitution brought to an end the existing land reform gained through the 1917 revolution. Article 27 set the legal framework for distribution of community-owned lands, which are called ejidos; by 1992, almost half of the land in Mexico was in the form of one type of collective or individual ejido status. It would not have been possible for the US agribusiness and meat industry to take over and penetrate the Mexican market if the ejidos remained intact as they provided a communal shield against massive transfer of land ownership. Before NAFTA, the community, through ejidos, held land titles in perpetuity. However, the Mexican president, in collusion with major business interests, moved to modify Article 27 of the constitution and limit or remove communal rights to the land.

NAFTA and the constitutional changes caused thousands of existing ejido land-claim petitions already on file with the agrarian reform commission to be thrown away, thus making the lands available for sale or for government transfer of ownership. The changes to Article 27 nullified all the pending petitions, and overnight farmers and communities were left landless with the government moving to auction the land in favor of agribusiness and US meat-producing companies. It is this constitutional change that was the primary cause of the Zapatista uprising, which launched its nationwide protest on January 1, 1994, the same day that NAFTA went into effect.[185] The connection between Article 27 and NAFTA was immediate and deliberate. More critically, the immigration from the Mexican countryside to US cities can be located in the changes made to Article 27 that caused the displacement of hundreds of thousands of poor farmers who, for generations, had no other source of income other than the land that was taken from them by the government because of NAFTA.

Mexican land was opened to US corporate interests, and rapid development took place to relocate agribusiness, factories, assembly plants, and toxic industrial production while making sure the existing peasants were driven out. The low income levels and high poverty rate made it possible to create some show-off pieces of progress and improvements in living standards for the select few while dispossessing and displacing the many. All types of deals were pursued to bring factories or assembly lines to various Mexican states with each offering every possible incentive to get one of these industrial-looking boxes in the hope of improving employment or, through it, managing to kick-start the dormant economy.

This illusory promise of growth and economic opportunity was packaged and sold by US corporate elites, who were looking for bigger profit margins and new ways to compete with cheaper Asian products. The maquiladoras were the initial answer whereby manufacturing was moved to Mexico, thus reducing costs and freeing corporations from any real environmental oversight or labor laws. On the American side of the border, the move to Mexico allowed corporations to extract wage concessions from labor unions, reduce or remove local and federal government regulations, and extend large loans and subsidies to keep production in the US.

In this context, NAFTA had its intended outcomes for corporations as it forced US labor to forgo higher wages and become ready to give away existing benefits in regular contract negotiations. US labor agreed more than once to forgo pay raises, improvement in work safety conditions, vacation time, and job protections. Furthermore, labor agreed to corporate plans to reduce health-care coverage, impose limits to company contributions to pension funds, and, at times, increase the retirement age. On both sides of the US-Mexican border, corporations were laughing all the way to the bank and making sizable returns each way.

As NAFTA took hold and displacement of farmers occurred, a

flood of Mexican immigrants headed north, to the US, where their farming skills and manpower in labor-intensive jobs were needed. The arrival of Mexican immigrants added further downward pressure on wages at the lower levels of the economy. This arrival of immigrants, which was predictable, made it possible to pressure US labor forces further, as well as create racial and class tensions between the new Mexican arrivals and African Americans on the one hand, and poor and middle-class whites on the other.

❧ Free Trade and Right-Wing Politics

Through exploiting these heightened tensions, the political right, in both Mexico and the US, was able to rally patriotic and at times xenophobic sentiments and ride it back again and again into political office. For the US, the racial and ethnic divide is an important one that shaped and continues to influence the direction of political discourse. And by fanning white poor and middle-class resentment, the right wing was and continues to be able to cast itself as a defender and promoter of national values and win elections on that basis. Fueling resentment among communities of color was an equally important tool deployed by the democrats after presiding over the signing of NAFTA and shifting into embracing neoliberal economics.

What develops in this period is a global political system divided between the corporate left and corporate right, but to be sure, it is a corporate political system. Indeed, we have a world for corporations and made by corporations, with the good life for the few at the expense and over the bodies and souls of the many. We, the corporations, hold these truths to be self-evident, that all corporations are created equal, endowed by the 1 percent, to unleash poverty unto the world, endless thievery of natural resources, maximization of profits through privatization schemes, and pursuit of death and destruction through war and militarism. We must "ask not what your country can do for you" but what you can steal and rob from it by buying politicians and controlling the media at all times.

What started in Mexico after a short period of time became a model to be pushed out to the whole Global South, which became one massive and extended maquiladora system. Country after country, and state after state, was ready to jump into offering its land and people for the sake of a few jobs through the maquiladora system. We are all presently situated in a never-ending maquiladora system that dehumanizes all while producing resentment among the impacted people in the Global South and the inner cities and rural regions in the Global North. A bidding war ensued across the postcolonial South to locate the next assembly plant to supply Walmart, Nike, Apple, HP, Microsoft, Kmart, et cetera with the cheapest labor cost input, free land and build-to-suit schemes, local tax breaks or no taxes for thirty or fifty years, and of course no environmental policies or protection for workers.

Indeed, a type of "hunger games" for the cheapest labor costs was offered to multinational corporations with each state offering its own people, lands, water, and dignity as commodities to be sacrificed in the deadly manufacturing-efficiency game. Someone is always ready to do it cheaper and more efficiently, which makes the multinationals more emboldened in running these real "hunger games" that cost real lives and destroy many societies along the way.

We are all in agreement that large sections of Africa, Asia, and the Middle East are in total collapse with many failed or about to fail states in these regions. Take your pick of a country to include in this category: Afghanistan, Central African Republic, the Congo, Iraq, Liberia, Libya, Mali, Myanmar, Nigeria, Somalia, and Syria, to name the obvious but more could be added. From the US and Europe's perspective, the crisis of failed or failing states is strictly an internal problem to each state, and the immigration crisis is disconnected from the long pre- and postcolonial histories altogether or the never-ending interventions. From the Cold War to neoliberal economic structures, privatization and downstream processing entrenched an already corrupt elite and shifted additional resources to their accounts while pushing the middle class and poor to the breaking point.

The six features of the colonial period discussed earlier got a new lease on life by being incorporated into the postcolonial structure where the failure and conflict in each state required civilizational rehab and further intervention. Let's accept as a fact that we are all vested equally in making the world a better place, and not only for the few running the world economy but for everyone in the world. Central to this is a much-needed unequivocal declaration that every life matters equally, regardless of skin color, origin, religion, or geographic location, but we know that it has never been the case, and more so today than any other time. A black, brown, or Asian life is not equal and does not matter as much as a white life! A life in the northern hemisphere is not more valuable than in the southern, but as we all know, all lives are not equal, and some lives matter, count, and are recorded more than others.

Immigration is not a root cause but an outcome and a by-product of failed economic, social, political, military, and educational policies set in place over a long period of time. Everywhere we turn, we come into contact with colonial history that continues to impose itself on the present. If addressing the immigration problem is what the US's and Europe's leadership are interested in pursuing with the hope of maintaining the Global North purity of "race and culture," then the already discussed causes that brought us to this point and the response so far has been in the form of slogans for election campaigns.

Why do people emigrate in the first place? Is it because deep down they despise their own countries, or are they simply seeking to explore and "discover" the world like Marco Polo and Columbus did in the past? Or maybe, as the Islamophobes insist without evidence, they have a hidden agenda to convert and Islamize the US and Europe because deeply they loathe "our" freedom. Maybe all the Salvadorans and Mexicans are coming to America to change and replace all the whites with Latinos! People in the past and the present emigrate in pursuit of economic opportunities, livelihood, and in search of security for self and family. The search for security and economic opportunities away from home is the primary engine for immigration and movement from one part of the world to another.

Immigrants to the US and Europe are seeking safety and economic opportunities away from home due to the collapse and total fragmentation of southern postcolonial economies and the crumpling political and social orders that have caused insecurity, which is directly connected to Western powers' military and economic interventions. The postcolonial economic structure is the colonial economy but with new local and indigenous-looking district managers operating the colonial franchise, which has run into a dead end.

Certainly, the countries in the southern hemisphere gained their independence—all are United Nations voting members in the General Assembly and are active in global institutions. However, do not let the official trappings distract attention from a sound political and economic power analysis. While the colonial forces and troops indeed were forced out forty to fifty years ago, nevertheless the economic, political, social, military, and educational infrastructure remained colonial at root. The colonial companies that controlled the raw materials never left, banking institutions and finance remained intact, the educational epistemology never strayed away from Eurocentric frames, social relations remained governed by a racial hierarchy, and a military trained in the Global North presided over the system to control and crush the population and keep them away from contesting the vested colonial system. An aggravating factor was the forty-to-fifty-year Cold War that recruited states as subcontractors to the US or USSR, conflicts that likewise reinforced the colonial structure but under modified constraints to be followed by the destructive neoliberal, and privatization schemes that took the last vestiges of protection present in the Global South.

The postcolonial economy in the newly independent states was kept as a satellite, maintained in a dependency and at a controlled radius from the ex-colonial motherland. How this was made possible in the postcolonial and independent period was discussed earlier, and little attention is paid to it. Indeed, the elites in the southern hemisphere who were educated, trained, and nurtured in the colonial bosom and suckled into an epistemic postcolonial maturity, then set up to manage the existing franchise with all the trappings of independent statehood such as flags, stamps, currency, et cetera, have managed to transfer massive wealth to the Global North. The training was successful and intended to reproduce the normative colonial patterns so that the postcolonial state could never structurally break away from the motherland.

As I have argued earlier, the colonial project was vested in the mind as much as in direct geographical and territorial control. The economic order never ceased being colonial, and the agreements to remove colonial troops were always connected to, if not made conditional on, keeping the financial and economic interests intact and privileging companies, corporations, and banks originating in the ex-colonial motherland and the Global North. The independent postcolonial state structure was managed by colonially educated elites trained to maintain unfettered access to markets, flow of raw materials, and resources to the North while using colonially trained and equipped military forces to keep the system uninterrupted.

The economy is connected financially at the hip to the ex-colonial motherland as well as to the global financial policing institutions, such as the World Bank and the IMF, and the designed trade distortions set in place through successive GATT and WTO negotiations. Emerging in this process is higher levels of domination, dependency, and control since the visible signs of the colonial structure were obfuscated through the presence of the local elites, who managed and maintained the system for a handsome fee from the ex-colonial motherland. They were called upon often as neutral experts or mediators to fix "native" problems, which the motherland put in place to begin with, such as exaggerated existing tribal and sectarian tensions. As consequence, the local southern economies never stopped being colonial and were set up as a service, raw material, and cheap labor feeder to the ex-colonial motherland. Thus, collectively, the southern populations and material resources have helped keep the northern hemisphere's financial well-being intact in the postcolonial period at the expense of people in the Global South.

In addition, the door that was opened to train the colonized elites resulted in a constant and deliberate brain drain from the Global South, which produced the multilayered dependencies as well as put a constraint on future development horizons by sequestering future indigenous intellects in the Global North. Of course, the benefits are greater, and the opportunities for the intellectuals and highly skilled labor are immeasurable compared with the south, which is precisely what produces generational dependency, the present cycle of a never-ending colonial structure, and the steady stream of immigrants and refugees.

Europe's and the US's right-wing political leaders declare "go back home and stop trying to change our culture, values, and society with your backward cultures that are turning our cities into third-world zones and bankrupting our economies." This is the daily message directed at the ex-colonial subjects working as restaurant cooks and dishwashers, taxi drivers, and garbage collectors in the northern colonial motherlands, negating their belonging and contribution. We do have a link between immigration and instability in the south. The Global South economies and political structures were colonially designed to be in constant chaos and a state of "relative" instability, which would facilitate the selling of raw materials for cheap in exchange for guns and the Global North's financial and political protection. In addition, the lack of stability forced the migration of the intelligent and skilled to the north, thus helping the north maintain its qualitative edge in development and constant buildup of the human capacity while depriving the south of it.

The problem is structural and can no longer be dealt with by building walls or increasing border patrols. As long as the Global South economies and resources are ravaged to benefit the 1 percent, then there is no hope of ending the immigration and refugee crisis. Furthermore, the postcolonial economy is not sustainable, and collapsing states in the south will only accelerate the move to the north and with it the transplantation of existing crises from colonies and conflicts into the Global North.

The solution to this begins with a complete recognition of the problem as a shared one. It is no longer possible to isolate "troubles" from the south as Global South issues alone. A political and economic collapse in the south means massive migration and refugees to the north, and as such the problem is connected and must be approached in an integrated manner. Even today, we have a net outflow of capital from the south to the north, which must be reversed, and real investment in people and sustainable regional economies needs to take the lead, rather than protecting corporations' bottom lines and securing intellectual property rights. Destroyed economies, fragmented political structures, and conflicts may be reduced or prevented by a sustained decolonial program rooted in addressing people's needs first and foremost. The days of taking raw materials, capturing markets, and greasing the palms of handpicked dictators and elites, as well as toxic dumping and exploiting cheap labor in the south, must come to an end. The alternatives are at hand, but instead of xenophobic and racist electioneering specialists, we require real leadership, a collective vision, and sustained investment. Today is the time to make this shift and a global move toward addressing the real and structural challenges at hand.

Chapter Five

"I can't breathe."

If viewed accurately, "I can't breathe," the final plea of George Floyd, is the most painful and apt summation of the colonialization effects, with death, destruction, and erasure visited upon people of the Global South no matter the geography they inhabit and the immediate connection to the immigration-refugee crisis. The daily news gives the impression that what has taken place in Minneapolis, Minnesota—the killing of George Floyd by police—is an isolated event that is disconnected from history, be it domestic or international. But one can't approach the topic of Blacks in America without beginning with Columbus's journey across the Atlantic, which commenced multiple genocides against the Indigenous people in the New World and across the globe. Furthermore, European genocides in the New World brought about the market-driven slave trade that witnessed snatching millions of Africans from their homes, lands, and families and shipping them as commodified cargo for a trading route that lasted almost three hundred years.

I was planning on concluding the book with a link back to my initial introduction, followed by some overarching recommendations to begin addressing the impact of colonization and the postcolonial state. But unfolding events positively disrupted this plan and necessitated a different direction altogether. Making connections is critical in the context of understanding the world we all inhabit. The Minneapolis police's murder of George Floyd; the Israeli army's killing of the autistic Palestinian kid, Iyad el-Hallak, in Jerusalem; and the drownings of the Syrian toddler Alan Kurdi (Aylan Shenu) and the Salvadoran immigrant Oscar Alberto Martínez and his twenty-three-month-old daughter, Angie Valeria Martínez, are all connected to this book. At first look, one is more inclined to see each event speaking to a specific context and circumstance that are far apart to make any meaningful or straightforward connection. However, the disconnect is a direct outcome of examining unfolding events in isolation of each other. The more accurate approach is to consider all the forces and elements that coalesced to bring each one of these tragedies to the forefront, including the long colonial history, its imprint on the postcolonial horizons, immigration, refugees, and disruptions of lives across the globe.

All these traumatic events appear unrelated but, in reality, point to the coloniality entanglement in the contemporary world and are paradigmatic of all that it touches. I started to write this chapter on June 8, 2020, in the middle of a national rebellion after the on-camera police officers' murder of George Floyd. Then I spent a few days protesting and trying to see how to frame what is going on within the colonial and postcolonial epistemic while also organizing community and scholarly responses to the unfolding events. Critically, I wanted to write on the topic but to do so with the lens of the long history of slavery, colonization, genocide, erasure, and the specificity of police violence and brutality, which has its origins in slave patrols in the South.

George Floyd's murder is directly linked to the construction of race, the racial state, and the genocidal aspects of colonization that I discussed earlier, and points to its seamless continuities in the postcolonial and post-civil-rights movement. Interventions in postcolonial states in the Global South bring about wars, death, and the immigration-refugee crisis, while structural racism and police brutality in the Global North fills the prisons and graveyards. The colonial present regulates and governs the bodies and spaces of Blacks and people of the Global South, no matter the region they inhabit.

I will discuss George Floyd's murder in context of the US's settler colonialism and the heavy racial imprint that shapes and regulates everything while making links to the multiple erasures that connect it all to the collapse of the postcolonial state. Notedly, the murder of George Floyd ushered in an iconoclastic global moment that witnessed the tearing down, and at times the sinking in rivers and harbors, of the many symbols of "celebrated" colonizers, slave traders, and confederate figures. Statues across the world became the focal point for activists and the much-needed move to reclaim public space for social justice movements—a major development that sits at the crossroads of the colonial and postcolonial phase and becomes a stride toward rewriting history in real time despite the continuity of systematic and systemic structural racism.

After George Floyd's murder, the European Parliament passed a resolution (493 votes in favor, 104 against, and 67 abstained) declaring "Black Lives Matter" and the slave trade as "a crime against humanity," which is a step in the right direction.[186] However, the European Parliament is more progressive than each European state's parliament and governments, which have pursued policies that demonstrate a total disregard for Black lives and the daily death toll of African and Asian immigrants and refugees. European states must come to terms with the daily carnage on the Mediterranean, with thousands of Black and brown lives already lost at sea and those making it onto land ending up in dead-end camps that currently hold thousands of immigrants and refugees, who, for no other reason, are seeking safety and security away from wars, Western interventions, and economic destruction. Passing a resolution and declaring slave trade "a crime against humanity" is easy, but confronting the present colonial, structural racism and the erasure of Black and brown bodies across the continent would be the real test.

❧ The Colonial Knee on the Neck

On May 25, 2020, the world watched an eight minute and forty-six second video of Derek Chauvin, a Minneapolis police officer, murdering George Floyd,[187] a forty-six-year-old Black man, while two other officers assisted in holding his body down and another kept the crowd away. Initially, the police department fired the four officers without charging any of them with a crime. It took five full days of a national rebellion with thousands of people in the streets demanding justice before Mike Freeman, the Hennepin County attorney, "announced murder and manslaughter charges against Derek Chauvin, the officer who can be seen most clearly in witness video pinning Mr. Floyd to the ground."[188] The murder occurred as a result of Derek Chauvin pressing his knee on George Floyd's neck until he lost consciousness and keeping it in place "for a full minute after paramedics arrived at the scene."[189] The murder was captured on video, which showed George Floyd pleading for his life and saying many times, "I can't breathe," but to no avail:

It's my face, man. I didn't do nothing serious, man. Please, please, please. I can't breathe. Please, man. Please, somebody.

Please, man, I can't breathe. I can't breathe, please. Man, I can't breathe. My face. Just get up. I can't breathe, please. I can't breathe…I can't move.

Mama. Mama. I can't, my knee, my nuts. I'm through. I'm through. I'm claustrophobic. My stomach hurts. My neck hurts. Everything hurts.

Some water or something, please. Please. I can't breathe, officer. Don't kill me. They're gonna kill me, man. Come on, man. I cannot breathe. I cannot breathe.

They're gonna kill me; they're gonna kill me. I cannot breathe. I can't breathe. Please, sir, please, sir, please. I can't breathe.

While the video had sufficient evidence to arrest and charge Officer Chauvin, the mayor and city leadership did not act immediately to take the next steps to charge those responsible, which caused more legitimate, intense public anger and protest. After four full days of national and international protests and outright rebellion in over forty US cities, the Minneapolis city's leadership and the district attorney moved, on Friday, May 29, to arrest Officer Chauvin on a third-degree murder charge. The other three officers did not get charged or arrested until June 3, and only after the appointment of Keith Ellison, Minnesota Attorney General, to prosecute and oversee the case.

Initially, the protesters' demands focused on charging the four officers, but as police departments across the country acted upon President Trump's incitement to dominate[190] the streets, responding with brutality, rubber bullets, tear gas, and violence, the debate rapidly shifted to the nature of systemic and institutional racism. Critically, the problem of systemic and structural police violence and brutality against Black, Indigenous, and brown communities has been at the heart of the civil rights movement's demands from the end of slavery to the Trump era.

Race and systematic and structural racism are the colonial legacies that are baked into policing, governing, education, the economy, entertainment, and everything else in contemporary society. "I can't breathe" is the most-fitting epistemological orientation for settler colonialism and the police placement of a real knee on the necks and lives of so many people across the globe. The knee has always been there, controlling the bodies, the space, and the oxygen intake, frequently snuffing life itself of so many human beings around the globe. The eight minutes and forty-six seconds of the video are the difference between the human endowed with the meaning contained therein and the subhuman within the colonially crafted time, space, and body.

George Floyd's murder has all the strands of the crisis of the postcolonial world and the colonialism that shaped it. Just take a minute to consider that George Floyd is a descendant of enslaved Africans brought to this country in the hulls of ships; the owner of the store where the crime took place is a Palestinian immigrant himself, and his family is in America as a result of European and Zionist settler colonialism; the murderous officer, Derek Chauvin, is of Irish heritage, a community that was deemed inferior and only admitted into whiteness after the Civil War and the Chinese Exclusion Act.; and the participating officer Tou Thao is a member of the Hmong Vietnamese community that arrived as refugees after the long US war and intervention in the country. Adding more complexity to the picture is the fact that the Minneapolis Police Department and others around the country receive training in Israel on the exact brutal methods deployed against Blacks and communities of color in America.[191]

Derek Chauvin's murder of George Floyd brought forth an expression of solidarity by the Irish antiracism movement, which is best expressed by the Dublin musician Imelda May in a protest poem:

> You don't get to be racist and Irish
> You don't get to be proud of your heritage,
> plights and fights for freedom
> while kneeling on the neck of another!
> You're not entitled to sing songs
> of heroes and martyrs
> mothers and fathers who cried
> as they starved in a famine
> Or of brave hearted
> soft spoken
> poets and artists
> lined up in a yard

blindfolded and bound
Waiting for Godot
and point blank to sound
We emigrated
We immigrated
We took refuge
So cannot refuse
When it's our time
To return the favour
Land stolen
Spirits broken
Bodies crushed and swollen
unholy tokens of Christ, Nailed to a tree
(That) You hang around your neck
Like a noose of the free
Our colour pasty
Our accents thick
Hands like shovels
from mortar and bricklaying
foundation of cities
you now stand upon
Our suffering seeps from every stone
your opportunities arise from
Outstanding on the shoulders
of our forefathers and foremothers
who bore your mother's mother
Our music is for the righteous
Our joys have been earned
Well deserved and serve
to remind us to remember
More Blacks
More Dogs
More Irish.
Still labelled leprechauns, Micks, Paddy's, louts

we're shouting to tell you
our land, our laws
are progressively out there
We're in a chrysalis
state of emerging into a new
and more beautiful Eire/era
40 Shades Better
Unanimous in our rainbow vote
we've found our stereotypical pot of gold
and my God it's good.
So join us…'cause
You Don't Get to Be Racist and Irish.[192]

The Irish themselves have been colonized and struggled against the British for eight hundred years and just recently have been able to arrive at a peace settlement in Northern Ireland. What we have in Minneapolis is an entanglement of race, settler colonialism, violence, immigration, and refugee narratives. However, if the list does not provide enough entanglements, then consider the fact that Congresswoman Ilhan Omar, who represents the district, is herself an African Somali refugee, while the Minnesota attorney general, Keith Ellison, the person appointed to oversee the investigation and prosecution, is himself a Black Muslim.

If you wanted to put together a movie for a story about the long history of colonization, settler colonialism, enslavement, genocides, foreign interventions, race, racial profiling, whiteness, Blackness, communities of color, systematic neglect, inner-city business dynamics, militarism, neoliberal economics, militarized police and police brutality, and foreign links to the training—all taking place in the middle of a coronavirus (COVID-19) pandemic that up to this point has killed one hundred and twenty thousand Americans—then the killing of George Floyd brings all of these strands together in an eight minute and forty-six second opening scene.

Pouring salt into racism's deep wounds is the basic fact that "black Americans are 3.5 times more likely to die of COVID-19 than white Americans,"[193] which may be directly attributable to disparity in the availability of health care in Black communities, an outcome traced to compounded factors, including enslavement, Jim Crow laws, separate-but-equal segregation, never-ending disinvestment, toxic dumping, pollution, poisonous food, and police violence. Yes, many Blacks do have preexisting health conditions, like many of their white counterparts, but the only circumstance that matters, which is a natural one and determines all other elements in life, is their Blackness. Society time and time again dismisses, ignores, and refuses to tackle a color-blindness that kills daily!

❧ "Black Skin Boy…Born to Die" and America's Open Casket

"He was a black skin boy. So, he was born to die,"[194] goes Bob Dylan's song, "The Death of Emmett Till." The lyrics are as timely today with the murder of George Floyd as when they were first written and performed because Black skin remains a threat and the cause of death of far too many in the US and around the world.[195] The song narrates the story of Emmett Till, a fourteen-year-old Black youngster from Chicago, who was murdered while visiting relatives in Mississippi on August 28, 1955, by two white men because, supposedly, he flirted with a white woman.[196] At the time, Mamie, Emmett's mother, insisted on a public funeral in Chicago with an open casket for everyone to view America's racism and brutality that completely disfigured and mutilated the face of her beautiful boy. The motionless body was Emmett's, but the open casket is America's well-documented lynching history, racism, sanctioned police brutality, and erasure, structurally assigning subhumanness to Blacks.

America's soul continues to be burdened by the countless, motionless Black bodies that pile up daily in inner-city streets and alleyways and from police fomented violence. Not to leave behind the walking, living bodies made motionless and numbed into a lifeless existence through racism: filling prisons, shattering dreams, and creating permanent modern "civilized" slavery.

Multiple academic and professionally published research papers on police violence show that racial bias is the primary cause behind the differentiated treatment accorded to Black communities. In a detailed summary of eighteen national studies on police and racial bias, Kia Makarechi concluded that "taken together, the research paints a picture of a nation where a citizen's race may well affect their experience with police—whether an encounter ends with a traffic stop, the use of police force, or a fatal shooting."[197] A study by professor Cody T. Ross, an anthropologist at the University of California, Davis, cited by Makarechi, found "evidence of a significant bias in the killing of unarmed Black Americans relative to unarmed white Americans, in that the probability of being black, unarmed, and shot by police is about 3.49 times the probability of being white, unarmed, and shot by police on average." What was more interesting in the study is, "there is no relationship between county-level racial bias in police shootings and crime rates (even race-specific crime rates), meaning that the racial bias observed in police shootings in this data set is not explainable as a response to local-level crime rates."[198]

The study makes an association between police killings and the race of victims, but often people retort back with the fact that more white individuals are killed by police annually than Blacks or Latinos. Certainly, the raw numbers are correct, but it is a flawed measurement if not adjusted and balanced to population percentages. An article published by the *Washington Post* adjusted the police killing data to population size with "nearly 160 million more white people in America than there are black people" and constituting "roughly 62 percent of the US population but only about 49 percent of those who are killed by police officers."[199] On the other hand, "African Americans...account for 24 percent of those fatally shot and killed by the police despite being just 13 percent of the US population." The *Washington Post*'s study concluded that "black Americans are 2.5 times as likely as white Americans to be shot and killed by police officers."[200]

In the same study, the 2015 data shows that "police have shot and killed a young black man (ages 18 to 29)—such as Michael Brown in Ferguson, Mo.—175 times since January 2015; 24 of them were unarmed. Over that same period, police have shot and killed 172 young white men, 18 of whom were unarmed. Once again, while in raw numbers there were similar totals of white and black victims, blacks were killed at rates disproportionate to their percentage of the US population. Of all of the unarmed people shot and killed by police in 2015, 40 percent of them were black men, even though black men make up just 6 percent of the nation's population."[201]

Demagogues like Rudy Giuliani, former New York City mayor and currently Trump's lawyer, insultingly maintain, "if you want to deal with this on the black side, you've got to teach your children to be respectful to the police, and you've got to teach your children that the real danger to them is not the police; the real danger to them, 99 out of 100 times, 9,900 out of 10,000 times, are other black kids who are going to kill them. That's the way they're gonna die."[202] This assertion of Black-on-Black violence is used to rationalize and excuse away police violence and brutality. Certainly, data shows that Black-on-Black violence accounts for 90 percent of the murder in the Black community, but also white-on-white violence is responsible for 82 percent of the killing of whites. Taking this racist logic a step further, the overwhelming majority of pedophilia and serial killers come from within the white community in America, but no one frames it as a white issue or white crime, rather, as it should be, it is considered on a case-by-case basis, and no collective race guilt is assigned.

A study by Texas A&M University economist Mark Hoekstra looked at two million responses to emergency calls in two US cities, and "concluded that white officers dispatched to Black neighborhoods fired their guns five times as often as Black officers dispatched for similar calls to the same neighborhoods."[203] The issue is not only Black-on-Black violence, but the implicit bias and differentiated treatment directed at Black communities, and it shows a marked difference within each neighborhood, depending on the racial background of the responding officers.

A *Wall Street Journal* article by Heather Mac Donald pushed the same association of crime areas and police violence by insisting that "such a concentration of criminal violence in minority communities means that officers will be disproportionately confronting armed and often resisting suspects in those communities, raising officers' own risk of using lethal force."[204] Just as Giuliani pivoted to Black-on-Black violence, Donald shifts toward problematizing minority communities thus affirming and appealing to America's existing racial imaginary of these communities. These two assertions and other lines of argumentation are a clear example of the compounded and sophisticated type of racism. The notion that the high-crime area or threat posed by supposedly armed Blacks is used to gloss over the flimsy evidence to back these assertions.

The research shows that "the use of lethal force by police in 2015 found no correlation between the level of violent crime in an area and that area's police killing rates."[205] To put it another way, 69 percent of African Americans killed by police in 2015 were nonviolent and unarmed, which trumps the assertion that crime or presence of arms or lethal threat was the cause of the shooting. A published study by the Center for Policing Equity, which looked at nineteen thousand cases of police use of force from 2010 to 2015, found that "African-Americans are far more likely than whites and other groups to be the victims of use of force by the police, even when racial disparities in crime are taken into account."[206]

Another important study titled, "Protecting Whiteness: White Phenotypic Racial Stereotypicality Reduces Police Use of Force," conducted in 2016 by a team from Harvard; Portland State University; University of California, Los Angeles; and Boston University, tested the hypothesis of whether "the Whiter one appears, the more the suspect will be protected from police force." The team's findings were that the "police used less force with highly stereotypical Whites, and this protective effect was stronger than the effect for non-Whites."[207] Thus, the national debate on police violence and use of force against Blacks should be totally reframed away from association with the supposed criminal background or the high-crime area.

Existing research cited and other studies undermine claims of area association or criminal behavior, which brings us back to race as the primary differentiated factor that explains the propensity of police to frequently use lethal force when encountering Blacks. In today's America, on average, police kill a Black man or woman every twenty-eight hours, and on the rare occasion that charges are brought against officers, it is extremely extraordinary to have a court or jury convict the officer. The charges against the four Minneapolis police officers and other officers fired since May 25, 2020, across the country, point to possibly a new phase in confronting institutional racism, but this is still at the beginning of the road and a difficult struggle is ahead.

Rodney King, Eula Love, and Amadou Diallo are forgotten signposts on America's entanglement with racism and the constant willful denial of the serious problem of police use of deadly force and shifting the blame to the victims. The policing approach to Black and brown communities has developed over centuries, and it is not only a recent problem. For sure, the epistemic framework for policing originates in the slave institution with focus on the total control of Black bodies: regulating movement within and outside the plantations and extreme legally mandated punishment to prevent rebellion and challenge to the existing order.

Policing Black communities can be traced all the way back to slave patrols in the South, which, according to Dr. Marsha Coleman-Adebayo and Kevin Berends, "had three primary goals: (1) to chase down, apprehend, and return to their owners, escaped Africans; (2) to provide a form of organized terror to deter African armed revolts; and (3) to maintain a form of discipline for Africans who were subject to vigilante summary execution, outside of the law, if they violated any plantation rules or just ran afoul of any white person."[208] After the Civil War, the slave patrols were incorporated into police departments without ever altering the basic assumptions relating to Blacks centered on the need to control and discipline the targeted population.

Violence in the Internal and External Colonial

The control and violent structure inside the US can be better understood if we bring colonial discourse analysis into it and contextualizing the local as a subset of, and possessing epistemic continuity with, the global. Certainly, Malcolm X in the early 1960s spoke of Black communities as constituting the "internal colonies," which was an important and correct base of analysis on how African Americans are viewed and managed within the Global North. In the external colonies, the same mode of control and domination is instituted with the goal of driving maximum political, economic, and social benefits from it while controlling the colonized brown bodies, confining their movement, and regularly using maximum violence. Thus, violence is paradigmatic in colonial structures because it is based on achieving total control toward a population that is deemed to be inferior or subhuman (i.e., animallike and maliciously assumed to respond only to force and power, which is intended to "rationalize" the use of violence against it).

Violence is used in the same way against the colonized subject as an animal is trained to respond to the command of the trainer, who uses the whip to induce fear, then provides treats when a positive controlled response emerges from the animal. Violence in both plantation and colony is the preferred tool for inducing cooperation and bringing about total control and domination. White supremacy, a global phenomenon, normalizes violence by making it a constitutive and productive paradigm shaping the relationship in the internal and external colonial. Blacks in the US and colonized populations epistemologically are reproduced in this colonial discourse as mere biological subhuman material that has not yet emerged out of the hulls of slave ships into servitude of the modern civilizational project, and violence is a training instrument, even if it causes death! Indeed, America's inner cities are the epistemic hulls of the modern internal colonial slave ships navigating the oceans of unbeing and subhumanness.

Many factually point out that Black-on-Black violence takes more African American lives than police use of deadly force or white-on-Black violence. This statement is uttered daily by countless news talking heads, politicians, and embedded intellectuals who are engaged in systematic obfuscation and reductionism of the real and sustained causes of violence in Black communities at home and communities of color in the Global South. Indeed, the intention is to shift blame and direct attention away from the structural and systemic aspects of violence directed at Blacks and people of color at home and abroad. Today, we are focusing on George Floyd's case, but the history of violence directed at Blacks is deeply intertwined with America's history itself and defines the social, political, religious, and economic relationships over the past five hundred years.

Furthermore, and on the question of terminology, by using and insisting on the term "Black-on-Black violence," the public discourse affirms the racial categorization of the crime as the only defining character for the violence and not the act itself. The Blackness of the person is what drives the crime and not the motive. Consider when whites commit crime and they do so against other whites, the ascription is not their whiteness that drove the crime, rather a mere report on the crime itself and what happened.

More critically is the question as to the causes of higher rates of Black-on-Black violence or, for this matter, of colonized populations exhibiting the same symptoms, be it in Africa, Latin America, or the Middle East. For the racist, the answer is an obvious one: it is located in the Arab, Black, Indigenous, African, Asian, Latino, and Muslim nature that reproduces this irrational violence, and what is needed is an intervention to civilize them and a global rehab project to alter the biological and evolutionary defects witnessed daily. Racist violence is akin to chemotherapy directed at a supposed cancer present in the inferior races. Thus, the problem is not in colonial violence or discourse, internal and external; rather for the racist, it is located in the targeted populations themselves. Interventions, the white man's burden, and "shock and awe" are framed positively by the racist because they are intended to help civilize the savage. But if the savage is killed, permanently disfigured, or maimed in the process, then the killer should not be taken into account, just like a doctor administering a deadly medicine to cure the sick patient.

Blacks in the New World (Indigenous communities and populations in the Global South) have been living under a violent structure since the day they were captured and transformed into a commodity to be sold and bought. If one wants to locate the present violence in America's inner cities, then no need to go beyond a clear and unmistaken analysis of the torture, dehumanization, objectification, and commodification of tens of millions of Blacks, generation after generation until the present. The racist offers theology, pseudoscience, culture, or any other new fashionable dumbed-down contemporary-coffee-shop internet hypothesis to explain away "Black" and "colonized" violence, but never looking at the violent structure that became productive in plantations and colonies alike.

When the enslaved or the colonized took the whip or the gun from the slave or colonial master's hand, they could only reproduce the violence, which they have internalized in the epistemic and constitutive relationship in the plantation and colony. For sure, the master is shocked at the violent outcome because they believed all along that they have managed to "civilize" the savage and brought to them the "treats" of the good life in the same way the trainer related to the caged animal. The enslaved and colonized subject's violence is the master's own medicine that has been internalized and reproduced in reaction to the dehumanization. This type of violence tends to become more intense and, at times, random in a reversal of the "shock and awe" strategy deployed to bring maximum response and compliance from the enslaved and colonized subject.

Black-on-Black or colonized-on-colonized violence has to be understood in relation to the racist structure that was put in place at the inception of both projects. The setting in motion of a superior and a subhuman in the enslaved communities and the colonial structures results over time in an internalized devaluation and subhumanness in the subjects themselves, which further gets played out in internal relations within the group. When a Black person looks at another Black man or woman, or a colonized person looks at another colonized subject, the eye is seeing through the constructed and deeply internalized racial and colonial lens. Thus, it reminds them of their assigned inferiority and that which they are not: the society's assigned superior white, who is the master of the internal and external colonial. In this manner, killing another Black person or colonized subject does not have the same epistemic consequences in the mind of the one committing the crime within the same group. For as far as they are concerned, they are acting as the agent of the superior in eliminating the projected or historically constructed inferior, the self.

Black-on-Black or colonized-on-colonized violence is a process of killing that which reminds the self of its inferiority in the existing racial and global hierarchical structures. Just as the murdering of a Black person or colonized person by the superior slave or colonial master had no consequences, the same dynamic is internalized by the subjects themselves, who begin to act and display violence because it is the only way that meaning of self-worth has been internalized and transhistorically transmitted and affixed. '

The master's power is exhibited and demonstrated through violence, and an imitative and distorted sense of self-worth as a mirror image of it gets reproduced by the enslaved and colonized. In this context, the slave and colonial institutions not only managed to dominate and control the bodies of subjects in the past but also, through a mental process, have been able to control present and future conduct within the colonized communities. The perceived freedom of movement is no more than the conditioned animal that no longer needs the physical chains for control because the confinement and induced state of helplessness has been imprinted upon the mind. In this process, the response to Black and colonized violence is to bring in more violence and even greater deployment of "shock and awe" in order to reconstitute fear and control and to "dominate the streets."

Notice when violence among whites takes place—be it in school or random college shootings, workplace murders, or war crimes—it is dealt with as a unique circumstance specific to the individual or individuals involved and not projected on whites as a group or an investigation into the theology, biology, or culture traits. More critically, the discussion is led by psychologists who offer insights into the mental state of the individual, possible childhood trauma, divorced parents, accidents, and any other factors, including bullying or post-traumatic stress disorder. What we have is an examination of causes that led the normal human to act in an abnormal manner to cause the death of others. The approach to Blacks and the colonized populations is illustrative since those brought to speak on the issue focus on the subject's race, religion, culture, mode of dress, music, body size, "demon" looking characteristics, drug dealing, or just walking suspiciously with a hood. None of these items can explain motives or reasons for the supposed "crime" since all point to a constructed racial image on the basis of which violence against communities is rationalized by that which is irrational.

The shifting focus of George Floyd's murder to people burning down buildings, looting, and behaving "uncivilized" on live TV is yet another dimension of the colonial and racial structure. "Riots" and "rebellions" are the voice of the voiceless; however, as a way to empty it of any context, the coverage has laser focused on burning buildings, cars, and properties and failed to ask the important questions as to the reason behind the fires that are consuming the cities and toppling statues across the world. Could it be biological, genetic, and indicative of Blacks and colonized populations' "savage" nature? If this is the case, then what is needed is the animal trainer with the whip to put the "savage" back in the hulls of the inner-city cage; what is needed is law and order to teach all to know their place in society. Otherwise, and if left alone, they will roam the streets and undue "civilization" itself. The response is an internal "shock and awe" and law and order to force compliance and reconstitute control at the modern inner-city plantation, for too much money and property are at risk to leave it to the subhuman and "barbarians" to determine.

Law and the legal process are born out of social, political, and economic conditions. The Michael Brown verdict is an affirmation, if any is still needed, that the law is indeed blind to the structured and embedded effects of racism, and the grand jury more than anything else affirmed the epistemic foundations of America's just-us legal system. Blackness in America is ascribed with criminal intent and even when unarmed constitutes a threat and a danger to a fully armed police officer, and in the case of George Floyd four fully armed officers. It is certain that George Floyd will not be the last to be killed by a police knee or possible hail of bullets since the conditions that make this possible have yet to be addressed, making no attempt at scratching the surface of the problem.

Disbanding, abolishing, and defunding the police are all positive calls to bring about fundamental change in the relationship with Blacks and communities of color. However, a real and sustained effort must be also undertaken to challenge the structure at an epistemic level and bring about a reconfiguration of power relations in society, education, media, and the economy that empower police brutality. Racism and white supremacy are vested in power, and no evidence points to a change in the near future.

❧ Fair & Lovely and Understanding Racism

Certainly, we can't begin to comprehend America's history without taking a clear and unmistaken understanding of racism as an epistemic structure and organizing principle that permeates every aspect of society, which was set at the foundation in the first moments of colonization. Two deep evil rivers irrigate America's contemporary racist tree: the enslavement of millions of Blacks and the genocide committed against the Indigenous population. America has not yet dealt with either of them and continues to operate on the meaning and wealth generated from both at a structural level.

Settler colonialism built institutions and provided the structural racism, which is the type of racism perpetrated by police, health, educational, media, and religious institutions and the political system, which makes whole communities subject to its governing and controlling apparatus and assigns them into permanent erasure. Structural racism speaks of discriminatory attitudes and perspectives that are mobilized and sit at the intersection of several layers of societal institutions that have and are able to use power to back up racist practices in such a way that racism becomes normal and part of accepted daily life.[209]

In America, we can and are able to speak of apartheid South Africa with ease and celebrate that it came to an end, but approaching America's own racial segregation system and institutional racism that tacks, controls, and determines the life, place, and future horizons of so many Blacks in the country is a daunting task. We have the ability and the data to ascertain a Black person's future horizon and life expectancy based on their zip code. The segregation is maintained and furthered despite the adoption of the Civil Rights Act of 1964 because different modes of control are in place that bring about the same outcome from earlier periods.

The prison industrial complex is the institutional and structural racism response to the attempted empowerment of Black and brown communities post-1960s. Through use of the prison industrial complex, racial profiling, redlining, and hyperpolicing of Black and brown communities, the segregation goals were achieved to even better results than the separate-but-equal era. Why is it better? Because at present we can actually blame the victims for their condition and absolve white supremacy and the political-social-legal-economic-educational-prison systems and structures of any responsibility; the law prohibits racism and discrimination. Individuals who bring this uncomfortable subject into conversation are pushed to the margins and isolated from circles of opinion making with few selected alterative data points offered as evidence to the contrary.

In addition, many in civil society and the media have a ready response, stating authoritatively with anger that we have made major progress in this country—other places are more racist than America—followed by a nice quote from Martin Luther King Jr.'s "I Have a Dream" speech from 1963. But rest assured that no one in these circles will be citing lines from "The Three Evils of Society" speech that King delivered in 1967, a year before his death. The same people who cite the 1963 King are actually closer to the majority of Americans who turned against King in 1967–68, after he opposed the Vietnam War and delivered a series of speeches that focused on militarism, materialism, and racism. As a matter of fact, all the major newspapers around the country wrote editorials against King, as well as some of the mainstream Black publications, because he was making things difficult for everyone by asking serious questions and making a link between the domestic and global colonial discourses.

Indeed, everyone during King's time until now has been asked to go back to business as usual, to structural racism, which means Black lives don't really matter and we should learn to get along and accept it. Look, it is much better to live in America than in Russia, China, or the Middle East, is the refrain by many. The problem of comparatives is that it fails to measure the country in relation to its professed ideals and legal aspiration, which makes the deployment of any of these other places another element of structural racism because it denies you the agency to appeal to the moral and ethical foundations of your own society. What this type of argument is saying is, if you don't like America, then go to these other places so as to appreciate what you have. Mind you, this is never said to members of the Ku Klux Klan, or anyone that practices white supremacy, since the assumption is that they belong to this society, know none other, and it is inconceivable for a moment to ask them to leave despite killing and maiming thousands of Black citizens in the country.

Another type of victim blaming is the focus on behavior, Black single-mother households, the social environment, crime, drug dealing, and more, which is deployed to make the killing of Blacks a justifiable homicide in America, not only in the law and courts but in all of our minds. On the one hand, Black men are over-policed, watched, racially profiled, and sent to prison in greater numbers than any other group per capita (an exception would be Indigenous men on reservations). Then mothers are blamed for having to raise children alone, stigmatized for being poor, and made an example of for their supposed moral failings. Being poor is made into a crime in America, and the poor constantly pay in so many different ways for their poverty. The religious establishment, media, and "sophisticated educated circles" add insult to injury by blaming the victim anew and by deploying the moralistic arguments that target the poor, single mothers, the erased, maimed, and dispossessed people while letting those who created and profited from these conditions off the hook or, at times, joining them on panels and at events to rail against those that have been put deep inside the hulls of America's modern slave ships—the prisons and inner-city ghettos.

Certainly, I am a religious man and do have a moral and ethical compass of the world and society, but I refuse to engage in such a discourse that blames the poor, the dispossessed, and the racialized and use them as a way to monetize the institutional spiritual path. Religion and religious institutions should be rooted in uplifting the poor, healing broken hearts and lives, and restoring mercy, dignity, balance, and justice for all, which must include an examination of society's leadership and elite members' actions producing the conditions that result in making people poor and disposable on a daily basis.

Structural racism is what made the murder of George Floyd and countless others possible. It has to be traced to the emergence of European whiteness, the link to Christianity or racial theology, which ontologically grounded superiority and inferiority in the biblical text. Thus, when speaking of racism, we must confront the theological racist postulate, which originates racial hierarchies based on a literal reading of Genesis 9:25: "And he said, Cursed be Canaan; a servant of servants shall he be unto his brethren." Some downplay the text's significance in the development of racism; however, evidence points to its use in the early Reconquista, the expulsion of Muslims and Jews, and as a constitutive element of the Inquisition and colonization.

Indeed, race theory emerged critically on the scene pre- and post-1492, and the affirmation of a racial hierarchy that shaped the articulation of European identity then and now formed the basis of colonialism and postcolonialism around the globe. To be a "civilized" European meant to be a white Christian of "pure blood" not mixed with the darker-skinned "inferior" races—a fallacy that gets replayed on a daily basis in the streets of America, Europe, and across the Global South. No one should be surprised that the statues being taken down are connected to individuals who led the colonial expansion and made their wealth from the slave trade and genocides in the Global South and the Americas.

❧ Statues and Contesting the Present Colonial

The fictitious debate concerning taking down colonial and slave trader statues attempts to dismiss people's action as merely putting history on trial and to convince people that these individuals no longer represent the values of society or the center of honor or glorification. In addition, many in the political and elite circles call for protesters, or those who are taking down the statues, to resort to the legal process rather than attacking public property on their own. Putting history on trial is an interesting argument because it implies a distant, unconnected past and that whatever these statues stood for is a distant memory that no longer has a hold on American and European societies.

The thesis that the colonial is in the past must be challenged on several fronts. I maintain that the past has not passed, and we are still living and experiencing the colonial present, or the post-colonial that is rooted in the colonial itself. The racial dimension has not been dealt with at any serious level, and George Floyd's murder and countless others are very illustrative of this point. More importantly, the discussion earlier about France's role in the Francophone countries is further evidence that the past has not passed for it to be considered in the realm of distant history that is not directing and imposing on the present.

The US and North Atlantic Treaty Organization invasion of Iraq in 2003, the destruction visited upon the country, including taking down statues, stealing, and at times burning the cultural heritage, and the Iraqi people themselves did not produce the same type of official protestation on preserving the history, art, and legacy of the society. I am all for preserving and studying art and history, certainly in a museum that examines colonization, genocide, slavery, and destruction of Indigenous populations, but these statues are placed in the context of glorification and celebration of the past in public space. Public monuments and statues are edifices built to give societal recognition and infuse collective meaning to the contributions made by the individuals or groups that are included, but likewise it speaks to who is excluded and erased.

Essentially, putting history on trial is a little too easy and a lazy argument because if we really go down that path, then let's take a visit to the British Museum in London, the Louvre Museum in Paris, and every other European main museum to assess the pillaging of every treasure and artifact from the Global South. We have not yet begun to assess history to take the next step and put it on trial. What is the value of all these pieces that were ripped from the societies and cultures across the Global South and put out on display for generations without paying a penny for their true value in the past and the accrued benefits from the moment of theft to the present? Please, don't put forward the insulting argument that at least they are preserved in the hands and museums of Europe, which is yet another added insult to injury even if the position put forth has some merit, because it was only made so through a long series of colonial and postcolonial destruction and impoverishment of the Global South.

The statues on public display are not about the past but the continuation of the epistemological foundation for contemporary society and the connection to history. Had European and American societies undertaken a type of truth and reconciliation approach or restorative justice project, then the explosion that we are witnessing today might have been different or the public space could have been shaped away from the painful past. Moreover, the connection between the materially visible and what is embedded in the mind is immediate, which makes the statues part of the continued epistemic violence directed at Blacks, Indigenous people, and communities of color that lived through colonization, violence, and dispossession. What does a statue of Columbus mean to the Indigenous communities of the Americas, not in the past but at present, living in reservations and facing environmental destruction and disproportionate death from COV-

ID-19? The past is still being unlived daily! What does Robert E. Lee's statues across the South mean to Blacks in the South? Are their collective experiences in today's America not informed by the embedded racism that still glorifies the past and is being re-written into the present?

The second argument that has been put forth is a plea to the protesters to use the "legal" means and the official process to bring about change. Here, the legal process is often subject to the same structural racism that pervades society in general. Case in point is the Cecil John Rhodes statue at Oxford University, which has been at the center of contestation for a long time, and the demand to remove it hit a brick wall with the trustees, who opposed its removal and expressed racist sentiments against those calling for its removal. As the Black Lives Matter movement came to the fore with George Floyd's murder, a new push for removal took hold, and attempts to take the statue down became a major flash point with donors threatening the university if it agrees to remove Rhodes's statue.[210]

Putting Cecil John Rhodes's history on trial and the continued benefits accrued from his murderous colonial programs in southern Africa would be very much appropriate and not any different than taking those who benefited from the Holocaust to task and demanding all things stolen and pillaged to be returned. We have not yet even begun to actually document the past to be able to put it on trial. What about all the endowments, banks, insurances companies, and museums that directly benefited and made billions of profits from colonization and postcolonization? Have we been able to document and actually take stock of the crimes of King Leopold II in the Congo, and what past and present benefits have been acquired and damage visited upon southern Africa from policies that lasted centuries?[211]

More insulting is the mere fact that up to the present day, European countries have not expressed any apology to the colonized countries; rather you see the continued arrogance when the French and British retort back that they built hospitals, roads, and airports; opened schools; and made the trains run on time, and they having nothing to apologize for. Instead, they demand to be thanked and glorified for it, never stopping for a minute to address the issue of genocide of millions, the pillaging of all resources, and the destruction that continues unabated to the present. Europe and the US direct the Global South to appeal to international agencies, which they set up in the first place to make sure that the people go through a circular path to nowhere.

Indeed, the legal system around the globe was structured around settler colonialism and slavery, which was further ensconced by baking race and white supremacy into every element of society. In America, Europe, and other parts of the world, a Black life is expendable, erased, and assigned guilt for being visibly Black, a mere biological material, a "divine error" that inhabits the permanent subhumanness. Guilty for walking while Black; guilty for being Black; guilty for daring to speak, laugh, sing, play, and dance while Black; and guilty for having the audacity to want to be Black and for taking a knee in defense of the murdered Black. Walking, driving, shopping, sitting, working, playing video games in your own home, sleeping, and living as Black are dangerous and life-threatening endeavors in today's America, and indeed, it has always been the case for "non-Europeans" since Columbus landed on these shores. One can't separate the long and painful settler colonial history, which is really not yet history, with the continued unfolding erasure, murder, and structural control of Black and brown people in today's America and Europe, both in the streets and the prison system, the modern hulls of enslavement ships holding commodified and marked bodies.

❧ Commodifying Racism and Profits

America's open casket to the world is its racism that has been institutionalized and commodified into every part of society from the police force to the political order, court system, education system, corporate structure, economy, health care, environment, media, entertainment, and global relations. Some are quick to point to gains made by Blacks since the civil rights movement, and indeed, we can point to these noticeable advancements, including having a Black president in the White House for two terms—although this was followed by the white backlash that landed Trump, the leader of the birther movement (over Obama's birth certificate), to take the country back for white supremacy. "Progress" has been made, but much more needs to be done to undo five hundred years of settler colonialism.

The data on "progress" provides a different picture of a nation that is separate and profoundly unequal. Black unemployment and underemployment are almost twice that of whites.[212] Further, data shows that "by age 17, the average Black student is four years behind the average white student; Black 12th graders score lower than white 8th graders in reading, math, US history and geography."[213] Blacks in today's America are among the poorest, living in the most economically depressed areas in the country, have the largest prison population per capita anywhere in the world, and are far more likely to die young from violence, crime, and drugs than make it to college, get a good paying job, and build a home and raise a family. History has never ended to become the past because it is the present uninterrupted, and the changes over time should have made things better and different, but they did not, which is exactly the point and context of thinking of the colonial and postcolonial framing in approaching the current world.

Indeed, the murder of George Floyd represents the normative experiences and the structural positioning of Blacks in contemporary America: a country deeply seeped in structural racism yet blinded by a self-promoting narrative of color-blindness and progress. This narrative, in essence, assigns blame to Blacks and communities of color for the contemporary conditions they find themselves in and asserts they are incapable of lifting the community out of these self-inflicted wounds of violence, drugs, crime, or dependency on the state. Don't blame slavery or history; rather blame yourself for your own conditions. What America does in this context is take the symptoms of structural racism and make them into the disease that needs to be eradicated. Thus, in this racist and colonial "logic," the problem is located in the Blacks, Africans, and communities of color themselves, and the offered remedy is more police, prison, and rehabilitation programs intended to "civilize" the savage with more mental Fair & Lovely (skin whitening cream) applied to the victims.

George Floyd's murder must be understood correctly, otherwise we go back to the same starting point of blaming the victim one more time by misunderstanding the conditions that brought about the murder in the first place. The police officer killed George Floyd, but America's racism and settler colonialism are the guilty institutions that reload the guns daily and direct them at Blacks and communities of color. America, as a whole, is responsible for the murder of George Floyd and countless other Blacks, young and old, men and women, at home and abroad. How, you may ask, is America to be blamed? America is seeped to its ears with racism and genocide structurally organized around media productions, economic resources, social indicators, and for sure the political arena despite claims to the contrary.

What we have in today's America is a public-housing industrial complex, a food-stamps agribusiness industrial complex, a prison industrial complex, a police and security industrial complex, a social services industrial complex, a sports industrial complex, a medical industrial complex, and a music and entertainment industrial complex: all living off and making massive profits from structural racism, settler colonialism, and the generationally constructed misery of Blacks, communities of color, and poor and middle-class whites as well. Yes, we do allocate funds to "help" Blacks and the poor, but one has to see it differently and accurately and treat it as a massive transfer of wealth to the rich by using the constructed poverty in communities of color as a racist signpost to rationalize these programs. What we have is a massive trickle-up economics from the poor, the postcolonial Global South, to the pockets and bank accounts of the obscenely rich. At the end of the day, massive wealth is made off the backs of Blacks, communities of color, and poor and middle-class whites.

Furthermore, this supposed aid to Blacks and communities of color gets used once again in fomenting divisions with poor and middle-class whites to bring them into line with supporting structural racism by shifting the blame away from the white oligarchy, corporate powerhouses, banks, and the military industrial complex and toward Black and brown communities at home and abroad. For sure, the poor and middle-class whites do get benefits from their white privilege, but at the same time, they are victimized by the same elite structure that seeks to mobilize them on a racist basis and against their collective interest to confront the possibility of empowerment and transformation for Blacks and poor people in general. Slavery was an economic institution in the past, and today's racism directed again at Blacks and communities of color is no different. It is situated to use Black and brown bodies to drive economic benefits to white elites while stoking poor and middle-class white resentment and blaming the victims by pointing to the residual conditions accrued from this most demonic enterprise.

Some will point to cases of success and for sure they exist, but it was not the generosity of the racist or sudden awakening of colonial consciousness in white America and the colonialized Global South that made it possible. Rather, it was despite the shackles, miseducation, prison walls, and violence that Blacks and communities of color were able to overcome racism, and there still is a long way to go. Furthermore, the overemphasis and exposure in media of the few who made it but are wasting or abusing their success, mostly in the music and sports arena, serve the purpose of further stoking the resentment of poor and middle-class whites, which is yet again mobilized to support racist political discourses directed at Blacks in general. In essence, it is used to illustrate the basic epistemic racist notions of "uncivilized" Blacks due to their inability to even manage success for they are constructed more as childlike than fully developed human beings.

Considering what Blacks (past and present) have been through, they continue to believe in and struggle for a better world. We should remember the past while honoring the dignity, perseverance, and creativity of the people. Judge not what you see of the Blacks or communities of color today for they had to live with binds and spurs, not only in the past but in the modern system that inflicts upon them similar punishment in so many ways. For Blacks are still facing the iron masks of miseducation, collars of economic commodification, leg shackles in the modern prison industrial complex, and spears of all types to maintain America's racial structure. Indeed, only a mighty people can go through this and continue to live, love, laugh, teach, raise families, and be a global creative force like no other!

Yes, we have made a few strides, but we are in a marathon, and we have just come out of the starting gate and are not even in the middle of the race to abolish racism. Furthermore, we cannot begin to untangle domestic and internal colonial structures without making the necessary connection to the global and external colonial structures, for they are both self-reinforcing and constitute the epistemic foundation of the modern. The internal colonial city and power distribution is built and organized on a similar basis as the external one, including the type of weapons used and the clothing and training of police, as well as defining relations with communities of color on the basis of warfare.

❧ What Does "Normal" Mean?

America's entanglement with racism and genocides is a present-day amoral river steadily flowing underneath the nation's feet, but no one is ready to dig below the surface until it overflows and disrupts the "normal" and otherwise "peaceful" daily life routines. "Normal" means that race, settler colonialism, whiteness, prisons, brutality, erasures, and multiple genocides are not a topic of conversation or a factor to consider in the political, social, economic, and religious order. Don't be too difficult, rock the boat, or be harsh on your assessment of America. "Normal" means Blacks and communities of color are shot and killed with no serious investigation or response, then they are blamed for it. "Normal" means Blacks and minorities know their place in society and keep to it so as not to alter the layered and carefully structured whiteness that is formed in civil society. "Normal" is to act out on one's own dehumanization in the hope to be included in society's structural exclusion of who you are as Black or a person of color that is inhabiting a space and a time that negates who you are, what you value, and what aspirations you hold for yourself and community alike. "Normal" is seeking to humanize the human, a dehumanizing act, but nevertheless you must engage in it because it gives whiteness the "moral" meaning in such a way that the civilizational project and the white man's burden is still unfolding. Meanwhile, the Black community and communities of color are striving to become fully "human," which in reality can never occur under these conditions. "Human" is only ascribed to whiteness, and all others can only partake in imitation of whiteness so they can be recognized as upwardly mobile toward the white shining city upon a hill; the double consciousness is always present.

"Peaceful" is another term calling for clarification—it refers to the absence of disruption in "society's" sense of "normal," centered on the abnormal status and conditions of Blacks and communities of color at home and abroad. Why is the Global South not peaceful? Why are the Congo, El Salvador, Iraq, and other places not peaceful? Is it biology, culture, religion, or just plain lack of appreciation of what colonization has brought them or could have developed in them had they not revolted against the superior, the white European? "Peaceful" means that the pain and suffering of Blacks and communities of color goes unnoticed, unreported, and totally rationalized as "cultural" or, more accurately, because of their race—

the inferior and the subhuman. "Peaceful" means that the bodies of Blacks and people of color are made motionless through violence, but no one cares or has empathy for the daily body count, which is insultingly called African-on-African, Black-on-Black, Salvador-an-on-Salvadoran, and Muslim-on-Muslim violence or some other dehumanizing drivel masquerading as a "legitimate point" by a slick "expert" epistemically struck with a whiteness "think tank" in the Global North to explain the deep suffering at hand. "Peaceful" means the victim is victimized once more by ascribing the cause of harm to something that is inherent in the character or the racial identity of the person being victimized—maybe the search for a DNA marker to discover and reconstitute biological racist interventions to address it.

When race bursts into the open to disrupt "normal" and "peaceful" life, we first get the shock about what happened, then everyone is ready to speak on how nonexistent, mistaken, and misplaced the emphasis is on this constructed race issue. Everyone comes on TV to say how racism does not exist, we are all the same, "all lives matter," and there is something else that is causing the protests (Antifa, the left, Russians, Chinese, billionaire investor George Soros,[214] right-wing conspiracies, and other distractions) while never discussing the real cause. Talking heads come out of the woodwork to inform everyone how race is a socially constructed category, how much progress we have made, and how the real issue is the victimization attitudes that are keeping Blacks, people of color, and the Global South from moving forward, all mixed with a heavy load of moral arguments of taking responsibility to pull oneself up by the bootstraps. But what if you don't have boots in the first place because they have all been stolen and pillaged for the past five hundred years and, presently, any leather and raw materials are shipped to the north to be made into high fashion for the sophisticated upper crust.

Pontification, along with all types of armchair secular and religious quarterbacking that rewards past and present colonization, victimizes the victim anew and cooks up a rebranded Fair & Lovely epistemic to offer to the minds of the colonized and all those that are challenging structural racism. If they would just let this race thing go—"all lives matter"—then we could go back to further building the "normal" and "peaceful" society that we have been developing until it was disrupted by the misguided, unsophisticated, and indeed violent actions of Blacks and communities of color that came out to the streets. It is when the "normal" and "peaceful" get punctured that Martin Luther King Jr.'s "I Have a Dream" gets airtime, replayed and quoted nonstop, to imply the arrival—if not already the passing—of the hoped-for society referenced in the famous March on Washington speech. Are we a color- or race-blind society? Does someone's skin color impact their economic and social standing? What is the criterion by which to measure the progress in confronting race and racism in society? Who should determine this arrival at a racism-free society, assuming it is a possibility under the current opposition to any real attempt at fundamentally confronting the race issue?

America and Europe carry the moral burden of settler colonial history on their shoulders, and race and racism are the water mixed with mortar that formed the building blocks for the political, social, economic, and religious order we inhabit. At times, people confuse different categories when attempting to speak about race and racism, which leads to further difficulties in approaching the subject. Often, mere attitudes of discrimination are used to define race and racism, which is actually a marker rather than the actual definition. Indeed, this focus on the marker leads to simplistic arguments that every human group engages in racism and at a certain level considers themselves better than others outside their group. In this context, discrimination is a universal phenomenon, and few are shielded from it. However, discrimination is not the same as racism or the construction of racial categories within the colonial epistemic since the former is an outcome or a marker of the latter.

Does race exist? How do we define and engage in a serious, sustained discussion about it? More importantly, how race factors into our political, social, economic, and religious order, what we call structural, systemic, and systematic racism, are the starting points before we substitute a racial category in place of another to claim the lack of existence of race, racism, and the made-invisible suffering of Blacks and minorities at home and across the globe.

❧ Undoing the 1960s

I am writing about racism again because of the increased tensions in today's America and Europe. The increasing polarization is a direct outcome of the political process that is witnessing a sustained effort at rolling back the gains of the civil rights movement of the 1960s. The Civil Rights Act, Immigration and Naturalization Act, and Voting Rights Act are the three pillars around which a societal compromise was reached in the 1960s in the hope of transforming Jim Crow's America into a more perfect union. A similar moment is present across Europe, where the end of World War II and colonization brought attempts at reforms, but since the early 1980s, a move away from serious reforms has been under way, and an emboldened racist right wing has captured seats of power across the continent. In America, in response to the three major civil rights legislations, southern democrats abandoned the Democratic Party and shifted into the republican fold, and a new campaign to "take our country back" was afoot (no democrat has won the majority of white votes since the 1964 presidential election).

The assault on the civil rights movement's gains started in the late 1960s, with the first challenge to affirmative action coming as early as 1968, and ten years later the US Supreme Court handed the Bakke decision that narrowed the scope of its use in college admission. Indeed, the Bakke decision on June 28, 1978, should be considered as the official end of the civil rights compromise, which means the remedy to structural exclusion lasted a mere fourteen years before it was heavily curtailed. While the

US Supreme Court ruled that affirmative action is constitutional, nevertheless, it struck down the important tool of quotas. The Bakke case began at the Davis Medical School of the University of California, which, at the time, had reserved 16 percent of its admission places for minority applicants. What this means is that 84 percent of the medical school's seats were wide open to everyone, and 16 percent had been set aside to open opportunities to Blacks and other minorities, who have been excluded from admission for generations while paying taxes to support the establishment of California's higher education system. The stoking of white resentment did not start with Trump—it manifested itself throughout the period of the civil rights movement and all the way to the present. Similarly, the arrival of Boris Johnson in the United Kingdom did not begin the shift back on issues of race; it can actually be traced to the early 1980s.

The suffering of poor whites and lack of economic and educational opportunities were the same themes that confronted Martin Luther King Jr. and civil rights advocates in the 1960s and 1970s. While organizing activities in defense of the educational access for Blacks and minorities at the University of California, Berkeley, in the early 1990s, I was confronted with the same arguments from poor and working-class whites in even more dire conditions, who needed opportunities in the same way as the minorities. Here, I agreed on the overall principle of needing to help everyone and advocate access for all, but at the same time, I asserted the need to remedy cumulative and generational exclusions that disproportionately impact Blacks and minorities.

It is not surprising to see the Trump administration going back to the same tool kit by targeting the affirmative action in college admission in a way to further consolidate the assault on civil rights gains from the 1960s and using law and order, a frame that is laced with racism and is a powerful node to the right wing that understands what is meant by it.[215] We can see this strategy on TV shows, as the arguments around the rise of the alt-right,

Ku Klux Klan, and neo-Nazis are immediately shifted to a discussion of the economic disparities and poverty faced by whites in America, and the issue is not about Blacks or race! Here, we have the immediate shift into white suffering, itself a racial category, while denying the existence of racial categories in society altogether, a sophisticated process for mainly silencing the suffering and experience of Blacks in particular. Stating that Blacks experience racism does not mean that whites don't experience poverty or economic, political, and social marginalization; they certainly do, but the topic is always inserted as a counter thesis to raising the question of racism and Black suffering.

Economic problems and dislocation affect all middle-class and poor Americans, but within this broad statement, some suffer more than others. It is a certainty that when the economy is good, Blacks, Indigenous peoples, Latinos, and some segments of the Asian American community are the last to benefit, and when a recession or depression hits, then they are blamed for being dependent on social welfare or government handouts. Mind you, on a purely numerical basis and as a percentage, whites access social welfare benefits more than communities of color and immigrants, but they are never stigmatized for it. The state should uplift and help those less fortunate in society and provide a safety net to those who are left behind due to a variety of economic, social, and political causes—building institutions that can attend to the weak and vulnerable is what makes us human and civilized.

If you lost your job, ended up on the streets with mental health issues, and had more opportunities to end up in jail than in Yale, then look no further than the combined effects of Reagan's and Clinton's policies, followed by Bush's seven trillion dollars spent on wars in the Middle East, with the funds going to the rich and powerful, to be followed by billions, if not trillions, to bail out banks and corporations under Obama's presidency. Who is to blame? The poor, Blacks, Muslims, immigrants, China, or Russia? Yes, Black Lives Matter activists and protesters are pushing a "radical" leftist agenda that will undermine "Western civilization" and family values! I really wish that those who use and deploy the silencing term "family values" actually believe and act on it!

Now, family values were not at play by sending hundreds of thousands to die in a foreign land while killing and maiming people they had no business to fight in the first place, only to come back home to face post-traumatic stress disorder with no services and funding from the government that sent them to fight abroad. Family values were not a topic of discussion when thirteen million Americans got thrown out of their homes after the 2008 financial crisis bailout that gave taxpayers' money to the banks and investment firms that created the crisis in the first place rather than to the people or the families that struggled to make ends meet. Family values were not a topic of discussion when welfare programs got cut, educational funding slashed, and a massive tax break given to the rich at the expense of the poor and middle class.

Family values were not a topic when Trump destroyed the last fig leaf of modesty and decency and showed the obscenity of right-wing elites (left wing as well) and lay bare the duplicity of the religious right in embracing a president that is the antithesis to every moral and ethical fiber or text that religion puts forth. Family values are also not a topic of discussion for the democrats who embraced a lighter version of the right-wing neoliberal agenda, supported free trade for corporations, and voted to expand prisons, cut welfare, provide open-ended funding for the military for the never-ending war, offer bank bailouts, and keep company with all the same set of shady corporate and elite characters. Family values for Black and brown communities are locked up in prison or imprisoned by society's neglect, criminalization, and total disregard in cities and towns across America.

All of these sentiments, and what I mentioned in earlier chapters, paved the way for the current crop of dead-end politics that is delighted to blame Black Lives Matter activists for those lives that no longer matter in the macro and micro calculus of America's domestic and global racial politics. More insulting and utterly despicable is when religious people enter into the family value discourse and breach success capitalism theology, keep company with all those pushing antifamily values, and offer prayers to the dispossessor while milking the pockets and squeezing the last dollar and drop of moral meaning from the dispossessed.

❧ Burning Churches and Targeting Black Institutions

George Floyd's murder opens the door to examine deeper wounds from enslavement and lynching, from the massacre of three hundred Blacks and the burning of Black Wall Street[216] in Tulsa, Oklahoma, to the constant attacks on Black churches. After the murder of nine Blacks in the Mother Emanuel African Methodist Episcopal Church in Charleston, North Carolina, at least eight different Black churches in the South got torched, with three confirmed as an arson attack. The last one in this string was the Mount Zion African Methodist Episcopal Church in Greeleyville, South Carolina, only sixty miles north of Charleston. The burned churches were mostly in the South and include Charlotte, North Carolina; Knoxville, Tennessee; and Macon, Georgia. White supremacists in the South have historically targeted African American churches, which continue to be used as a primary site to terrorize Black communities, but no one in the political establishment, media, and mainstream white religious institutions referred to them as such nor mobilized at an institutional level to counter it.

Burning Black churches did not disrupt the "normal" in America but speaking about it does! The burning of Black churches is a terrorist act intended to intimidate and instill fear in Black communities and through it make it possible to maintain the racist and white supremacist structure intact. The church is a visible public collective symbol and an affirmation of belonging to the shared civil society space. Therefore, burning a church is a terrorist act intended to contest and physically remove the institution and, more importantly, the Black bodies that it houses from civil society and the shared meanings connected to it. The church-burning phenomena is a racist act intended as a collective lynching and an attempt to permanently remove the Black institution from civil society and through it the Black community itself.

Here, a connection must be made between the lynching of Blacks in America's history and the never-ending burning of Black churches, since both are ideologically connected to white supremacy and institutional and systemic racism. The burning of Black churches strategy dates back to the early nineteenth century as these institutions began to be set up. Lynching was intended to keep the freed slaves in the same economic, political, social, cultural, and special relations that existed during the enslavement period. Lynching was used to terrorize Blacks and to draw racial boundaries and maintain institutional inequalities intact in the face of rising demands for economic and political rights by the freed slaves.

A study by the Equal Justice Initiative (EJI)[217] "documented 4,084 racial terror lynchings in twelve Southern states between the end of Reconstruction in 1877 and 1950, which is at least 800 more lynchings in these states than previously reported. EJI has also documented more than 300 racial terror lynchings in other states during this time period."[218] The report included the story of Jesse Thornton, who was lynched in Alabama for not uttering "Mister" when addressing a white police officer. Another case in the report was that of Jeff Brown, who was lynched for accidentally bumping into a white girl as he ran to catch a train.

Lynching was a tool to keep Black people "in their place" and to terrorize them into submission to white supremacy in the post-enslavement period. Moreover, "racial terror lynching was a tool used to enforce Jim Crow laws and racial segregation—a tactic for maintaining racial control by victimizing the entire African American community, not merely punishment of an alleged perpetrator for a crime."[219] The website and project by James Allen and John Littlefield, Without Sanctuary,[220] documented how widespread the phenomena was as people shared and sent each other greeting cards bearing photos of lynched individuals. What a deeply sick and vile society it was that sanctioned this activity. Considering the protesters taking down statues of slave traders and Columbus, the EJI report correctly states: "There are very few monuments or memorials that address the history and legacy of lynching in particular or the struggle for racial equality more generally. Most communities do not actively or visibly recognize how their race relations were shaped by terror lynching."[221]

The Black church was established to serve the needs of freed slaves and ministers who set up these institutions and provided a much-needed space for prayers and education as well as a site for rallying against institutionalized racism. The church was the first and primary site that gave a visible, collective, and public face to freed slaves and from its inception was firmly committed to an emancipatory agenda. Black churches were liberation churches from their inception. As the number of Black churches increased, the attacks by white supremacists intensified and, in the process, employed extreme terror and violence against the institution and the people who attended the services. As a matter of fact, Malcolm X's father was a minister and, likewise, according to Malcolm X's biography, was killed by the Ku Klux Klan. Furthermore, over sixty different churches were burned during the civil rights movement period, including a number of deadly bombings.

If we take the church burning, lynching, and police brutality together, then we arrive at a structured and institutionalized regime of violence and terror that has been historically deployed to keep Black people "in their place" and under control, which was exactly what was done to George Floyd in Minneapolis. Police violence becomes a civil-society-sanctioned lynching since the rate of conviction for officers involved in the deadly use of violence against Blacks is dismal, and even when guilt is established, they end up with a light sentence. The Black subject is constantly facing real and metaphorical lynching acts that contest their ability to live a "normal" life in America. Burning churches is a lynching act directed at the institutional backbone of the Black community and should be treated as a terrorist activity intended to sow fear and intimidation.

In all honesty, Black lives don't matter at all, and if evidence is needed, then go no further than your daily news cycle or a short visit to city streets, schools, universities, corporate boardrooms and upper management, jails, and hospitals. They will provide you more detail than going to a daylong session in any congressional hearing on race or racism or watching any TV special centered on whiteness while bringing on Black- and brown-supporting props to recenter themselves in the narrative. The cruel reality is that white working-class lives don't matter either, and cops' lives might matter a little more, but it boils down to different segments of America's gladiator arena set for the pleasure of a ruling class that is criminally indifferent to the racial and dispossessed edifice it built. Confronting race means coming to terms with America's multilayered industrial complexes that benefit from, and are enriched by, the operative racial matrix that informs, regulates, and nurtures every part of society inside and outside.

Policies have ramifications, and Blacks have been the permanent canary in the perpetual racial-colonial coal mine, at home and abroad, through which the results can be measured, witnessed, and ignored. Here, a significant point needs to be made that no one ever asks: "How does the canary feel being doomed to death to warn others about an impending death?" When will we make the needed shifts in policies and solutions that make the metaphorical societal mine safer for the canaries and let them fly free inside and outside the mine? Today, America's racist engine is exuding toxic racial fumes that are killing and disfiguring everyone in society, and the time is now to reimagine a new civil and human rights movement centered on confronting race, settler colonialism, and the legacy of slavery, making it possible for Blacks to breathe again.

A "radical revolution of values" was what Martin Luther King Jr. called for in Chicago during his 1967 "The Three Evils of Society" speech, and it is the same message that must be delivered in this day and age:

> So we are here because we believe, we hope, we pray that something new might emerge in the political life of this nation which will produce a new man, new structures and new institutions and a new life for mankind. I am convinced that this new life will not emerge until our nation undergoes a radical revolution of values. When machines and computers, profit motives and property rights are considered more important than people, the giant triplets of racism, economic exploitation and militarism are incapable of being conquered. A civilization can flounder as readily in the face of moral bankruptcy as it can through financial bankruptcy. A true revolution of values will soon cause us to question the fairness and justice of many of our past and present policies. We are called to play the good Samaritan on life's roadside, but that will only be an initial act.

Conclusion

Erasures and the Military Industrial Complex

Immigrants and refugees from the Global South coming to Europe and the United States are viewed in terms of the tail end of their journey, with no interest in the start of it and the causes that pushed them out. Moreover, addressing the crisis by focusing mainly on the challenges facing the Global North and never going beyond the outer layers of the unfolding calamities that brought these refugees and immigrants out of their homelands is shortsighted and disgraceful. The fomented racist public-discourse crisis in Europe and North America focused on the Syrian refugees and problematizing their arrival but not on the reasons why they left their country in large numbers and what role France, the United Kingdom, and the US, among others, played to create the crisis in the first place.

On September 2, 2015, TV screens and the front pages of newspapers across the world displayed the picture of Alan Kurdi (Aylan Shenu), a three-year-old Syrian toddler wearing a red T-shirt, lying face down motionless on the shore of a Turkish resort in the town of Bodrum. The toddler was one of twelve Syrians who drowned on that day attempting to reach Greece and make their way to Europe after escaping the raging civil war in their country. Even before the Syrian war, the Mediterranean Sea had become a graveyard for many who risked their lives in the hope of landing on a safer shore. No one is sure of the exact numbers of those who crossed and made it to Europe versus those who ended up at the bottom of the sea, nameless, faceless, and totally erased from the records and from our collective consciousness.

I began the book with the narrative focusing on Yousif, a story that is all too common for immigrants and refugees seeking safety in Europe. The European Union's adoption of restrictive immigration, refugee, and asylum regulations is directly connected to Alan's death on the shore and Yousif's erasure in the hope of arriving at a safe location in France. As I write these lines, thousands of immigrants and refugees are being held in modern-day prisons and camps across southern Europe and in local jails in western Europe for no crime other than being a human in search of safety and security.

The image of Alan's small body on the Mediterranean shore is so similar to the lifeless bodies of Oscar Alberto Martínez and his twenty-three-month-old daughter, Angie Valeria Martínez, face down in murky waters of the Rio Grande after drowning in their attempt to reach the US while escaping the ongoing unrest in El Salvador. The two images are thousands of miles apart from each other and emerge from different ethnic, religious, and national contexts, but they are connected in the reasons that made each one of them a painful news item—the plight of the immigrant and refugee across the globe, who are, more critically, subject to multifaceted erasure. In more than one way, the two are connected to US and European colonial history, interventionist records, and postcolonial policies that are disruptive and rooted in the fusion between the military industrial complex, multinational corporations, and the civilizational racist discourses that inform and give impetus to the unfolding crisis at hand—all of which are not included in discussions on the immigration-refugee crisis and only amplify the racial and ethnic makeup of the arriving person to stoke fear.

Europe's colonial past, which still regulates the postcolonial south in Asia and across Africa, is directly responsible for the misery, death, and confinement experienced by thousands, if not millions, of people. Colonization was not a single event, and postcolonization is not a single day of raising the independence flag and putting the clock back to precolonization so that we are back to "normal" times. Postcolonization has maintained the colonial apparatus governing the economy, society, education, politics, and religious discourses, which sits at the root of the current unfolding crisis. In the post-Cold War era, the postcolonial world experienced an accelerated privatization scheme, a push for neoliberal economic models, and a heavy dose of interventions from the US and western European states that emerged triumphant, asserting the validity of their history by winning the war against the communist USSR and emphasizing anew the exceptionalism of Eurocentrism and Western epistemology, the foundation of human progress and the "only true" enlightenment.

From the early 1990s to the present, a robust interventionist push into the Global South took place in total partnership with postcolonial ruling elites, multinational corporations, the military industrial complex, and hyperprivatization-oriented capitalism. which in a short period of time devastated what limited scope of economic and social cohesion existed across Africa, Asia, and Latin America

The domestic view is not disconnected from the global, and both reinforce each other at every turn in the same way the colonial period witnessed this dynamic relationship. The domestic framework in the US and Europe shapes the livelihoods of millions of people in distant lands and makes the flow of immigrants and refugees to the Global North an "acceptable" cost for entrenched and dead-end economic and political policies.

Often, the refrain from the political right and the interventionist humanitarian left is that the problems of colonization are long gone, major strides have been made to address racism, the white man's burden and manifest destiny is a historical relic, militarism is defending civilization itself from terrorism, and capitalism has lifted so many from poverty and overall is a force for good. Yes, we do have problems here and there, but if anyone does not like

Europe or America, then, as President Trump put it on Twitter, "Why don't they go back and help fix the totally broken and crime infested places from which they came. Then come back and show us how it is done. These places need your help badly, you can't leave fast enough. I'm sure that Nancy Pelosi would be very happy to quickly work out free travel arrangements!"[222] Indeed, the sentiment expressed by President Trump is widely shared among a sizeable segment of whites in the US and Europe and even a fragment of minorities that, and for a variety of reasons, have adopted a similar view.

In Trump's post, and among those who adopted this perspective, is the major disconnect between the colonial legacy and the postcolonial interventions that made for the unfolding political, economic, social, and humanitarian disasters that brought the immigrant and refugee to the US and Europe in the first place and landed a few of them in congressional, parliamentarian, and government seats. In the marches that followed George Floyd's murder, many protestors in the US and Europe carried signs stating, "We are here because you were there," which is an accurate summation of the causes that brought about the immigration-refugee crisis in the first place. Names like Cheney, Churchill, Columbus, Cromer, King Leopold II, Kissinger, McNamara, Nixon, Reagan, Rhodes, Rumsfeld, and Sykes-Picot and are celebrated figures with books, statutes, buildings, and institutions bearing their names, but for much of the Global South they are known for supporting wars, low-intensity conflicts, genocides, coups d'etat, and destruction of lives for many while making immigrants and refugees out of the lucky ones.

I have highlighted throughout the chapters the immediate nexus between the US and European interventionist foreign policy in the postcolonial Global South and the steady stream of immigrants and refugees arriving in cities, towns, and fields in the Global North. Erasure of the problem from public discourse and policy-making circles does not mean that the problem is solved or can be wished out of existence. It is not possible to address the tail end of the crisis without doing the much-needed work at the root cause of the problem, the disruption and continued political, economic, and military interventions in the Global South. Interventions do bring massive financial benefits to political elites in the Global North who are vested in the military industrial complex's death economy, for which the production of quick and industrial-scale death is its major commodity.

❧ Commodifying Death

The military industrial business is war: its marketing tools involve glorifying modern killing machines, its growth is achieved through manipulation of the political process and corruption, and its real product is the motionless and lifeless human bodies brought into instantaneous and industrial-scale death across the globe. Part of the problem is that domestically we don't see or think of the military industrial complex because we use racism, sexism, and antipoor discourses to obfuscate its impact. Moreover, when we say, the Global North economy is a military industrial complex, often this is not understood and is narrowly thought of when war is at hand, rather than thinking of all the resources that are directed at research, development, academic institutional investments, testing, and then commodifying death as a growth industry. In America, family values are introduced at every turn, while the backdrop is a society built on pernicious capitalism, weapon sales, armaments, militarism, interventions, and death—a reality which has been intertwined into every aspect of the domestic and global economies. Don't let a good gun go to waste, and defend the Second Amendment one body bag, one school mass shooting, and one hospital emergency room crisis at a time while making sure to raise the level of patriotism and fly the flag high when questions arise.

In the past year alone, the world has spent $1.64 trillion on buying and selling death machines that have no purpose other than death itself. The faster they can deliver death, the better and more expensive they are, and the more profit margins are generated. Added to this mix is the overwhelming financial services infrastructure that facilitates the death economy for the Global South, including the entertainment enterprise itself, which captures the imagination of the living and makes it possible for them to pursue and imagine the death of others and themselves as well. The scope of the death economy must include prisons, gun violence, homelessness, domestic violence, and drugs, both legal and those perceived to be illegal, that keep all numb to the mass production of death as a growth industry. Death and destruction abroad mean refugees and immigrants at the borders!

The military industrial complex's death economy is the type that commodifies postcolonialism, racism, and fear; stokes resentment among people; raises racial tensions; fosters ignorance; manufactures conflicts; urges interventions (humanitarian and military alike); and marshals resources to snuff out life itself. It is an economy that spends a million dollars to produce a "smart bomb" to kill a man, woman, or child in the Global South that barely survives on one dollar a day and with it murder human potential many generations over. Producing "smart bombs" is more important and has more "meaning" than nurturing smart and caring human beings!

Martin Luther King Jr.'s speech on August 31, 1967, "The Three Evils of Society," delivered at the National Conference on New Politics, is still prophetic: "But our moral lag must be redeemed; when scientific power outruns moral power, we end up with guided missiles and misguided men. When we foolishly maximize the minimum and minimize the maximum, we sign the warrant for our own day of doom. It is this moral lag in our thing-oriented society that blinds us to the human reality around us and encourages us in the greed and exploitation which creates the sector of poverty in the midst of wealth." The "thing-oriented" society is built on death machines and uses interventions as a way to maintain and preserve "our" living standards, which is built on the death of others to achieve it.

The military industrial complex's death economy, which is supported by Global North governments, corporations, and institutions, uses the Global South as a testing ground and the competitive market for putting more wealth in the coffers of merchants of death. Indeed, it is the type of economy that cuts childcare, health care, education, agriculture research, storytelling, libraries, schools, the arts, and social uplifting in favor of maximum and unlimited expenditures for militarized police at home and storm troopers abroad. "Smart bombs" and killing machines have limitless budgets, yet we are unable to save people from the global COVID-19 pandemic that is decimating our elders, Black communities, and other communities of color.

The military industrial complex's death economy has a bottomless pit of resources that are readily marshaled to produce faster, bigger, and supposedly "smarter" death machines and uglier police cars and outfits intended to bring about the end of many lives at a time. But these same tools are unable to rescue people like Alan Kurdi, Oscar Alberto Martínez, Angie Valeria Martínez, and the thousands of others across the globe held in camps, prisons, jails, and countless other facilities that produce mountains of wealth for the military industrial complex, security, and surveillance archipelago structures.

Asking for resources to save human lives is a difficult and arduous task, and walls of ignorance are offered to rationalize the lack of funding and the impossibility to shift resources away from national security. Death machines are funded with no questions asked and wrapped in the flag of patriotism and nationalism while marketing fear of darker bodies to secure public consent and increasing the national debt. Death machines are paraded on the national stage and celebrated as if they are objects of religious veneration giving spiritual meaning to an empty edifice that has become accustomed to the nauseating smell of death and destruction. Witnessing religious people offering prayers atop death machines is repulsive and criminal, while they stay away from the victims of such machines or offer to assuage their pain by a distorted and mind-numbing theology set in service of the empire.

The death economy is one that produces a national cult of death that sends its own to graveyards near and far for no other purpose than to pad profit margins for a Dracula-type bloodsucking private country club of morally bankrupt CEOs and their political delivery boys at the helm of governments. Governments borrow massively to fund the production of death machines and keep the addiction of the military industrial complex's death economy moving no matter the consequences.

What is the worst possible outcome for the death economy? Normally, death would be the worst outcome for anyone, but from a death economy's perspective, it actually translates into an opportunity for market growth by means of predictable rates of organized and mechanized killing. The US's and Europe's military industrial complex death economies are humming along and have not missed a beat since Columbus sailed the ocean blue (I am not against including other periods in human history, but we are in a class unto ourselves, and no one can even come close to the type of infusion of economy and death that has been produced). Whether in peace or war times, the spending and production never ceases and with it the long lines of skulls and bones that are left behind or displayed in museums, some of which are photographed, but many face the structured erasure, even when they are made visible.

The military industrial complex and the death economy posit defending the nation from domestic and foreign enemies as the rationale for developing the needed weapons and armaments, which if not undertaken correctly would result in loss of status and position on the world stage. Death machines are needed to protect the nation and its entire people from a possible attack by a group or a state using better or more tested death machines. We need them to protect ourselves, but to do that, we must surrender to the death economy itself, which kills all at home and abroad many times over. The military industrial complex's arms race that is put forth to the human family is calling for an infinite cycle of producing bigger and better death machines to protect "us" from their bigger and better death machines, which ends up causing all of our deaths by means of poverty, environmental destruction, mental disease, post-traumatic stress disorder, suicides, and societal fragmentation. An economy vested in destruction and testing our human capacity to end life itself is offered as the only present and future horizon by the merchants of death.

The military industrial complex's death economy is rationalized through the deployment of failed many times over colonial political theories, racist "scientific" studies of the cultural and biological types based on survival of the fittest, religious claims rooted in distorted and speculative or success theologies as well as imperial theologians blessings bombs and death, and a host of other circularly constructed reasons that lead straight to the graveyards. At the core, the military industrial complex's death economy points to its capacity to end life at an industrial scale as the needed proof of its veracity and urges the society to continue to build and expand its scope and investments. Death itself is the "measure of success" for the death economy!

Alarmingly, the military industrial complex's death economy depends on a sophisticated cadre of warmongers that peddle their views on the airwaves, on TV screens, and in major print media, as well as through internet advertisers, scholars at universities, and think tank experts. Media coverage of wars and the buildup for them is an art form that gets deployed to rally the nation into accepting the use of death machines and mobilize the death economy against a defined and ready-made-for-TV enemy, and the darker the bodies of the enemy, the better it is for fomenting the needed fear and rallying nationalist and patriotic sentiments. Rockets and missiles rain death and destruction on helpless people, while TV news ratings shoot skyward for war-mongers and journalists embedded with the frontline troops and the well-dressed and handpicked "experts" in the studio.

Live from Vietnam, Live from Baghdad, Live from Panama City, Live from Beirut, Live From Haiti, Live from El Salvador, Live from Grenada, and Live From Zaire (Congo) means only one thing: our death machines have hit their target, and we have the embedded journalist to provide the framing and get the need-ed B-roll footage for future marketing purposes. Even when ev-idence is lacking, the warmongers never miss an opportunity to produce the needed threats, on-air manufactured evidence, and concocted attacks on "our" troops that must be responded to with death machines, never divulging that the same company that owns the media outlet is likewise heavily invested in the death economyitself.[223]

Death and destruction sell and make a significant return on investment. Moreover, the relationship between the military in-dustrial complex's death economy and movie production studi-os is well-established, which works to formulate the latent death epistemic in the minds of the population.[224] Just like a scientific experiment in a lab produces results, the latent military industrial complex's death economy plays out daily on TV, as entertainment on the movie screens, and in video games in kids' hands, which is easily transformed into manifest popular support to fund, produce, and use death machines on human beings. Behind every immi-grant and refugee arriving from the Global North in the postco-lonial era is a military industrial complex involvement and a sales campaign that produced heavy returns on investments, while the stream of humans is an "acceptable" cost for doing business.

❧ Postcolonial Entanglements

A few days after George Floyd's murder, the Israeli army killed an autistic Palestinian kid, Iyad el-Hallak, in Jerusalem, in a hail of bullets despite his caretaker alerting the officers to his disability but to no avail. What is taking place in Palestine has a direct connection to George Floyd's murder because, as it turns out, the Minneapolis Police Department's officers receive training in Israel on various tactics, including how to subdue suspects and the use of the knee on the neck restraint for individuals.[225] Postcolonial entanglements brings together all types of state and non-state actors to maintain dispossession and structural erasures of communities across the globe.

Indeed, since the September 11 attacks, Israeli security, with its know-how and trainings, has been promoted as the go-to expert to provide the needed combat skills, which helped accelerate the militarization of the local police, making an immediate connection between the local and transnational. Not to imply that Israel acted alone; rather, Israeli political and military leadership acted swiftly post-September 11 and refocused their strategy to become even more of a utilitarian state for the US's expanding global war on terrorism and through this tactic managed to direct massive resources to their coffers. As an outcome or part of the strategy, the Palestinians, Arabs, and Muslims became expandable and targeted internally in the US, while Israel was granted total freedom in using violence and brutality in the region. The US's war on terrorism became a massive financial faucet for the military industrial complex at home and abroad, from which Israel and other global actors benefited and jumped on Uncle Sam's gravy train.

In this context, the dubious global war on terror became embedded into local policing through the Joint Terrorism Task Forces, Urban Shield trainings, countering violent extremism programs, and other types of projects that connected and entrenched Israel's connection and interests at the local level. This pushed the clock farther back on all civil rights reforms and the deployment of racially targeted surveillance and violence. The City of New York's stop-and-frisk policing tactics, mapping, surveillance, and placement of informants in Muslim community spaces[226] have a direct link to Israeli security training programs. Furthermore, the Transportation Security Administration's security teams in Boston Logan airport received Israeli training for the Screening of Passengers by Observation Techniques and ended up adopting and implementing it for traveler screening, including the intrusive background checks, which were celebrated at the time as a major step forward despite being highly racist and stereotypical.[227] A similar strategy was afoot in Europe, infusing Israel and its security interests into every aspect of "counterterrorism" training, strategy, and targeting of Muslims and immigrant and refugee communities.

The postcolonial entanglements include the neoliberal economic crisis that brought the world economic system to the brink of collapse. The global war on terror, coupled with the 2008 great recession, accelerated the collapse of the postcolonial global order and brought about massive social, political, and economic disruption, which translated into immigrants and refugees streaming to the Global North. This included the emergence of a complex right-wing, ultranationalist, racist, Islamophobic, and highly militarized network to supposedly confront the threat to Western civilization. Concurrently, the military, economic, social, religious, and political interventions in the Global South intensified and more so over the past twenty years, causing further disruptions and distortions at every level of society, which managed to obfuscate the causes behind people's movement to the Global North. In addition, the focus on the Syrian immigrants and refugees arriving in the US and Europe allowed the clash of civilizations warriors and white nationalists to fuse their global interventionist campaigns to domestic fears and through it ascend the ladder to political power and dominate public discourses.

In France and other European countries, the focus on the Syrian refugees permitted the amplification and solidification of existing Islamophobic sentiments, which were easily packaged into campaign themes and electioneering across the political spectrum at a time of greater financial and social uncertainty. Across

Europe and North America, the state withdrawal of a social welfare safety net, reduction in funding for education and health care, environmental destruction, and attacks on organized labor were all projected on the costs and problems of immigrants and refugees, which allowed the ruling elites to escape scrutiny on their failed trickle-down and neoliberal economic policies as well as rationalizing an open assault on the marginalized and powerless in the society.

Hidden and totally obfuscated from the public discourse around Syrian immigrants and refugees is all the other Global South people that have been displaced due to the continued interventions and distortions arising from the colonial and the postcolonial entanglements. For example, in France, the Syrian refugees and immigrants accounted for no more than 2–5% of those arriving in the country, yet public discourse and political debate laser focused on them, which allowed for the Islamophobic and orientalist imaginary to run wild, with the immediate consequence being the heavy deployment of a security and counterterrorism state response rather than a humanitarian and civilian based one.[228]

What was erased from the public discourse and political debate are the 95–98% of the immigrants arriving from other parts of Europe and the postcolonial ex-French colonies due to the continued domination of France over all aspects of their internal affairs and the need for a cheap and unregulated labor force to put pressure on organized labor to accept reduced wages, less health care, and an extension of retirement age.[229] "Undocumented" does not mean unpurposed or unplanned; rather it is part and parcel of a perfectly constructed labor market in a global gladiator arena that functions to extract maximum returns from each participant before their eventual retirement or death. The difference between both is often a minor one.

Lastly, the culmination of the Cold War with the "victory" of the US and western Europe witnessed the end of "revolutionary" political programs and parties, which was followed by postcolonial elites' contestation and a rapid repositioning in the Global South. The wars in Afghanistan, Iraq, Libya, Somalia, Sudan, Syria, and Yemen are directly connected to post-Cold War realignment and attempts at reconfiguring the Middle East and North and East Africa in relation to US and western European priorities while making sure to push and contest China's ability to access oil and resources in the region. A similar case with different players can be traced in Africa, where access to oil, natural'resources, and controlling markets stoked local conflicts while using the region to reposition the West opposite China's desire to make inroads in the continent. In this context, the Arab Spring is as much a grassroots effort to change the nature of the postcolonial Arab state as a new form of intervention to reconstitute the US, western European, and postcolonial Arab monarchies that play a critical role in keeping the strategic flow of oil at a manageable price to sell to the Global North while recycling the revenues into the coffers of the military industrial complex.

Consequently, focusing on the ebb and flow of the immigration-refugee crisis without putting it within the broader colonial, historical, political, and economic contexts that gave rise to it in the first place makes the problem more acute. Thus, focusing on the European Union policies to address the number of immigrants and refugees to admit into EU countries, the US's building of the wall on the Mexican border and adoption of draconian measures to dissuade people from coming to America, the UN's attempts to alleviate the suffering though humanitarian aid, and the not-for-profit sector's rendering of services misses the fundamental cause of the unfolding problem—the collapse of the postcolonial state.

However, the discourses that often get amplified are the ones rooted in a racialized vision of the problem, or the so-called replacement theory, which indicts the Global South people and assigns malicious intent behind their flight to safety from the death and destruction that is visited upon them by the Global North in partnership with postcolonial elites in the Global South. The immigrant and refugee from the Global South arriving in the US and Europe is framed as a "civilizational criminal" intent on committing a future genocide against "Western civilization" and its people in the Global North, rather than as an ongoing victim of a colonial project that erased their existence for the past five hundred years. Thus, victims of multiple genocides from the Global South have to answer for the fomented fear produced by Global North elites, military industrial complex corporations, and media pundits.

"We are here because you were there" is the only way to understand the unfolding immigration-refugee crisis, and unless the causes at the source are systematically and holistically addressed, then the problem will persist and intensify. Due to rapid changes in technology, transportation, and ease of communication, the ability to insulate and keep the postcolonial world far away from the Global North is a failed policy, which will only lead to building higher walls and creating fortresses, and, indeed, is shortsighted. As much as it keeps some out, it also keeps those on the inside locked up.

Fortification in Europe and the US is a reversal of the dynamic of colonial expansion, where building a fort was the way to push the borders farther and claim more lands while emptying the territories from their Indigenous inhabitants; the opposite is at play now. Building walls and legal fortresses to keep Global South populations away will not be successful as long as the causes that drive people out are still in place and the Western world is still vested in extracting natural resources, intervening in the political and economic affairs of these states, and exploiting regional differences. The immigration and refugee literature addresses the push-pull factors that motivate people to move from one place to another, which for the most part is accurate but at the same time incomplete. What makes it incomplete is the propensity to amplify the symptoms while erasing the causes behind them, both the immediate and the historical ones.

The push-pull factors function within a global world system that is forged out of the colonial and into the postcolonial entanglements. Thus, the idea that we can develop programs and projects to address them in isolation of the overall structure is faulty at best and part of the problem at worst. Some might be tempted to ask for immediate solutions, which is in itself a tricky proposition to seek it before coming to terms with how we define the problem in the first place. Often, seeking immediate solutions puts an academic and intellectual market pressure to become engaged in what I call "colonial problem solving" or at our stage "postcolonial problem solving." Asking for immediate solutions is akin to inviting scholars and activists to clean the colonial and postcolonial litter box rather than undoing its foundation.

We should not be in the business of colonial problem solving and accept the role of embedded intellectuals or academics brought to bear to solve technical outcomes from colonization and postcolonization. Answering a colonial or postcolonial question is in itself a problem since the attempt is to bypass the needed steps of undoing or unlearning the structure that created the crisis in the first place before one gets into constructing the possible alternatives. Academic fields that partake in the problem-solving discourse or the "development" theories behind such efforts often reproduce the same type of erasures and problematics. Often, the development project fails to appropriately contextualize the issues it is attempting to solve and arrives in each region equipped with a neoliberal tool set if not completely funded by outfits that are committed to it.

The military industrial complex has a mirror image or a softer side that comes along at the same time or after the bombs are dropped, the not-for-profit industrial complex or the humanitarian industrial complex, which is a vast network that acts as the emergency ICU for direct and hardnose colonial and postcolonial powers. The not-for-profit industrial complex produces the same colonial contradictions and elevates the Global North's needs and worldview at the expense of the hopes and aspirations of the Global South. Critically, the massive amounts of funds raised to address the impacts of the invasions and interventions end up being spent on the staff and infrastructure of the Global North agencies that are the soft power partners of the military industrial complex.

This is not to tarnish the work of solid organizations and groups, but the record and evidence of the major institutions in the Global North running these programs leave much to be desired and end up, through their work on the ground, affirming the racial, economic, political, and religious colonial hierarchies. However, and in their defense, they never had to deal with undoing and challenging colonialism or countering the postcolonial structure since the mission was only funded to deal with the immediate and narrowly defined focus on water shortage, school playground construction, and malaria vaccines, and not the reasons, both contemporary and historical, that caused areas with vast wealth to be unable to provide a glass of clean water or afford to build a school!

A number of deep-seated stereotypical, racist, and implicitly biased views of the Global South are at work within the American and European social imaginary, which informs "the experts" and works to regulate their perceptions and responses to the immigration-refugee crisis on the one hand and the solutions offered to postcolonial states on the other. Here, we have to make a distinction between simple ignorance and the phenomenon of compounded or structural ignorance, which goes beyond the simple kind and into a deeper level that assigns blame to the victims of colonization for being victimized. It locates the causalities in something internal to the Global South itself rather than the interplay of the six features of colonization discussed earlier. Simple ignorance is bad enough, but the compounded and sophisticated type works to parcel out the supposed "barbaric, terroristic, criminal" or societal "disease" present in the Global South to justify or rationalize the ongoing dispossession, pillaging, and destruction vested upon the postcolonial states. Clearly, the mechanisms that regulated the Global South and kept "the order" have collapsed, and with it the postcolonial states themselves are no longer able to sustain what is unsustainable. The immigrants and refugees streaming out is the visible symptom.

The starting point for solutions and remedies to the multifaceted immigrant-refugee crisis must begin with taking the six features of colonization into account to initiate a sustained and systematic decolonization program. Offering solutions without undoing each of these elements will only put the work and crisis back into a status quo stage and preoccupation with countless symptoms. A holistic and integrative approach to the immigration-refugee crisis would seek to make a connection between what we teach and the need to dismantle the economic, political, racial, social, culture, religious, and, for sure, military industrial postcolonial edifice that prevents so many people around the globe from breathing.

Gone are the days of piecemeal solutions or welcoming "experts" from the colonial motherland to come fix the problem by rearranging the leadership rosters, renegotiating the debt noose that European and US governments and banking institutions have set in place, and concocting development schemes centered on sending more to the Global North, including millions of people importuned to plow the fields, cook the food, build the houses, and operate the assembly lines across cities and towns. Enough is enough! Sending "experts" or political, economic, educational, military, and religious hitmen to further dismantle, disassemble, and dismember what remains of the Global South and package it as a growth indicator or a path to afterlife salvation is no longer tolerable or defensible.

From Europe and the Arab world to Asia, South Africa, and North America, the immigration crisis today is a global one, and neoliberal or failed postcolonial remedies can't keep the problem away from every corner of this earth. At present, every human group and nation-state on earth are either immigrants or refugees themselves or a host destination and are, thus, facing myriad challenges to address the problem. The responses vary across the globe depending on the region, numbers, and internal economic, social, and political conditions. However, what is certain is that the current approach is not working for all concerned, and the Global North and South constitute one continuous chain—an event in one place is moments away from impacting every other location in the world.

At the policy level, the immigration-refugee crisis is being addressed at the tail end—that is, the arrival at the border or airport, be it documented or undocumented, and various structures are built to limit, exclude, and accommodate the arrivals at the moment of entry. In Europe, the crisis has become acute, with a weekly human avalanche making its way from Afghanistan, Iraq, Jordan, North and sub-Saharan Africa, Palestine, Somalia, and Syria, to name the well-known hot spots. But others from across Asia are fleeing adverse political, social, and religious conditions that are rapidly deteriorating due to US and European military interventions, neoliberal economic programs, and a new containment strategy directed at China.

In North America, the immigration-refugee debates have become a football tossed between republicans and democrats, with each attempting to craft a "patriotic" response that would not impact its electoral chances. The idea that the problem is external and can be solved by building walls and adding cameras and more border security is an illusion and not a solution since it focuses on the end result of the crisis and not the causes behind it. What is witnessed in this massive human movement is the collapse and coming to an end of postcolonial states and the pernicious globalized world system, with the immediate outcome being massive displacement and the immigration-refugee crisis.

I hope this work will generate more questions and further interest in the subject rather than a search for immediate answers. Not that answers are not needed; they are, but the task at hand was to reframe the current predicament away from the popular discourses centering on problematizing the immigrant and refugee themselves on the basis of race, ethnicity, and religion, on the one hand, and the intense focusing on securitization and exclusion by the US and European states, on the other. The other undertaking was to redate the current problem and locate its genesis to the emergence of the age of discovery, significantly accelerating it during the colonial and postcolonial periods. In so far as my own experiences that gave impetus to this book, the various chapters constitute a holistic narrative that locates the struggle for freedom and justice in Palestine within the continuities of settler colonialism, links to modernity, and Zionism's embrace of Eurocentricity and violence, which are themselves drivers for further creating a stream of Palestinian immigrants and refugees. The visible, the made invisible, and the erased narratives and fingerprints of immigrants and refugees in Europe and the US are part and parcel of the never-ending genocides that span more than five hundred years and the postcolonial structural displacements and deaths.

The global environmental crisis will bring about another cycle of immigrants and refugees escaping the consequences of climate change and other devastation accumulated over the past two hundred years. Colonization made it possible to "open" the world for capitalist and industrial exploitation of the whole earth, which resulted in the slow but methodical undoing of the ecological balance, the acceleration of global warming, melting ice caps, rising sea levels, and destruction of food supplies. Often, the colonial and postcolonial impacts on the world are isolated from being connected to the unfolding environmental and ecological destruction witnessed around the globe, which must be remedied in research and writing on the subject. The environmental immigrants and refugees will reshape the Global North and South relations, and movement of people across the world will impact existing food supplies; agriculture; and economic, political, and cultural norms in the near future. I did not write a separate chapter on this topic as it is not an area in which I have done primary work or research to make a major contribution, but I urge readers to contribute to the topic in the future and make the needed connection between the colonial, the postcolonial, and the world's environmental and ecological crisis.

On April 4, 1967, Martin Luther King Jr. delivered a speech in New York City upon becoming cochairman of Clergy and Laymen Concerned about Vietnam, titled "Beyond Vietnam," which is as prophetic today as the day it was delivered.[230] In this speech, King took on the Vietnam War and broke his silence on the subject, but more importantly, he called for a "radical revolution of values," which would be the only way America could change its future course. The choices we make in the near future will make a difference and decide whether our attachment to "things," objects, and material wealth will result in a "spiritual death" or bring about the needed changes to build a just, peaceful, and love-based society. Often, I find myself going back to read and listen to King's 1967 and 1968 speeches and find in them the clearest and groundbreaking analysis of the problems confronting the world and pointing to the needed change to be made, which is most appropriate to end the book with a long quote from "Beyond Vietnam":

A true revolution of values will soon cause us to question the fairness and justice of many of our past and present policies. On the one hand, we are called to play the Good Samaritan on life's roadside, but that will be only an initial act. One day we must come to see that the whole Jericho Road must be transformed so that men and women will not be constantly beaten and robbed as they make their journey on life's highway. True compassion is more than flinging a coin to a beggar. It comes to see that an edifice which produces beggars needs restructuring.

A true revolution of values will soon look uneasily on the glaring contrast of poverty and wealth. With righteous indignation, it will look across the seas and see individual capitalists of the West investing huge sums of money in Asia, Africa, and South America, only to take the profits out with no concern for the social betterment of the countries, and say, "This is not just." It will look at our alliance with the landed gentry of South America and say, "This is not just." The Western arrogance of feeling that it has everything to teach others and nothing to learn from them is not just.

A true revolution of values will lay hand on the world order and say of war, "This way of settling differences is not just." This business of burning human beings with napalm, of filling our nation's homes with orphans and widows, of injecting poisonous drugs of hate into the veins of peoples normally humane, of sending men home from dark and bloody battlefields physically handicapped and psychologically deranged, cannot be reconciled with wisdom, justice, and love. A nation that continues year after year to spend more money on military defense than on programs of social uplift is approaching spiritual death.

America, the richest and most powerful nation in the world, can well lead the way in this revolution of values. There is nothing except a tragic death wish to prevent us from reordering our priorities so that the pursuit of peace will take precedence over the pursuit of war. There is nothing to keep us from molding a recalcitrant status quo with bruised hands until we have fashioned it into a brotherhood.

Endnotes

1   Rawan Damen's work in Palestine Remix is an important project that provides a robust source for the Nakba and Palestine history in general, see https://interactive.aljazeera.com/aje/palestineremix/al-nakba.html#/17; also, Professor Ahlam Muhtaseb's documentary, *1948: Creation & Catastrophe*, coproduced and codirected with Andy Trimlett, is one of the best treatments of the subject with heavy dependence on primary sources, see https://www.factory-filmstudio.com/portfolio-item/1948-creation-catastrophe/.

2   See the UNRWA site, which lists the ten Palestinian camps that are served by the agency, at https://www.unrwa.org/where-we-work/jordan/jabal-el-hussein-camp.

3   Hawari Yara, "Palestine Land Day: A Day to Resist and Remember," *Al-Jazeera* (March, 30, 2017), see https://www.aljazeera.com/indepth/opinion/palestine-land-day-day-resist-remember-180330054113738.html.

4   See "Sabra and Shatila: New Revelations," *The New York Review of Books*, for further details and updates from primary documents, at https://www.nybooks.com/daily/2018/09/17/sabra-and-shatila-new-revelations/.

5   See the Richard Nixon Foundation report "President Nixon: First US President to Visit the Hashemite Kingdom of Jordan," at https://www.nixonfoundation.org/2014/06/president-nixon-first-u-s-president-visit-hashemite-kingdom-jordan/.

6   See the Monroe Doctrine text at https://avalon.law.yale.edu/19th_century/monroe.asp.

7   "Epitaph for Constructive Engagement," *New York Times* (February 14, 1987), see https://www.nytimes.com/1987/02/14/opinion/epitaph-for-constructive-engagement.html.

8   Samuel Huntington, "The Hispanic Challenge," *Foreign Policy* (October 28, 2009), see https://foreignpolicy.com/2009/10/28/the-hispanic-challenge/.

9   Murtaza Hussain, "The Far Right Is Obsessed with a Book about Muslims Destroying Europe. Here's What It Gets Wrong," *The Intercept* (December 25, 2018), see https://theintercept.com/2018/12/25/strange-death-of-europe-douglas-murray-review/.

10   The primary source of information on refugees, immigrants, and migrants is the Office of the UN High Commissioner for Refugees (UNHCR). This is due to the extensive and multiparty reporting infrastructure behind it, while being fully aware that certain gaps in the data exist and more work is needed. Indeed, the UNHCR figures do not fully account for all migrants or displaced populations due to limits or barriers set in place by member states of the UN. See https://www.unhcr.org/en-us/figures-at-a-glance.html.

11   Robert Mackey, "The Plot Against George Soros Didn't Start in Hungary. It Started on Fox News," *New York Times* (January 23, 2019), see https://theintercept.com/2019/01/23/plot-george-soros-didnt-start-hungary-started-fox-news/.

12   Ian Sherr, "Facebook, Cambridge Analytica and Data Mining: What You Need to Know," *CNet* (April 18, 2018), see https://www.cnet.com/news/facebook-cambridge-analytica-data-mining-and-trump-what-you-need-to-know/; also Hannes Grassegger, "The Unbelievable Story of the Plot Against George Soros," *BuzzFeed News* (January 20, 2019), see https://www.buzzfeednews.com/article/hnsgrassegger/george-soros-conspiracy-finkelstein-birnbaum-orban-netanyahu.

13   Martin Luther King Jr., "Address at the Fourth Annual Institute on Nonviolence and Social Change at Bethel Baptist Church," Montgomery, Alabama (December 3, 1959), see https://kinginstitute.stanford.edu/king-papers/documents/address-fourth-annual-in-

stitute-nonviolence-and-social-change-bethel-baptist-0.

14   Hatem Bazian, *Palestine...It Is Something Colonial* (Amrit Consultancy, November 2016).

15   Lance Bartholomeusz, "The Mandate of UNRWA at Sixty" (UN Publication, May 10, 2010), see https://www.unrwa.org/user-files/201006109246.pdf.

16   From 2004 to 2016, he served as chief of the International Law Division, Department of Legal Affairs, United Nations Relief and Works Agency for Palestine Refugees in the Near East.

17   Bartholomeusz, "The Mandate of UNRWA at Sixty."

18   Afghan, Cambodian, Rohingya, and Syrian refugee populations are large and may be considered for such designation. The intention is not to create a competition or comparison between the different groups that have suffered and been displaced from their homelands.

19   See the UNRWA's fact sheet on Palestinian refugees at https://www.unrwa.org/palestine-refugees.

20   Ibid.

21   See UN Resolution 194 at https://undocs.org/A/RES/194%20(III).

22   Nur Masalha, *The Palestine Nakba: Decolonising History, Narrating the Subaltern, Reclaiming Memory* (Zed Books: London and New York, 2012), 3.

23   Ibid, 12–13.

24   Ibid, 14.

25   Israeli citizenship is a different apartheid-structured enterprise because the state has two different categories for the construction of a modern nation-state. The Israeli Knesset adopted the Nationality Law in 1952, which cemented in law the discriminatory nature of the state. See https://www.knesset.gov.il/review/data/eng/law/kns2_nationality_eng.pdf. In 2018, the Knesset adopted another articulation of the earlier version, which stated, "(a) The Land of Israel is the historical homeland of the Jewish people, in which the

State of Israel was established; (b) The State of Israel is the nation state of the Jewish People, in which it realizes its natural, cultural, religious and historical right to self-determination; (c) The exercise of the right to national self-determination in the State of Israel is unique to the Jewish People." See https://knesset.gov.il/laws/special/eng/BasicLawNationState.pdf.

Thus, Israel has nationality and citizenship categories in defining belonging to and membership in the state. National or nationality law is slowly assigned to Jewish members of the Israeli society, which grant them all the rights and privileges accrued from the conceptualization of the state as a "Jewish State" belonging exclusively to all Jews, those inside and outside the country, while Arabs only have residency under the citizenship law. As such, Jewish nationality gives access to state land, marriage rights, residency and building permits, loan rights, service in the army, living in settlements (not that I support the settlements but rather point to these exclusive rights), and over 65 other laws that discriminate against the Palestinian citizens of the state. See https://www.adalah.org/en/content/view/7771.

Palestinian citizens of Israel are living under a carefully crafted apartheid system that relegates them into third- or fourth-class members of a society that rejects their membership altogether and sets barrier to their formative legal and practical equality. Thus, Israel is not a liberal democracy, but an apartheid state structured around elevating an ethnic-religious identity of one group, Jewish members of the society, at the expense and the determinant of Palestinians, which includes Muslims, Christians, Palestinian Jews, and Druze.

26   Nimer Sultany, "The Making of an Underclass: The Palestinian Citizens in Israel," *Israel Studies Review* 27, No. 2 (Winter 2012): 190–200.

27   "Jericho Declaration," *Palestine Post* (December 14, 1948), see https://archive.vn/20120710043504/http://jpress.tau.ac.il/Default/Scripting/ArticleWin.asp?From=Archive&Source=Page&Skin=TAU-En&BaseHref=PLS/1948/12/14&PageLabelPrint=1&Entity-

Id=Ar00106&ViewMode=HTML.

28   Avi Shlaim, "The Rise and Fall of the All-Palestine Government in Gaza," *Journal of Palestine Studies* 20 (1990): 37–53.

29   Avi Shlaim, *Collusion Across the Jordan: King Abdullah, the Zionist Movement, and the Partition of Palestine* (Columbia University Press, July 1, 1988).

30   See Department of State Communications, Foreign Relations, 1969–1976, Volume XXIV, at https://2001-2009.state.gov/documents/organization/113360.pdf.

31   Richard A. Mobley, "US Joint Military Contributions to Countering Syria's 1970 Invasion of Jordan," *Joint Force Quarterly* 55, No. 4 (2009), see https://pdfs.semanticscholar.org/a07a/9b28db30d5e5a-b40a253683c6d7224670eea.pdf.

32   "According to a 1973 memorandum that summarized the events and meetings relating to the Jordan crisis of 1970, the 4:30 p.m. meeting with President Nixon included Kissinger, Rogers, Laird, Mitchell, Hoover, Sisco, Helms, and U. Alexis Johnson. At the meeting, Helms remarked, 'Unless someone goes in and cleans up the situation, there is no chance of peace in the Middle East.' Laird noted that the United States would have to send in ground forces to help Hussein if he decided to fight the fedayeen. Nixon then asked what Jordan would do if Israel assisted it. Sisco responded that an Israeli intervention would 'be a cause of death for Hussein' and that it would lead to a united Arab front against Israel and the United States.' Nixon concluded that 'US intervention is better than Israeli intervention.' Rogers also warned that 'we'd pay an enormous price, and it is essentially useless.'" Source: *Foreign Relations, 1969–1976*, Volume XXIV (Library of Congress, Manuscript Division, Kissinger Papers, TS 31, Geopolitical Files—Jordan, Jordan Crisis—September 1970 Notebook, 1970–73), see https://2001-2009.state.gov/documents/organization/113360.pdf.

33   See "Middle East: Gaza Strip," Central Intelligence Agency World Factbook, at https://www.cia.gov/library/publications/the-world-factbook/geos/print_gz.html.

34 Anne Joseph, "Incitement: The Film about the Man Who Murdered the Israeli Peace Process," *The Guardian* (October 11, 2019), see https://www.theguardian.com/film/2019/oct/11/incitement-assassination-yitzhak-rabin-yigal-amir.

35 Rebecca Stead, "Remembering Hebron's Ibrahimi Mosque Massacre," *Middle East Monitor* (February 25, 2019), see https://www.middleeastmonitor.com/20190225-remembering-hebrons-ibrahimi-mosque-massacre/.

36 David Rose, "The Gaza Bombshell," *Vanity Fair Magazine* (March 8, 2008).

37 See "Gaza Crisis," United Nations Office for the Coordination of Humanitarian Affairs, at https://web.archive.org/web/20150725191044/http://www.ochaopt.org/content.aspx?id=1010361.

38 See full report at https://blackfriday.amnesty.org/

39 For coverage of the Amnesty International report release, see "Israel Accused of War Crimes during Campaign in Gaza," *The Guardian* (November 5, 2014), available at https://www.theguardian.com/world/2014/nov/05/israel-accused-war-crimes-gaza--amnesty-international.

40 See full report at https://blackfriday.amnesty.org/

41 Patricia Luna, "Chile: Palestinians Gather to Forge Unified Diaspora," *Al-Jazeera* (January 15, 2017), see https://www.aljazeera.com/indepth/features/2017/01/chile-palestinians-gather-forge-unified-diaspora-170115081651493.html.

42 Patricia Luna, "Chile: Palestinians Gather to Forge Unified Diaspora," *Al-Jazeera* (January 15, 2017), see https://www.aljazeera.com/indepth/features/2017/01/chile-palestinians-gather-forge-unified-diaspora-170115081651493.html.

43 Ibid.

44 "Judge Throws Out Charges in 'Los Angeles Eight' Case," Center for Constitutional Rights (October 23, 2007), see http://ccrjustice.org/newsroom/press-releases/judge-throws-out-charges-"los-angeles-eight"-case.

45 See Michael Suleiman's *Arabs in America: Building a New Future* for a longer history of Arabs in American and the challenges they faced over the generations; see Paul Findley's *They Dare to Speak Out: People and Institutions Confront Israel's Lobby* for an examination of targeting individuals and organizations in the US for speaking and taking a public position in support of the Palestine struggle; see Alfred M. Lilienthal's critical work *The Zionist Connection: What Price Peace?* for an insight into a long history of defamation and erasure of Palestine in America's public and political discourses; and see Alex Lubin's chapter looking at the Black Panthers and the PLO in *Geographies of Liberation: The Making of an Afro-Arab Political Imaginary.*

46 See the full examination of the Holy Land Foundation case in Miko Peled's *Injustice: The Story of the Holy Land Foundation Five* (Just World Books, February 1, 2018).

47 Chip Gibbons, "FBI Opened Terrorism Investigations into Non-Violent Palestinian Solidarity Group, Documents Reveal," *The Intercept* (April 5, 2020), see https://theintercept.com/2020/04/05/israel-palestine-fbi-terrorism-investigation/.

48 Watch Democracy Now interviews on FBI raids on Palestinian activists' homes in the Chicago area, at https://www.democracynow.org/2010/9/27/fbi_raids_homes_of_anti_war.

49 Adam Entous, "How a Private Israeli Intelligence Firm Spied on Pro-Palestinian Activists in the US," *The New Yorker Magazine* (February 28, 2018), see https://www.newyorker.com/news/newsdesk/how-a-private-israeli-intelligence-firm-spied-on-pro-palestinian-activists-in-the-us.

50 See congressional bill HR 6451 - UNRWA Reform and Refugee Support Act of 2018 at https://www.congress.gov/bill/115th-congress/house-bill/6451.

51 Samuel Huntington, *The Clash of Civilizations and the Remaking of the World Order* (Simon & Schuster, 2011).

52 The notion of "discovery" is problematic and has been deployed often as a tool of silencing and erasure of the history, culture, and so-

cieties that existed before European arrival or contact. At the same time, "discovery" was used to constitute "rights" over the territories and regions that the European's arrived at and settled, which were crystalized in the issuing of the doctrine of discovery, a principle that is incorporated into the body of international law. "Discovery" is what Europeans did, and those "discovered" became defined through this process, and henceforth, their entry into the "known world" was by means of this act and definition. To be "discovered" is to be known by Europe and the West, which means that prior to this moment, "you" and your society did not really exist, or if you did, then it is merely as objects in a state of nature, uncivilized, and subhuman in all that term means.

While many think that the term "discovery" is in the distant past, I argue that it is still used in a variety of ways, least of which is how writers and intellectuals from the Global South are "discovered" and brought into Western awareness by means of individual Western scholars, publishing houses, and systems of knowledge that are rooted in the Global North, whose function is to make the Africans, Asians, and Latin Americans knowable, touchable, and understandable to the Western audience. The act of "discovery" is not simply the arrival to a land unknown to the one who is arriving; rather it is an imposition of an epistemic that negates the existence of the people themselves, their history, their culture, and more critically their rights to their own lands.

53 Hamid Dabashi, "Whence and Wherefore 'Europe'?" In *Europe and Its Shadows: Coloniality after Empire* 51–81 (London: Pluto Press, 2019), 55, accessed May 28, 2020, at https://www-jstor-org. libproxy.berkeley.edu/stable/j.ctvr0qtvb.7.

54 Ramon Grosfoguel, "What is Racism?" *Journal of World-Systems Research* 22, No. 1 (2016), 9–15, at https://doi.org/10.5195/jwsr.2016.609.

55 Ibid.

56 Ibid.

57 Ibid.

58 Dabashi, "Whence and Wherefore 'Europe'?" 65.

59 Hannah Devlin, "First Modern Britons Had 'Dark to Black' Skin, Cheddar Man DNA Analysis Reveals," *The Guardian* (February 7, 2018), see https://www.theguardian.com/science/2018/feb/07/ first-modern-britons-dark-black-skin-cheddar-man-dna-analysis-reveals.

60 Ibid.

61 Ibid.

62 Ibid.

63 Jules François Camille Ferry, "Speech Before the French Chamber of Deputies, March 28, 1884," *Discours et Opinions de Jules Ferry*, ed. Paul Robiquet (Paris: Armand Colin & Cie., 1897), -1, 5, 199–201, 210–11, 215–18. Translated by Ruth Kleinman in Brooklyn College, see https://sourcebooks.fordham.edu/mod/1884ferry.asp.

64 Ibid.

65 Ibid.

66 Ibid.

67 Edward G. Bourne, (Ed.), *The Northmen, Columbus and Cabot, 985–1503: The Voyages of the Northmen, The Voyages of Columbus and of John Cabot* (New York: Charles Scribner's Sons, 1906), 265–266.

68 "Top 5 Atrocities Committed by Christopher Columbus," *The Rapid City Journal* (October 9, 2019), see https://rapidcityjournal.com/ lifestyles/people/top-atrocities-committed-by-christopher-columbus/collection_76ebb2b8-f63d-11e3-a137-001a4bcf887a.html#1.

69 Angelique Chrisafis, "Macron Asks Experts to Investigate French Role in Rwandan Genocide," *The Guardian* (April 5, 2019).

70 Bourne, (Ed.), *The Northmen, Columbus and Cabot, 985–1503*, 111–112.

71 "Top 5 Atrocities Committed by Christopher Columbus."

72 Thomas Southey, *Chronological History of the West Indies* (Vol. 1) (London: Longman, Rees, Orme, Brown, and Green, 1827), 21, ac-

cessed through Google Books on April 27, 2020.

73   "An American Secret: The Untold Story of Native American En-slavement," Interview on *Hidden Brain*, NPR Radio, see https://www.npr.org/2017/11/20/565410514/an-american-secret-the-un-told-story-of-native-american-enslavement.

74   Southey, *Chronological History of the West Indies*, 22.

75   Ibid, 21.

76   Bourne, (Ed.), *The Northmen, Columbus and Cabot, 985–1503*, 33.

77   This raw material focus has changed recently with the emergence of the information technology (IT) sector and moving industrial manufacturing to China and other states. Manufacturing compa-nies shifted production offshore in the desire to reduce labor costs; escape environmental, health, and tax regulations; and drive max-imum profits. IT has caused a change in the centrality of manufac-turing in the Global North, and much of the products currently are being made in the Global South. China's economic power might begin to change the global landscape in the next decade, but the Global North's role in IT will continue to impact the flow of capital and resources globally.

78   Bill Tomson, "Ebola Threatens Chocolate," *Politico* (November 12, 2014), see https://www.politico.com/story/2014/10/ebola-choco-late-industry-africa-effects-111809.

79   See the full report on the crisis: E. De Buhr and E. Gordon, *Bitter Sweets: Prevalence of Forced Labour & Child Labour in the Cocoa Sectors of Côte d'Ivoire & Ghana* (Tulane University & Walk Free Foundation, 2018).

80   Peter Whoriskey and Rachel Siegel, "Cocoa's Child Laborers," *The Washington Post* (June 5, 2019), see https://www.washington-post.com/graphics/2019/business/hershey-nestle-mars-choco-late-child-labor-west-africa/.

81   Ibid.

82   Ibid.

83   Amnesty International Report, "Amnesty Challenges Industry Leaders to Clean Up Their Batteries," (March 21, 2019), accessed May 11, 2020, at https://www.amnesty.org/en/latest/news/2019/03/amnesty-challenges-industry-leaders-to-clean-up-their-batteries/.

84   Ibid.

85   See the critical work of Jenna M. Loyd and Alison Mountz, *Boats, Borders, and Bases: Race, the Cold War, and the Rise of Migration Detention in the United States* (University of California Press, 2018).

86   Matt Simon, "Who's Burning the Amazon? Rampant Capitalism," *WIRED* (August 28, 2019), accessed May 11, 2020, at https://www.wired.com/story/whos-burning-the-amazon-rampant-capitalism/.

87   "Refugees in South Africa: 'Give Us a Place Where We Can Be Safe,'" *BBC News*—Africa (February 2, 2020), see https://www.bbc.com/news/world-africa-51284576.

88   Giorgio Spagnol, "Is France Still Exploiting Africa?" European Institute of International Relations (February 10, 2019).

89   The fourteen countries account for 14 percent of Africa's population and 12 percent of the continent's GDP and are sources of raw materials. Only twelve of these states were ex-French colonies, and two joined the French monetary-controlled program.

90   Spagnol, "Is France Still Exploiting Africa?"

91   Ibid.

92   Currently there are twenty-nine Francophone countries that have economic, political, and cultural ties to France, and among these are the fourteen African states.

93   Ibid.

94   Megan Specia, "The African Currency at the Center of a European Dispute," *New York Times* (January 22, 2019), see https://www.nytimes.com/2019/01/22/world/africa/africa-cfa-franc-currency.html.

95   Ibid.

96   Ibid.

97 Ibid.

98 Ibid.

99 Ndongo Samba Sylla, "The CFA Franc: French Monetary Imperialism in Africa," *African Review of Political Economy* (blog) (August 11, 2015), accessed May 9, 2020.

100 Spagnol, "Is France Still Exploiting Africa?"

101 Ibid.

102 John Perkins, *Confessions of an Economic Hit Man* (Plume, December 27, 2005).

103 Ibid.

104 Warren C. Whatley, "Guns-For-Slaves: The 18th Century British Slave Trade in Africa," Conference Paper (August 15, 2008), accessed on May 9, 2020, at https://conference.nber.org/conferences/2008/si2008/DAE/whatley.pdf.

105 Spagnol, "Is France Still Exploiting Africa?"

106 Patrick J. McGowan, "African Military Coups D'état, 1956–2001: Frequency, Trends and Distribution," *The Journal of Modern African Studies* 41, No. 3 (2003): 339–70, accessed May 12, 2020, at www.jstor.org/stable/3876235.

107 Ibid.

108 See Albert Memmi, *The Colonizer and the Colonized* (Beacon Press; Expanded edition, July 8, 1991); also see Aimé Césaire, "Discourse on Colonialism," *Monthly Review Press* (2001); Edward W. Said, *Culture and Imperialism* (Vintage Books, May 31, 1994); and Frantz Fanon, *Black Skin, White Masks* (Grove Press; Revised edition, September 10, 2008).

109 Perkins, *Confessions of an Economic Hit Man.*

110 "Crisis Deepens as Global South Debt Payments Increase by 85%," Jubilee Debt Campaign report (April 3, 2019), accessed May 12, 2020, at https://jubileedebt.org.uk/press-release/crisis-deepens-as-global-south-debt-payments-increase-by-85.

111 Elizabeth Olson, "Swiss Resist Disclosing Any Mobutu Bank Funds," *New York Times* (May 6, 1997), accessed May 9, 2020, at https://www.nytimes.com/1997/05/06/world/swiss-resist-disclosing-any-mobutu-bank-funds.html.

112 "UK Banks 'Exposed to Money Laundering in South Africa,'" *BBC News* (October 19, 2017), accessed May 9, 2020, at https://www.bbc.com/news/business-41672793.

113 "Banks and Dirty Money: How the Financial System Enables State Looting at a Devastating Human Cost," Global Witness report (June 18, 2015), accessed May 9, 2020, at https://www.globalwitness.org/en/campaigns/corruption-and-money-laundering/banks-and-dirty-money/.

114 Perkins, *Confessions of an Economic Hit Man.*

115 "25 Corruption Scandals That Shook the World," Transparency International report (July 5, 2019), accessed May 9, 2020, at https://www.transparency.org/news/feature/25_corruption_scandals.

116 Darien Cavanaugh, "The CIA and KGB Both Tried to Blackmail This World Leader with Sex Tapes," *Medium—War Is Boring* (October 30, 2016), accessed on May 12, 2020, at https://medium.com/war-is-boring/the-cia-and-kgb-tried-to-blackmail-this-world-leader-with-sex-tapes-927fc7ddbd48.

117 Perkins, *Confessions of an Economic Hit Man.*

118 See the article by Tim Hyde, "Are Colonial-Era Borders Drawn by Europeans Holding Africa Back? How the 'Scramble for Africa' May Still Be Fueling Ethnic Conflict," *American Economic Association* (July 13, 2016), accessed May 12, 2020, at https://www.aeaweb.org/research/are-colonial-era-borders-holding-africa-back.

119 See the material on the School of the Americas, which the US used to train and provide the needed support for military strongmen and dictators across Latin America, at https://soaw.org/about/.

120 Paul Orogun, "'Blood Diamonds' and Africa's Armed Conflicts in the Post-Cold War Era," *World Affairs* 166, No. 3 (2004): 151–61, accessed May 10, 2020, at www.jstor.org/stable/20672689.

121   See the work of Amar Farooqui, "'Divide and Rule'? Race, Military Recruitment and Society in Late Nineteenth Century Colonial India," *Social Scientist* 43, No. 3/4 (2015): 49–59, accessed May 10, 2020, at www.jstor.org/stable/24372935.

122   Richard Morrock, "Heritage of Strife: The Effects of Colonialist 'Divide and Rule' Strategy upon the Colonized Peoples," *Science & Society* 37, No. 2 (1973): 129–51, accessed May 10, 2020, at www.jstor.org/stable/40401707.

123   Ibid, 129.

124   See the history of waterboarding as a torture method on *Encyclopaedia Britannica* at https://www.britannica.com/topic/waterboarding (accessed May 12, 2020).

125   See Ramon Grosfoguel, "The Structure of Knowledge in Westernized Universities Epistemic Racism/Sexism and the Four Genocides/Epistemicides of the Long 16th Century," *Human Architecture: Journal of the Sociology of Self- Knowledge* 11, Issue 1 (September 22, 2013), 73–90.

126   European capitals hosted human zoos, whereby populations from the colonies were placed in enclosures and visitors would come to see, touch, and feed these "exotic" creatures. Also, the 1904 World's Fair in the US included similar exhibits, which were one of the most visited parts of the fair. Read the articles by Shoshi Parks, "These Horrifying 'Human Zoos' Delighted American Audiences at the Turn of the 20th Century," *TimeLine* (March 20, 2018), accessed June 2, 2020, at https://timeline.com/human-zoo-worlds-fair-7ef0d0951035; Julian Robinson, "The Horrifying Human Zoos: Shocking Photos Reveal How Zoos Around the World Kept 'Primitive Natives' in Enclosures as Westerners Gawped and Jeered at Them Just 60 Years Ago," *DailyMail.com* (March 17, 2017), accessed June 2, 2020, at https://www.dailymail.co.uk/news/article-4323366/Photos-reveal-horrifying-human-zoos-early-1900s.html; and Brittany Rosen, "Human Zoos Are One of Europe's Most Shameful Secrets, and Only Ended in the '50s," *Plaid Zebra* (February 20, 2015), accessed June 2, 2020, at https://theplaidzebra.com/human-zoos-one-europes-shameful-secrets-ended-50s/.

127 See the League of Nations text granting British mandate authority over Palestine, accessed June 6, 2020, at https://avalon.law.yale.edu/20th_century/palmanda.asp.

128 See full text of League of Nations mandate, "French Mandate for Syria and the Lebanon," *American Journal of International Law* 17, No. 3 (1923): 177–82, accessed June 6, 2020, at https://www-jstor-org.libproxy.berkeley.edu/stable/2212963.

129 See Wm. Roger Louis, "The United Kingdom and the Beginning of the Mandates System, 1919–1922," *International Organization* 23, No. 1 (1969): 73–96, accessed June 6, 2020, at www.jstor.org/stable/2705765.

130 See Adam Gopnik, "Trial of the Century: Revisiting the Dreyfus Affair," *The New Yorker* (September 21, 2009), accessed June 6, 2020, at https://www.newyorker.com/magazine/2009/09/28/trial-of-the-century.

131 Jackie Bischof, "Nearly 2 Million Africans Were Pulled into World War I, Their Reward Was Even More Colonization," *Quartz Africa* (June 27, 2018), accessed June 6, 2020, at https://qz.com/africa/1316060/nearly-2-million-africans-were-pulled-into-world-war-i/. Also, see the BBC article on the topic of colonial troops, "The African Soldiers Dragged into Europe's War," (July 3, 2015), at https://www.bbc.com/news/magazine-33329661.

132 Gary K. Busch, "The Forgotten African Soldiers in WWII Celebrations," *Pambazuka News* (June 18, 2014), accessed June 6, 2020, at https://www.pambazuka.org/governance/forgotten-african-soldiers-wwii-celebrations.

133 See Bülent Kaya, "The Changing Face of Europe Population Flows in the 20th Century," Council of Europe Publishing (February 2002), accessed June 6, 2020, at https://rm.coe.int/1680494249.

134 One area that does not get much attention is the link between debt and environmental destruction, which continues to this day as much of the land and resources came under international control in this process. See Raymond E. Gullison and Elizabeth C. Losos, "The Role of Foreign Debt in Deforestation in Latin America," *Con-*

servation Biology 7, No. 1 (1993): 140–47, accessed June 7, 2020, at www.jstor.org/stable/2386650.

135 Lucy Clarke-Billings, "Panama Papers: Top Ten Tax Havens— Where the Money Is Hidden," *Newsweek* (April, 6, 2016), accessed on June 6, 2020, at https://www.newsweek.com/panama-papers-top-ten-tax-havens-where-money-hidden-444512; also see Jørgen Juel Andersen, Niels Johannesen and Bob Rijkers, "Elite Capture of Foreign Aid Evidence from Offshore Bank Accounts," Policy Research Working Paper 9150, World Bank Group (February 2020), accessed on June 6, 2020, at http://documents.worldbank.org/curated/en/493201582052636710/pdf/Elite-Capture-of-Foreign-Aid-Evidence-from-Offshore-Bank-Accounts.pdf.

136 See the structural adjustment programs case study on the Philippines by Jiah L. Sayson, "Structural Adjustment Programs: Whose Colonizing Instrument?" *Philippine Quarterly of Culture and Society* 34, No. 1 (2006): 53–64, accessed June 6, 2020, at www.jstor.org/stable/29792583.

137 Ray Bush, "Coping with Adjustment and Economic Crisis in Egypt's Countryside," *Review of African Political Economy* 22, No. 66 (1995): 499–516, accessed June 7, 2020, at www.jstor.org/stable/4006295.

138 See Robin A. King and Michael D. Robinson, "Assessing Structural Adjustment Programs: A Summary of Country Experience," In *Debt Disaster?: Banks, Government and Multilaterals Confront the Crisis*, edited by John F. Weeks and Michael P. Claudon (NYU Press, 1989), 103–24, accessed June 6, 2020, at www.jstor.org/stable/j.ctt9qg11q.16.

139 Nancy C. Alexander, "Paying for Education: How the World Bank and the International Monetary Fund Influence Education in Developing Countries," *Peabody Journal of Education* 76, No. 3/4 (2001): 285–338, accessed June 7, 2020, at www.jstor.org/stable/1493253.

140 Fantu Cheru, "Debt, Adjustment and the Politics of Effective Response to HIV/AIDS in Africa," *Third World Quarterly* 23, No.

2 (2002): 299–312, accessed June 7, 2020, at www.jstor.org/stable/3993502.

141 Mark Duffield, "Absolute Distress: Structural Causes of Hunger in Sudan," *Middle East Report*, No. 166 (1990): 4–11.

142 Haider Ali Khan, "Economic Modeling of Structural Adjustment Programs: Impact on Human Conditions," *Africa Today* 37, No. 4 (1990): 29–38, accessed June 6, 2020, at www.jstor.org/stable/4186691.

143 F. F. Clairmonte, "Third World Debt: Anatomy of Genocide," *Economic and Political Weekly* 23, No. 8 (1988): 357–58, accessed June 7, 2020, at www.jstor.org/stable/4378137.

144 Ibid.

145 Wonder Guchu, "Impoverishing a Continent," In *The Gods Sleep Through It All: A Collection of Essays* (Chitungwiza, Zimbabwe: Mwanaka Media and Publishing, 2018), 85–95, accessed June 7, 2020, www.jstor.org/stable/j.ctvgc615k.24.

146 Clairmonte, "Third World Debt: Anatomy of Genocide."

147 Guchu, "Impoverishing a Continent."

148 See Farhad Noorbakhsh and Paloni Alberto, "Structural Adjustment Programs and Industry in Sub-Saharan Africa: Restructuring or De-Industrialization?" *Journal of Developing Areas* 33, No. 4 (1999): 549–80, accessed June 6, 2020, at www.jstor.org/stable/4192889.

149 See the discussion on Argentina by J. Patrice McSherry, "Strategic Alliance: Menem and the Military-Security Forces in Argentina," *Latin American Perspectives* 24, No. 6 (1997): 63–92, accessed June 7, 2020, at www.jstor.org/stable/2634307. Also, see the discussion on Egypt by Simon Bromley and Ray Bush, "Adjustment in Egypt? The Political Economy of Reform," *Review of African Political Economy* 21, No. 60 (1994): 201–13, accessed June 7, 2020, at www.jstor.org/stable/4006205.

150 Juha Y. Auvinen, "IMF Intervention and Political Protest in the Third World: A Conventional Wisdom Refined," *Third World*

Quarterly 17, No. 3 (1996): 377–400, accessed June 7, 2020, at www.jstor.org/stable/3993197.

151   Caroline A. Hartzell, Matthew Hoddie, and Molly Bauer, "Economic Liberalization via IMF Structural Adjustment: Sowing the Seeds of Civil War?" *International Organization* 64, No. 2 (2010): 339–56, accessed June 7, 2020, www.jstor.org/stable/40608018.

152   Clairmonte, "Third World Debt: Anatomy of Genocide."

153   See the work of Andres Velasco and Felipe Larrain, "The Basic Macroeconomics of Debt Swaps," *Oxford Economic Papers*, New Series, 45, No. 2 (1993): 207–28, accessed June 7, 2020, at www.jstor.org/stable/2663635.

154   Clairmonte, "Third World Debt: Anatomy of Genocide."

155   See a full discussion on the origins of neoliberalism by Richard Lachmann, "Neoliberalism, the Origins of the Global Crisis, and the Future of States," In *The Sociology of Development Handbook*, edited by Richard Lachmann, Gregory Hooks, Shushanik Makaryan, Paul Almeida, David Brown, Samuel Cohn, Sara Curran, Rebecca Emigh, Hi-fung Hung, Andrew Jorgenson, Linda Lobao, and Valentine Moghadam (Oakland, California: University of California Press, 2016), 463–84, accessed June 7, 2020, at www.jstor.org/stable/10.1525/j.ctv1xxwbg.23. Also, Naomi Klein's book *The Shock Doctrine: The Rise of Disaster Capitalism* (Picador, June 24, 2008) provides another important analysis of neoliberal economics and how it came to dominate the globe.

156   Ibid.

157   See Frank Stricker, "Reagan, Reaganomics, and the American Poor, 1980-1992," In *Why America Lost the War on Poverty—And How to Win It*, 183–206 (Chapel Hill: University of North Carolina Press, 2007).

158   David Farber, "Ronald Reagan: The Conservative Hero," In *The Rise and Fall of Modern American Conservatism: A Short History*, 159–208 (Princeton; Oxford: Princeton University Press, 2010).

159   James E. Cronin, "Cold War Ironies: Reagan and Thatcher At

Large," In *Global Rules: America, Britain and a Disordered World* (Yale University Press, 2014), 148–79, accessed June 7, 2020, at www.jstor.org/stable/j.ctt1bhkp54.9.

160 Ibid.

161 Ibid.

162 The arrival of Afghan refugees to different parts of the world is directly connected to the Cold War and using the country as a site for a protracted US-USSR confrontation through proxies. Elaheh Rostami-Povey, "Afghan Refugees in Iran, Pakistan, the UK, and the US and Life after Return: A Comparative Gender Analysis," *Iranian Studies* 40, No. 2 (2007): 241–61, accessed June 7, 2020, at www.jstor.org/stable/4311892.

163 Esther Howard,, "Arms Suppliers to the Dictators," *Journal of Palestine Studies* 12, No. 3 (1983): 224–30, accessed June 7, 2020.

164 US farm and agriculture subsidies create adverse conditions for farmers and the poor across the Global South, causing collapse of prices and with it the livelihood of so many people. Furthermore, US foreign aid in the form of food products is intended to help American farmers and then make countries in the Global South dependent for their food on this supply, thus having a chokehold over their national security and decision-making.

165 Alison Brysk, "Recovering from State Terror: The Morning After in Latin America," *Latin American Research Review* 38, No. 1 (2003): 238–47, accessed June 7, 2020, at www.jstor.org/stable/1555442. Also, see Neil C. Livingstone, "Death Squads," *World Affairs* 146, No. 3 (1983): 239–48, accessed June 7, 2020, at www.jstor.org/stable/20671988, and Justus M. Van Der Kroef, "Terrorism by Public Authority: The Case of the Death Squads of Indonesia and the Philippines," *Current Research on Peace and Violence* 10, No. 4 (1987): 143–58, accessed June 7, 2020, at www.jstor.org/stable/40725074.

166 Matthew F. Jacobs, "The Perils and Promise of Islam: The United States and the Muslim Middle East in the Early Cold War," *Diplomatic History* 30, No. 4 (2006): 705–39, accessed June 7, 2020, at www.jstor.org/stable/24915081.

167 Casting Christianity not only as anticommunist but as procapitalist can be seen in the case of Nicaragua. Adolfo Miranda Sanez, "The Political Metamorphosis of Evangelicals in Nicaragua," *Transformation* 9, No. 3 (1992): 20–25, accessed June 7, 2020, at www.jstor.org/stable/43053059.

168 See the "Mythical Portrait of the Colonized" and "Situations of the Colonized" chapters in Albert Memmi's *The Colonizer and the Colonized* (Beacon Press; Expanded edition, July 8, 1991).

169 For a good discussion on British efforts in India that impacted the role and status of Islam, including the responses to counter such measures, which ended up impacting the subsequent developments in Pakistan, see Muhammad Qasim Zaman, "Islamic Identities in Colonial India," In *Islam in Pakistan: A History* (Princeton; Oxford: Princeton University Press, 2018), 14–53.

170 Joseph P. Chinnici, "The Cold War, the Council, and American Catholicism in a Global World," *US Catholic Historian* 30, No. 2 (2012): 1–24, accessed June 7, 2020, at www.jstor.org/stable/23362867. Also, the work of the Evangelical churches in Eastern Europe point to the recruitment of religious institutions in the Cold War. See Joe Gouverneur, "Underground Evangelism: Missions During the Cold War," *Transformation* 24, No. 2 (2007): 80–86, accessed June 7, 2020, at www.jstor.org/stable/43052695.

171 Tariq Amin-Khan, "The Rise of Militant Islam and the Security State in the Era of the 'Long War,'" *Third World Quarterly* 30, No. 4 (2009): 813–28, accessed June 7, 2020, at www.jstor.org/stable/40388151.

172 Ibid.

173 Ibid.

174 Cheryl A. Rubenberg, "Israeli Foreign Policy in Central America," *Third World Quarterly* 8, No. 3 (1986): 896–915, accessed June 7, 2020, at www.jstor.org/stable/3991928.

175 A must read on this subject is the work of Jane Hunter, *Israeli Foreign Policy: South Africa and Central America* (South End Press, July 1, 1999); also see the report by Jane Hunter, "South Africa: Through the

Back Door," *NACLA Report on the Americas* 22, No. 4 (1988): 4–6, D OI: 10.1080/10714839.1988.11723297.

176 Ibid.

177 Read the full report, "Deadly Exchange," which provides important research on this subject considering the current development in the US with police brutality: https://deadlyexchange.org/deadly-exchange-research-report/.

178 Peter Andreas, *Killer High: A History of War in Six Drugs* (Oxford University Press, January 2, 2020). Also, allegations of CIA involvement in drug trafficking was subject to a congressional hearing on March 16, 1998: https://www.c-span.org/video/?102219-1/cia-drug-trafficking-allegations.

179 Mark Ames, "The Kings of Garbage, Or, The ADL Spied on Me and All I Got Was This Lousy Card," *Pacific Standard*, May 3, 2017, accessed June 7, 2020, at https://psmag.com/news/kings-garbage-76228.

180 John Dobson, "TNCs and the Corruption of GATT: Free Trade versus Fair Trade," *Journal of Business Ethics* 12, No. 7 (1993): 573–78, accessed June 9, 2020, at www.jstor.org/stable/25072437.

181 Alex Isenstadt, "Bill Clinton Defends DLC Role, Legacy," *Politico* (June 16, 2009), accessed June 9, 2020, at https://www.politico.com/story/2009/06/bill-clinton-defends-dlc-role-legacy-023833.

182 John Fairhall, "Jackson Raps Clinton, Accuses Him of Trying to Divide Voters Singer's Remarks Rekindle Animosity," *Baltimore Sun* (June 6, 1992), accessed June 9, 2020, at https://www.baltimoresun.com/news/bs-xpm-1992-06-16-1992168022-story.html.

183 See Paul Ciccantell, "NAFTA and the Reconstruction of US Hegemony: The Raw Materials Foundations of Economic Competitiveness," *Canadian Journal of Sociology* 26, No. 1 (2001): 57–87.

184 Arthur Schmidt, "Globalization, Neoliberal Ideology, and National Identity: The Historical Uncertainties of NAFTA," *Caribbean Studies* 29, No. 1 (1996): 67–105, accessed June 9, 2020, at www.jstor.org/stable/25613324.

185 Leonard Cavise, "NAFTA Rebellion," *Human Rights* 21, No. 4 (1994): 36–46, accessed June 9, 2020, at www.jstor.org/stable/27879870.

186 Read the press coverage on the European Parliament vote, "EU Declares 'Black Lives Matter,' Condemns Racism," at https://www.dw.com/en/eu-declares-black-lives-matter-condemns-racism/a-53878516.

187 Evan Hill, Ainara Tiefenthäler, Christiaan Triebert, Drew Jordan, Haley Willis, and Robin Stein, "8 Minutes and 46 Seconds: How George Floyd Was Killed in Police Custody," *New York Times* (May 31, 2020), accessed June 7, 2020, at https://www.nytimes.com/2020/05/31/us/george-floyd-investigation.html.

188 Ibid.

189 Ibid.

190 Fadel Allassan, "Trump Lashes Out at Governors, Calls for National Guard to 'Dominate' Streets," *Axios* (June 1, 2020), accessed June 20, 2020, at https://www.axios.com/trump-george-floyd-protests-crackdown-cd5e3b62-db90-4f0b-beea-145a55c9ab8b.html.

191 See *Deadly Exchange*, a report by Researching the American-Israeli Alliance in partnership with Jewish Voice for Peace (September 2018), at https://deadlyexchange.org/wp-content/uploads/2019/07/Deadly-Exchange-Report.pdf.

192 Jack Beresford, "'You Don't Get to Be Racist and Irish'—Imelda May Pens Powerful Anti-Racism Poem," *The Irish Post* (June 6, 2020), accessed June 14, 2020, at https://www.irishpost.com/news/imelda-may-protest-poem-186373.

193 See the *Medical News Today* website on the latest information on COVID-19 cases, accessed June 14, 2020, at https://www.medicalnewstoday.com/articles/racial-inequalities-in-covid-19-the-impact-on-black-communities#Making-sense-of-incomplete-data.

194 Read the lyrics of Bob Dylan's song "The Death of Emmett Till," at https://www.bobdylan.com/songs/death-emmett-till/.

195 W. Ralph Eubanks, "What the Face of Emmett Till Says about Every

Brutalized Black Body—Then and Now," *Vanity Fair* (June 4, 2020), accessed June 11, 2020, at https://www.vanityfair.com/style/2020/06/emmett-till-represents-every-brutalized-black-body.

196 Sheila Weller, "How Author Timothy Tyson Found the Woman at the Center of the Emmett Till Case," *Vanity Fair* (January 26, 2017), accessed June 11, 2020, https://www.vanityfair.com/news/2017/01/how-author-timothy-tyson-found-the-woman-at-the-center-of-the-emmett-till-case.

197 Kia Makarechi, "What the Data Really Says about Police and Racial Bias," *Vanity Fair* (July 14, 2016), accessed June 20, 2020, at https://www.vanityfair.com/news/2016/07/data-police-racial-bias.

198 Ibid.

199 Wesley Lowery, "Aren't More White People Than Black People Killed by Police? Yes, but No," *Washington Post* (July 11, 2016), accessed June 20, 2020, at https://www.washingtonpost.com/news/post-nation/wp/2016/07/11/arent-more-white-people-than-black-people-killed-by-police-yes-but-no/.

200 Ibid.

201 Ibid.

202 Nick Gass, "Giuliani: Black Parents Should 'Teach Children to Be Respectful of the Police,'" *Politico* (July 10, 2016), accessed June 20, 2020, at https://www.politico.com/story/2016/07/giuliani-black-parents-should-teach-children-to-be-respectful-of-the-police-225342.

203 Lynne Peeples, "What the Data Say about Police Brutality and Racial Bias—and Which Reforms Might Work," *Nature* (June 19, 2020), accessed June 20, 2020, at https://www.nature.com/articles/d41586-020-01846-z#ref-CR3.

204 Heather Mac Donald, "The Myths of Black Lives Matter," *Wall Street Journal* (July 9, 2016), accessed June 20, 2020, at https://www.wsj.com/articles/the-myths-of-black-lives-matter-1468087453.

205 Timothy Williams, "Study Supports Suspicion That Police Are More Likely to Use Force on Blacks," *New York Times* (July 7, 2016),

accessed June 20, 2020, at https://www.nytimes.com/2016/07/08/
us/study-supports-suspicion-that-police-use-of-force-is-more-
likely-for-blacks.html?auth=login-facebook.

206 Ibid.

207 Ibid.

208 Marsha Coleman-Adebayo and Kevin, Berend, "Code Black
Alert: Slave Patrols Alive and Well across America, Killing of
Vonderrit Myers—Part II," Black Agenda Report (October 23,
2014), accessed June 20, 2020, at https://blackagendareport.com/
node/22136?page=4.

209 See the report published by the Office of the United Nations High
Commissioner for Human Rights in cooperation with the United
Nations Educational, Scientific and Cultural Organization, "Di-
mensions of Racism" (February 19–20, 2003), accessed June 19,
2020, at https://www.ohchr.org/Documents/Publications/Dimen-
sionsRacismen.pdf.

210 Ben Quinn and Richard Adams, "Rhodes Statue: Tech Boss Pledges
to Cover Funds Pulled by 'Racist donors'" The Guardian (June 18,
2020), accessed June 20, 2020, at https://www.theguardian.com/
world/2020/jun/18/rhodes-statue-tech-boss-pledges-to-cover-
funds-pulled-by-racist-donors.

211 Paula Froelich, "Belgian Prince Defends Slave Trader King Leopold
II: 'He Built Parks,'" The New York Post (June 13, 2020), accessed
June 20, 2020, at https://nypost.com/2020/06/13/belgian-prince-
defends-slave-trader-king-leopold-ii-he-built-parks/.

212 Valerie Wilson, "Black Unemployment Is at Least Twice as High
as White Unemployment at the National Level and in 14 States
and the District of Columbia," Economic Policy Institute (April 4,
2019), accessed June 20, 2020, at https://www.epi.org/publication/
valerie-figures-state-unemployment-by-race/. Also see Olugbenga
Ajilore, "On the Persistence of the Black-White Unemployment
Gap," Center for American Progress (February 24, 2020), accessed
June 20, 2020, at https://www.americanprogress.org/issues/econ-
omy/reports/2020/02/24/480743/persistence-black-white-unem-

ployment-gap/.

213   Alan Vanneman, Linda Hamilton, and Janet Baldwin Anderson, "Achievement Gaps: How Black and White Students in Public Schools Perform in Mathematics and Reading on the National Assessment of Educational Progress," Statistical Analysis Report, US Department of Education, National Center for Education Statistics (2009), accessed June 20, 2020, at https://nces.ed.gov/nationsreportcard/pdf/studies/2009455.pdf.

214   Robert Mackey, "The Plot Against George Soros Didn't Start in Hungary. It Started on Fox News," *The Intercept* (January 23, 2019), accessed June 21, 2020, at https://theintercept.com/2019/01/23/plot-george-soros-didnt-start-hungary-started-fox-news/. Also see Hannes Grassegger, "The Unbelievable Story of the Plot Against George Soros," *BuzzFeed News* (January 20, 2019), accessed June 20, 2020, https://www.buzzfeednews.com/article/hnsgrassegger/george-soros-conspiracy-finkelstein-birnbaum-orban-netanyahu.

215   Grassegger, "The Unbelievable Story of the Plot Against George Soros."

216   Kimberly Fain, "The Devastation of Black Wall Street," *JSTOR Daily* (July 5, 2017), accessed June 20, 2020, at https://daily.jstor.org/the-devastation-of-black-wall-street/.

217   Read the Equal Justice Initiative report, *Lynching in America: Confronting the Legacy of Racial Terror*, accessed on June 20, 2020, at https://lynchinginamerica.eji.org/report/.

218   Ibid.

219   Ibid.

220   Visit the Without Sanctuary website at https://withoutsanctuary.org/.

221   Read the Equal Justice Initiative report.

222   See President Trump's Twitter post at https://twitter.com/realDonaldTrump/status/1150381395078000643.

223   See Glenn Greenwald, "The Spirit of Judy Miller Is Alive and Well at

the NYT, and It Does Great Damage," *The Intercept* (July, 21, 2015), accessed July 2, 2020, at https://theintercept.com/2015/07/21/spir-it-judy-miller-alive-well-nyt-great-damage/; also Eric Boehlert, "How the Iraq War Still Haunts *New York Times*," *Media Matters for America* (January 7, 2014), accessed July 2, 2020, at https://www.mediamatters.org/new-york-times/how-iraq-war-still-haunts-new-york-times; and Claire Cozens, "*New York Times*: We Were Wrong on Iraq," *The Guardian* (May 26, 2004), accessed July 2, 2020, at https://www.theguardian.com/media/2004/may/26/pres-sandpublishing.usnews.

224 CBC Radio series, "How Hollywood Became the Unofficial Prop-aganda Arm of the US Military," accessed July 2, 2020, at https://www.cbc.ca/radio/ideas/how-hollywood-became-the-unoffi-cial-propaganda-arm-of-the-u-s-military-1.5560575.

225 See "Deadly Exchange," a report by Researching the American-Is-raeli Alliance in partnership with Jewish Voice for Peace (Septem-ber 2018), available at https://deadlyexchange.org/wp-content/up-loads/2019/07/Deadly-Exchange-Report.pdf.

226 Diala Shamas and Nermeen Arastu, "Mapping Muslims: NYPD Spying and Its Impact on American Muslims," The Creating Law Enforcement Accountability & Responsibility (CLEAR) Project, CUNY School of Law, accessed July 14, 2020, at https://www.law.cuny.edu/wp-content/uploads/page-assets/academics/clinics/im-migration/clear/Mapping-Muslims.pdf.

227 Jana Winter and Cora Currier, "Exclusive: TSA's Secret Behavior Checklist to Spot Terrorist," *The Intercept* (March 27, 2015), ac-cessed July 13, 2020, at https://theintercept.com/2015/03/27/re-vealed-tsas-closely-held-behavior-checklist-spot-terrorists/; also see Israel21c Staff, "US Airport Security Enters a 'New Age' Thanks to Israeli Expertise," *Israel 21c* (September 10, 2006), accessed July 13, 2020, at https://www.israel21c.org/us-airport-security-enters-a-new-age-thanks-to-israeli-expertise/.

228 See France's asylum cases for 2019 in the Asylum Information Da-tabase, accessed July 14, 2020, at https://www.asylumineurope.org/reports/country/france/statistics; for a longer view of France's ref-

ugee data from 1990 to 2020, see Macrotrends, accessed July 14, 2020, at https://www.macrotrends.net/countries/FRA/france/refugee-statistics.

229 See "Immigration in France in Ten Stats that Matter," *The Local*, accessed July 14, 2020, at https://www.thelocal.fr/20141201/immigration-in-france-10-key-stats.

230 See the full text of Martin Luther King Jr.'s "Beyond Vietnam" speech and recording, accessed July 21, 2020, at https://www.americanrhetoric.com/speeches/mlkatimetobreaksilence.htm.